BAHAISM
AND ITS CLAIMS

LECTOR HOUSE PUBLIC DOMAIN WORKS

BAHAISM AND ITS CLAIMS

SAMUEL GRAHAM WILSON

ISBN: 978-93-90215-40-9

Published: -

LECTOR HOUSE LLP
E-MAIL: lectorpublishing@gmail.com

BAHAISM
AND ITS CLAIMS

A STUDY OF
THE RELIGION PROMULGATED BY
BAHA ULLAH AND ABDUL BAHA

BY

SAMUEL GRAHAM WILSON, D. D.

Thirty-two Years Resident in Persia Author of "Persian Life and Customs," etc.

**TO
MY WIFE**

*whose love and appreciation
are a constant inspiration
in our far-away home*

CONTENTS

INTRODUCTION

AMONG movements in the Mohammedan world in modern times Babi-Baha-ism is one of the most interesting. It is a definite revolt from Islam within its own fold. It has won its way in Persia amid considerable persecution to a position as a separate religion. It has added another to the permanent sects of the Near East. There Christian missions, inspired to long-postponed effort to convert Mohammedanism, have come face to face with Bahaism as a new and aggressive force. It has laid out a program as a universal religion, has crossed the seas and aspires to convert Christendom. Interest in it has been increased by this propaganda in the West and by the visits to Europe for this purpose of its present head, Abdul Baha Abbas, in 1911 and 1912.

Besides those who are interested in Bahaism as students of history and comparative religions, there are several classes who have shown marked favour to Bahaism.

(1) One class are simply bent on seeking some novelty. They are well described by the *Egyptian Gazette*, of Alexandria, in speaking of the reception of Abdul Baha in London: "About the London meetings there was a certain air of gush and self-advertisement on the part of Baha's friends, which was quite patent to all who are familiar with that kind of religion which will listen to anything so long as it is unorthodox, new, and sensational."[1]

(2) Another class are believers in the truth of all great religions, and, with a vague pantheistic notion, recognize all great men as God-inspired. They are willing to put Baha Ullah and Abdul Baha on the list of true religious leaders. Such is Rev. R.J. Campbell, who, in receiving Abdul Baha in London, spoke of the "diverse religious faiths that are all aspects of the one religion," and of the services as "a wonderful manifestation of the Spirit of God." He said to the congregation: "We as followers of the Lord Jesus Christ, who is to us and always will be the Light of the World, give greeting to Abdul Baha."

Mr. Campbell gives opportunity to the Bahai propaganda in the *Christian Commonwealth*, and has enlisted Abdul Baha as a contributor.

(3) Another class look on Bahaism as an ethical system, and Baha and Abdul Baha as world teachers. Their relation to Christ has been only that of a disciple to a teacher of morals. They recognize in Baha a new schoolmaster. Being Bahais to them consists in admiration of certain principles on which Abdul Baha is in the habit of dilating. But these are not Bahaism any more than Romans xii.-xv. are Pauline Christianity. Paul's gospel is Romans i.-viii. In its moral precepts and so-

[1] Nov. 16, 1911, quoted in *Star of the West*, Dec. 11, 1911.

cial principles, Bahaism is a borrower from Christ's teaching, and sometimes from Mohammed. However, Bahaism is a religion, not a system of morals.

(4) Some adherents regard Bahaism as Christianity continued or renewed by the Second Coming of Christ, whom they recognize in Abdul Baha. Most American Bahais are of this class, with faith in Baha Ullah as God the Father.

How can I classify the late Prof. T. K. Cheyne of Oxford? This widely known critic in his last work (1914), "The Reconciliation of Races and Religions," bewilders me by his credulity. It is only charitable to excuse it as the product of his dotage. How otherwise could an Oxford scholar take pride in adopting the "new name" and titles given to him by Abdul Baha, sign his preface "Ruhani," Spiritual, and have pleasure in being called the "divine philosopher," "priest of the Prince of Peace (Baha)," and being compared to St. Paul as a herald of the Kingdom, and write himself a "member of the Bahai community." At the same time Doctor Cheyne wrote himself down as a "member of the Nava Vidhan, Lahore" (Brahma-Samaj).

At present there are Bahai congregations in sixteen of the United States, in Canada, Hawaii, South Africa, England, Germany and Russia, as well as in India and Burmah. The future of its propaganda in Christendom lacks promise. Yet its measure of success makes it desirable to examine its claims and the facts regarding them.

Fortunately besides the older Babi books, there is an abundance of Bahai literature. There are (1) Treatises of Baha Ullah, (2) Tablets (Letters) and Addresses of Abdul Baha, (3) Persian Narratives, (4) Evidential books and tracts by its propagators, (5) Narratives of pilgrimages to Acca. From an independent point of view, little has been written. Nearly all of the many articles which have appeared in periodical literature have been from the pens of Bahais, though often not so ostensibly. Prof. E. G. Browne of Cambridge University, England, has translated and edited important Babi-Bahai works. His Introductions, Notes and Appendices to these books are storehouses of erudition and enable the reader to correct the biased information of the text. They pertain for the most part to the Babi period. So do the able contributions of Mr. A. L. M. Nicolas, the Consul of France, with whom, as my neighbour at Tabriz, I have had the pleasure of valuable conversations on this subject on which he is such an authority. I have had as sources of information also a manuscript "Life of Baha Ullah" by Mohammed Javad Kasvini, the "Kitab-ul-Akdas," Most Holy Book, translated by Dr. I. G. Kheiralla, in manuscript, and various unpublished letters and documents. Besides all this, I have been in personal contact with Bahais in Persia for a generation. My language teachers were Bahais, one of them a convert to Christianity. I have found their journal, the *Star of the West*, a prolific source of information. I may claim not to be of the class referred to by Abdul Baha when he says, "Baha Ullah will be assailed by those who are not informed of his principles."

After sketching, in brief, the history of Bahaism I will examine its religious, moral, political and social doctrine and life. In doing this I shall quote for the most part from the words of the "Revelation" and its adherents, in order to insure fairness and justice. In the course of the investigation, the history and character of the founders will be considered. Finally I shall describe its propaganda in the Occident.

Bahais declare that Babism is abrogated and superseded. In reality it is dead and I do not treat of it, except as it throws light on the history or doctrines of Bahaism. To all intents and purposes, the Bab is as much an obsolete prophet as Mani or Babak.

I am to deal with Bahaism in its latest phases. The term Babi is not appropriate to the religion of Baha nor to his followers. Of the "revelation," it may be said as Jacob said of his wages, they "have changed them ten times." The Bab altered his declarations regarding himself and his statements of doctrine. Subh-i-Azal made further changes. Baha's standpoint in the "Ikan," at Bagdad, differs greatly from that in the "Kitab-ul-Akdas," at Acca. Abbas gave the kaleidoscope another whirl and added his interpretations and emendations. Besides all these, it has been given a Western aspect for Christians. The Rev. H. H. Jessup, D. D., compares it very aptly to the town clock in Beirut, which has two kinds of dial plates. The face turned towards the Moslem quarter has the hands set to tell the hour according to Oriental reckoning; the face towards the Christian quarter, according to the European day. It is the face towards the Christians that I shall look at specially in the present investigation. However historical facts are the same and the main doctrines taught in the West have no essential difference from those of Persian Bahaism.

Acknowledgment and thanks are hereby tendered to *The Bibliotheca Sacra, The Bible Magazine, The East and the West, The Church Missionary Review, The Missionary Review of the World, The Moslem World, The Union Seminary Review,* and The *Princeton Theological Review* for the use of materials which I have previously published in their pages.

I

HISTORICAL SKETCH

The East productive of religions—Imamat—Shiahism, its sects—Sheikhiism—The Bab-Subh i Azal—Baha Ullah—His policy—His haram—Abdul Baha—Journey to Occident—Education—Number of Bahais

Does it often happen that the earliest records of a religious movement ... pass, within a short time after their completion, into the hands of strangers who, while interested in their preservation, have no desire to alter them for better or worse. So far as my knowledge goes, it has never happened save in the case of the Babi religion. — *"The New History of the Bab," p. xi, by E. G. Browne.*

Persia is, and always has been, a very hotbed of systems from the time of Manes and Mazdak in the old Sassanian days, down to the present age, which has brought into being the Babis and the Sheikhis. — *"A Year Among the Persians," p. 122.*

Outside of a certain mixture of Occidental science and philanthropy, introduced largely for foreign consumption and in order to give an up-to-date stamp or colouring to the movement, there is scarcely anything that distinguishes Babism from its predecessors. The materials are inextricably interwoven with the whole course of Persian history in all its departments, political, religious, social, and philosophical. Time has pronounced its verdict again and again in the most unmistakable manner. So deep a hold have the ideas, which lie at the foundation of Babism and similar sects, taken of the minds and hearts of the people, that it may be said that as every American is a possible president, so every Persian is a possible murshid. For every sect that makes its appearance on the page of history, there are hundreds of embryo sects, of whose existence no one knows outside of a very limited circle.—*P. Z. Easton, quoted in Speer's "Missions and Modern History," Vol. I, p. 121.*

For the Bahais, the Bab became a sort of John the Baptist, sent to announce to the world the coming of Mirza Husain Ali, Baha Ullah, and perhaps of Abbas Effendi—a pitiable result of martyrdom. This thesis is essentially false. Reading of the book (the

"Bayan") will convince every one of this.—*A. L. M. Nicolas, "Béyan Persan," Vol. I, p. 11.*

THE soil of the East has been fertile of religions. Montanus, Manes, Mazdak, Babak, Mukanna—familiarized in Lalla Rookh as the Veiled prophet of Khorasan,—Hasan Sabah chief of the Assassins, Hakim the cruel God of the Druses, each of these propagated his doctrines, exerted a wide influence, and left his mark on the people of the Orient. Saad-i-Doulah the Jew, Argoon Khan the Mongol, Ala-i-Din al Khalig, king of Delhi, and many others attempted to found new religions. In our own day the Mahdi of the Sudan, Ahmad Quadiani of India and Sheikh Ali Nur-i-Din of Tunis entered the lists. In the West, too, in America a land unbridled by traditions, Mormonism, Dowieism and Christian Science have flourished. To all these must be added Babism and Bahaism.

As an introduction to a discussion of Bahaism and its claims, I will sketch briefly and simply its origin and history. Bahaism is derived from Babism. Babism has its roots in Shiahism, a soil impregnated with the doctrines of the Imamate and Mahdiism. The atmosphere is filled with millennial hopes and dreamy mysticism, with Sufi philosophies and allegorical fancies of its poets. This soil has been fruitful of many sects. The Shiahism of Persia is called the "Religion of the Twelve" because its fundamental doctrine is that the twelve Imams, the lineal descendants of Ali and Fatima, the daughter of Mohammed, were the rightful Caliphs of Islam, in succession to Mohammed. In the tenth century (329 A. H. or 940 A. D.) the Twelfth Imam disappeared into a well, and still lives in Jabulka or Jabulsa whence he is expected to reappear as the Mahdi or Kaim. After his concealment, four persons in succession were channels of communication between him and the faithful. The title given to these was Bab or the Gate.

Among the sects which sprang up among the Shiahs or were related to them were the Ismielis, Carmathians, Druses, Hurufis, Ali-Allahis or Nusairiyeh, Assassins, Batinis and many others. A group of these were called Ghulat, because they rendered excessive honour to the Imams, believing them to be incarnations of the attributes or essence of God. Those holding this view anticipated that the Imam Mahdi would be a divine Manifestation.[2] At the beginning of the nineteenth century, a sect arose in Persia, called Sheikhis. It received its name from its founder, Sheikh Ahmad of Ahsa, 1752-1827. He taught that there was always in the world a "perfect

Shiah," who held communication with the absent Imam and revealed his will. Sheikh Ahmad was that "perfect one." He was favoured by the Kajar Shahs and had a considerable following. His successor, Haji Kazim of Resht, near the time of his death, announced to his disciples at Kerbela that the Manifestation was at hand. One of his disciples was Mirza Ali Mohammed of Shiraz. When twenty-four

---

[2] Prof. E. G. Browne says ("A Literary History of Persia," p. 311), "The resemblance between these numerous sects, whose history can be traced through the last eleven centuries and a half, is most remarkable and extends even to the minute details of terminology." "The doctrines appear to be endemic in Persia, and in our own days appeared again in the Babi movement."

years of age in 1844, he laid claim to be the "promised one." He took the title of "Bab," the Gate or Door of communication of the knowledge of God. His followers were called Babis. He soon advanced his station and claimed to be the Kaim or Mahdi. Still advancing he took the title of *Nukta* or Point of Divine Unity and announced his "Revelation" or "Bayan" as the abrogation of Islam and the Koran. From Shiraz he went to Mecca and proclaimed his manifestation. On his return he was imprisoned. Many of the Sheikhis became his zealous followers and by their active propaganda caused great agitation throughout Persia. The Bab was transferred to the extreme northwest of Persia and confined in prison at Maku and Chirik. His sectaries, oppressed and persecuted, rose in arms against Mohammed Shah, anticipating victory through divine interposition. The Bab was executed at Tabriz in 1850. The insurrections were put down and many of the brave captives were treacherously slaughtered. A few Babis, seeking revenge, attempted to assassinate the new Shah, Nasr-ud-Din. This led to cruel reprisals. Four score Babis were executed at Teheran. Others fled into exile, especially to Bagdad. Among these was Mirza Yahya whom the Bab had appointed his successor. His title was Subh-i-Azal, the Dawn of the Eternal, or His Holiness the Eternal.

A special point of the Bab's teaching was the announcement of the coming of "Him whom God should manifest." After his death a number of the Babis claimed to be the promised incarnation. There was a "chaos of divine manifestations," including Hazret Zahib, Janab-i-Azim, Nabil and others. Among these claimants was Mirza Husain Ali, a son of Mirza Abbas, surnamed Buzurk, and his concubine. The father was steward or "vizier" of the household of Imam Werdi Mirza, Governor of Teheran. He was half brother to Mirza Yahya and thirteen years his senior. His title was Baha Ullah, the splendour or glory of God. For many years Baha acted in Bagdad (1852-67) as factotum for Azal, and acknowledged him as supreme. Then he announced that he himself was "He whom God should manifest," and took active measures to supplant Azal. About this time the Turkish Government transferred them to Adrianople. Here developed bitter jealousies, quarrels and foul play. The Sultan intervened and sent Subh-i-Azal to Famagusta, Cyprus, and Baha Ullah to Acca[3] (Acre), Syria, August 1868. Both were granted pensions and kept under police surveillance as parties dangerous to religion and the state. Azal continued to be the head of the Babis, called henceforth also Azalis. Baha attracted most of the Babis to himself, and they became known as Bahais. Baha relegated the Bab to the position of a forerunner, and declared the "Bayan" and other books of the Bab to be superseded by his own "Revelations." He changed in a measure the doctrines and laws of Babism, liberalizing its provisions. He put himself forward as the Lord of a new dispensation, the founder of a new religion.

During the next quarter of a century Bahaism made little stir in Persia. Its advancement was by no means as rapid as during the earlier years of the Bab. The zeal and devotion of the followers sensibly slackened. *Tagiya* (dissimulation regarding one's religion) was allowed and practiced. The fierce warriors turned to professing the doctrines of expediency, condemning as unwise zealots the fighting

[3] At that very time the chief of the Vashratis, who held that Sheikh Ali Nur-i-Din, of Tunis, was a Manifestation of Mohammed, and his essence divine, was in exile in Acca. He was in friendly relations with Baha.

Babis of the previous generation. During these years they escaped bloody persecutions except in rare instances. They tried to make their peace with the Shah, constantly emphasizing their loyalty, expurgating their books to suppress condemnation of the dynasty, and inducing the Sadr-Azam, the Prime Minister of Nasr-i-Din Shah, to tolerate and befriend them.

In Acca, too, Baha soon acquired considerable freedom, built a palace, called Bahja, in a delightful garden and freely received the pilgrims. He sent out many tablets, composed his Books of Revelation and had them published in Bombay. He died at Acca in May, 1892, in his seventy-fifth year. His temple tomb is near the Bahja.

Baha's haram consisted of two wives and a concubine. After his death, the sons of the different wives quarrelled regarding the succession. Abbas Effendi, the only son of the oldest wife, proclaimed himself the successor, the Interpreter, the Centre of the Covenant, the Source of Authority. Mohammed Ali and his brothers strenuously opposed Abbas and intense animosity was engendered which divided the followers in Acca and Persia. Abbas drew the greater number with him. He assumed the title of Abdul Baha (Servant of Baha). He has the ambition to make the faith a world religion and has inaugurated a propaganda in the West. After the proclamation of constitutional liberty in Turkey, he resided in Egypt. Later he made several journeys to Europe and one to North America. His visit to the Occident brought him into the lime-light. He was given good opportunity to present his cause.

The addresses of this "Infallible Interpreter" of the cult did not reveal clearly the real doctrines and aim of the movement. Abdul Baha confined himself mainly to the utterance of popular platitudes such as are stock-in-trade for a multitude of social and religious reformers, and most of which are original and accepted principles and precepts of Christianity. The real claims of Bahaism are set forth in the Books and Tablets (Epistles) of Baha Ullah and Abdul Baha, and in a considerable literature by Persian and American Bahais.

Abdul Baha is an intelligent, well informed man, of fair sagacity. He was educated at home after the custom of Persia. He says of himself, "I have studied Arabic profoundly and know the Arabic better than the Arabians themselves. I have studied the Persian and Turkish in my native land, besides other languages of the East. But when I visit the West I need an interpreter."[4] He said to Doctor Jessup, "Yes, I know your Beirut Press and your books." His references to ancient and modern philosophers, to historical events and to European writers, quoting from the same, show some familiarity with literature.[5] He repudiates the claims of some of his disciples that he has no literary culture, as that of Abul Fazl[6] or of M. A. Lucas who says:[7] "He has had no access to books, yet his knowledge is unbounded." On this point Professor Cheyne remarks:[8] "His public addresses prove that through

---

[4] *Star of the West*, April 9, 1913, p. 35.
[5] Phelps' "Life of Abbas Effendi," p. 227.
[6] "Bahai Proofs," pp. 94, 109.
[7] "My Visit to Acca."
[8] "The Reconciliation of Races and Religions," pp. 155, 159.

this and that channel he has imbibed something of humanistic and even scientific culture. He must have had some one to guide him in the tracks of modern inquiry. I venture to hope that his expounding may not, in the future, extend to philosophic, philological, scientific, and exegetical details. Abdul Baha may fall into error on secular problems, among which it is obvious to include Biblical and Koranic exegesis." "I am bound to say that Baha Ullah has made mistakes and the almost equally venerated Abdul Baha has made many slips."[9]

A word should be said about the number of Bahais. I have many data on this point, but can here give only a summary. Regarding their numbers, the Bahais have indulged in gross exaggeration. "Millions" is the usual figure used by American Bahais. Thus Phelps[10] speaks of "the millions of Bahais in Persia." MacNutt, in "Unity through Love," declares that "His followers number millions from all the religious systems of the world." Kheiralla[11] says: "Abdul Karim, 1896, assured me that the believers in Baha were fifty millions. I wrote to Syria to ask. Sayid Mohammed, secretary of Abbas Effendi, said that the number was fifty-five million souls." Kheiralla afterwards denounces it as a gross deceit. As to Persia, they place the proportion at one-third or one-half. Dreyfus writes,[12] "Probably half the population of Persia is Bahai." Some judicious non-Bahai writers allow them half a million or less in Persia on a basis of ten millions of population. American missionaries, as Jordan at Teheran, Frame at Resht and Shedd at Urumia, calculate that the number in Persia does not exceed 100,000 to 200,000. After careful inquiry I agree with this estimate.

As to other races and countries, let us see. Abul Fazl claims[13] that "Jews, Zoroastrians, and Nusaireyah by thousands" are Bahais. M. Haidar Ali[14] says: "The majority of Zoroastrians are recognized as Bahais in all sincerity." On the contrary Professor Browne writes:[15] "I had been informed that Zoroastrians were accepting Bahaism. However after much intercourse with the Zoroastrians of Yezd and Kerman for the space of three and a half months, I came to the conclusion that few, if any, had adopted the Bahai creed." In India the proportion of Parsee-Bahais is very small.

As to Jews:—Remey says: "In Hamadan there is a large Israelitish following of Baha." A census made by a European Jew showed exactly 59 parents and with their children 194 persons out of a population of 6,000 Jews. As to the United States, I give some particulars in the closing chapter. The census of 1906 reported 1,280 Bahais, which may have increased to two or three thousand. In the Turkish empire they are few, for Sunni Moslems are utterly indifferent to Bahaism. The Egyptian *Gazette* says of Egypt where Abdul Baha resided for two years, "The new religion has made little perceptible progress; Islam remained indifferent, and the Christian

---

[9] "The Reconciliation of Races and Religions," p. 181.
[10] "Life of Abbas Effendi," p. 100.
[11] "Three Questions," p. 22.
[12] Page 42.
[13] Page 64.
[14] "Martyrdoms in 1903."
[15] *Jour. Roy. As. Soc.*, p. 501, 1889.

community was ignorant of his presence." Of Syria, Mr. Phelps wrote:[16] "All the Bahais in Acca are Persians. No other nationalities are among them." The inference is plain that no native of Acca had become Bahai through forty years of contact with Baha and his seventy followers. Bahais outside of Persia are probably all told not more than 15,000 and one-third of these are Persians in Russia. Abdul Baha gave the impression that many of the Christians of Persia are converts to Baha. Dr. J. H. Shedd wrote, 1894, "I have heard of no case of a Christian conversion to Bahaism." Dr. G. W. Holmes wrote, 1903, "I do not know of a single Christian in Persia, who has been converted to Bahaism. Some Bahais who made a profession of Christianity turned back to Baha." Rev. J. W. Hawkes declares that in his observation none of the members of the Syrian (Nestorian) or Armenian churches in Persia have become Bahais.[17] I have known of one Armenian family in Resht and two men in Maraga, one of whom was a notorious ne'er-do-well, who kept up his opium using as before.

---

[16] Page 109.
[17] R. E. Speer's "Missions and Modern Hist.," pp. 157, 181.

II

THE GENERAL CLAIMS OF BAHAISM

(I) New religion needed—(II) Bahaism that new religion—To supersede Christianity—Doctrines—Baha God—His Revelation—The Akdas—Conditions of discipleship—Position of Abdul Baha—(III) Claims superiority to former religions—In founder, books and doctrines—Not superlative—(IV) To be a universal religion—Defects in rites, regulations, calendar, civil government—House of Justice—Alphabet—Universal language.

The conception on which Bahaism bases its claim is false. Truth does not grow old, nor is it possible to change the religion with the growth of the race. A universal religion must present truth in a form that will reach men in every stage of civilization, for the reason that in every period of the world since the dawn of history there have been simultaneously men in every stage of intellectual development.—*W. A. Shedd in "Miss. Review of the World."*

It (Bahaism) has not enough assurance of personal immortality to satisfy such Western minds as are repelled by the barren and jejune ethical systems of agnostics, positivists, and humanitarians who would give us rules to regulate a life which they have rendered meaningless.—*Professor Browne in Phelps' "Life of Abbas Effendi," p. xviii.*

The essence of being a Bahai is a boundless devotion to the person of the Manifestation and a profound belief that he is divine and of a different order from all other beings.—*Professor Browne, Art. "Bab" in Ency. of Religion and Ethics.*

THE claims of Bahaism are many and varied. They cover a wide range. I will first consider its general claims and of these the most significant.

I. First of all, Bahais claim that a new religion is needed. All the great religions, they say, were true in their day; not only Moses, Christ, and Mohammed, but Zoroaster, Confucius, and Buddha were Divine Manifestations, and revealed God's truth. But now the old religions are dead. Abdul Baha[18] says: "The Spirit has passed away from the bodies of the old religions. While the forms of their doc-

[18] Phelps' "Life of Abbas Effendi," p. 144.

trines remain, the Spirit has fled." "The principles of the religion[19] of Christ have been forgotten. It is then clear and evident that in the passage of time religions become entirely changed. Therefore they are renewed." "There is to-day[20] nothing more than traditions to feed upon.... The world of humanity is in the dark." One chapter in Thornton Chase's "The Bahai Revelation" is headed "The Bahai Revelation is needed." This he argues, stating (1) that Christianity is condemned because after 1900 years it has not been accepted by all people; (2) because it refuses to reject miracles and the blood atonement and will not confine itself to the "principles of Jesus," as the Brahma Samaj; (3) because it tends to separate peoples, holding itself to be the only religion authorized by God; (4) because people are dwelling in bondage and are no **longer** satisfied. Tares are many and Baha Ullah must come and uproot them.[21]

"The old order of things is passing away," says Sprague;[22] "people are being tossed about with every wind of doctrine." "True religion is forgotten," says Phelps,[23] "or has become a hollow name; faith has waned, men are wandering in the dark." This decay, they teach, is inevitable and in accord with divine arrangement. They deny the belief of Christians that Christianity is the permanent religion of humanity; and that of Moslems, that Mohammed was the "seal of the prophets," and hold that Christianity was succeeded by Islam, Islam by Babism, and Babism by Bahaism. Abdul Baha says: "Time changes all things. Transmutation and change are requirements of life. All religions of God are subject to the same law. They are founded in order to blossom out and develop and fulfill their mission. They reach their zenith and then decline and come to an end." "A new cycle must begin, for the world needs a new luminary."

It is not necessary to refute the fundamental fallacy of this first claim, for it is patent that Christianity is alive and growing. Its manifold spiritual activities, its varied and progressive efforts for righteousness and peace among men, for social and moral reforms, its zeal for Missions and their marvellous success, show that Christianity is neither stagnant nor dead. It has a forward triumphant movement. The Church renews its strength from its divine Head; He, alive forevermore, is its Light and its Life.

II. Bahaism claims to be the divine Revelation in this new cycle—a new Dispensation or Covenant. It disclaims being a new religion, affirming rather that it is a renewal of religion or religion renewed. One writes: "The Revelation is not a new religion, but the very essence of God's word as taught by Christ (and Moses and Mohammed), but not perceived by Christians at large" (nor by Jews nor Mohammedans). Baha Ullah[24] says: "Of the utterances of the prophets of the past we have taken the essence, and in the garment of brevity clothed it." Abdul Baha says: "The same basis, which was laid by Christ and later on forgotten, has been renewed by Baha Ullah." "All that is true in all religions will stand; by the new Dispensation,

[19] "Some Answered Questions," by Barney, p. 19.
[20] *Star of the West,* May 17, 1913, p. 68. Abbreviated hereafter as *S. W.*
[21] Page 158 f.
[22] "Story of the Bahai Movement," p. 23.
[23] Phelps, *ibid.,* p. 256.
[24] Phelps, "Jewels of Wisdom," p. 237.

new spirit is infused into these teachings."[25] Phelps[26] says: "The body of doctrine which Bahaism teaches is not put forward in any sense or particular as new, but as a unification and synthesis of all other religions." Of its system of morals the same is true. It is a restatement in unsystematic form of common ethics. It reiterates the second table of the Mosaic Law, and the New Testament principles of brotherly love and unity. Yet in some of his addresses Abdul Baha names certain principles as new in the Bahai faith, such as universal peace, the unity of humanity, arbitration, compulsory education of both sexes, the harmony of science and religion, the evil of prejudice and fanaticism, need of investigating the truth, etc. Not one of these is new; not one owes its position in the world of thought or activity to the Bahai propaganda.

But whether Bahaism claims to be new in its principles or disclaims it, in fact it is a new religion. The disavowals are, no doubt, made for the sake of obtaining easier access to the followers of the old religions, and are only a temporary expediency. In this they are simply following the example of Mohammed, who proclaimed his message to the people of Arabia as the religion of Abraham, and as the same as that of the Law and the Gospels. But it is evident that Bahaism is inconsistent with Christianity, as indeed with Islam. Bahais' claims, if admitted, would lead to the superseding of Christianity. This will appear when I state its doctrines. The present attitude of Bahais in maintaining connection with Christian Churches and at the same time worshipping Baha and propagating Bahaism is one of intellectual stultification or of moral blindness.

In the same way, in Moslem lands, Bahais conform to the externals of Islam. In the case of the latter the cause of this is often moral obliquity or fear; with deceived Christian brethren it is probably ignorance; by the Bahai propagandist it is allowed from astute policy. It is an intellectual impossibility for one to accept the teachings of Baha Ullah and to be his disciple and at the same time to be an intelligent disciple of our Lord Jesus Christ. The one excludes the other. Bahaism is a distinct religion. It is not even a sect of Islam. It abrogates and annuls it. Professor Browne says: "As Christianity is a different religion from Judaism, and as Islam is distinct from Christianity, so Bahaism is a separate religion, distinct from Christianity or Islam." It even superseded and abrogated Babism. The Bab has been relegated to the background, and put into the position of a John the Baptist. His book, the "Bayan," is long ago neglected to such an extent that Professor Browne had difficulty in obtaining a copy in Persia. Remey[27] says: "Babism fulfilled its purpose, and when this was accomplished in the appearance of Baha Ullah, it, as such, ceased to exist." Mirza Abul Fazl[28] says: Babism "is not the same religion or creed as Bahaism."

A statement of the fundamental doctrines of Bahaism will suffice to show that it is a distinct religion.

(1) The fundamental assertion of Bahaism is that Baha Ullah is the Manifesta-

---

[25] *Ibid.,* p. 145.
[26] *Ibid.,* p. 144.
[27] "The Bahai Movement," p. 20.
[28] "Bahai Proofs," p. 78.

tion or Incarnation of God the Father. Baha Ullah says of himself in his letter to the Pope: "O Pope! This is indeed the Father of whom Isaiah gave you tidings and the Comforter whom Christ promised." Abdul Baha affirms: "The Father, foretold by Christ, has come amongst us." "The Father of Christ is come among you."[29] "The manifested God Himself has come."[30] He is called the "Lord of Hosts," "the Lord God Almighty," "Creator of whomsoever is in the world," also "the Ruler." Abdul Baha cabled back to America after his voyage: "Thanks to Baha Ullah, we arrived safely at Liverpool."[31] Instead of beginning a book, as the Moslems do, "In the name of God," the Bahais begin, "In the Name of our Lord El Baha."

The Persian Bahais accept this teaching. One of them in Tabriz declared to me: "Baha is very God of very God." M. Abdul Karim delivered the doctrine in this form to the disciples in America[32] and said: "Upon the Day, when God Almighty, in the form of man known as Baha Ullah declared Himself and said, 'I am God and there is no God but Me,' the old heavens and old earth passed away, all things became new." So it continues to be preached.

Mr. Remey[33] says in the Bahai monthly (the capitals are his): "This one is THE FATHER Himself, The Manifested GOD *Himself* BAHAULLAH."

(2) The Revelation of Baha is contained in his Books and Tablets (Epistles). Some of these are the "Ikan," the "Surat ul-Haykal," the "Hidden Words," the "Seven Valleys," and the "Kitab-ul-Akdas." Remey[34] pronounces them "The latest and greatest of God's revelations to the world." "They contain knowledge which was sealed and closed up by the prophets of bygone cycles, so that the minds of the wisest of men were unable to comprehend it." Thornton Chase, exceeding the others in his extravagant language, declares that "were all the books of former days lost and forgotten, the whole of true religious teaching could be found in the 'Bahai Revelation.'"

The "Kitab-ul-Akdas," "The Most Holy Book," is called by M. Abul Fazl the "greatest" and "most important." It consists of 146 pages of manuscript, about 10,000 words. It was written at Acca in Persian and Arabic. It has been translated into Russian, and a synopsis of it is given by Professor Browne,[35] of Cambridge University, in the *Journal of the Royal Asiatic Society*, 1892, of which I make use. The "Kitab-ul-Akdas" warns the learned against criticizing it, and in imitation of Mohammed challenges them to produce the like of it. It is similar in its teachings to the "Bayan" of the Bab, though less fantastic and mystical. Its contents are confused and unsystematic. It has laws—ceremonial, moral, civil, criminal—min-

[29] Chase, "The Bahai Revelation," p. 178.

[30] *S. W.*, March 2, 1913, p. 10.

[31] See *S. W.*

[32] Addresses in New York and Chicago, 1900.

[33] *S. W.*, p. 10, March 2, 1913.

[34] *S. W.*, 1913, p. 267.

[35] Prof. E. G. Browne has translated various books of the Bahais; among them are "The Episode of the Bab," or the "Traveller's Narrative," and the "New History." His investigations and comments have given offense to the Bahais, while his praises of them often wound the Christian reader. I have been kindly permitted by Doctor Kheiralla to examine his English translation of the "Kitab-ul-Akdas" in manuscript.

gled with rhapsodies, exhortations, addresses, and various digressions. After an introduction and some laws, follow addresses to the Emperor of Germany and to the Sultan of Turkey, to the cities of Teheran and Kirman, and to the province of Khorasan. After more laws there is a digression about revelation; then more laws and a digression about the Bab; again sundry laws, followed by a denunciation of Subh-i-Azal, and this by various civil laws, ending with a command to select a universal language.

The book is a medley, and bears internal evidence of the truth of the tradition that it was written piecemeal in answer to various questions from believers. The fragments were jumbled together without order. The learned are reminded by Baha that he never studied the sciences, and there is too abundant evidence in the book itself to confirm the statement. It ranks far below Deuteronomy as a system of laws or a literary composition.

The opening words of the Book of Akdas state the conditions of entrance into the religion of Baha: (1) "Verily the first thing which God hath ordained unto His servants is the knowledge of the Dawning-Place of the Revelation [*i. e.*, of Baha]. Whosoever hath attained thereunto hath attained unto all good; and he who is deprived thereof is indeed of the people of error—even though he bringeth all good actions." (2) "It behoveth every one to follow that whereunto he is commanded. These two things are inseparable." Acceptance of Baha as the Manifestation of God and following Him in obedience are the two conditions of discipleship. (3) A third condition has been added since the death of Baha—namely, adherence to Abdul Baha Abbas as supreme Head, "the centre of the covenant." This assumption of authority by Abbas caused a bitter and angry schism at Acca.

Remey[36] says: "He [Baha] has pointed to the one who should be looked upon as authority by all, and has closed the doors to outside interpretation. Therefore obedience and submission must be shown completely to him." Mirza Asad Ullah[37] says: "Whosoever turns away from Abdul Baha is one of the companions of the left hand [a goat], and one of the letters of hell-fire." The rejectors of Abdul Baha are termed Nakazeen—"the violators." They are "cut off," are "no longer of the Kingdom." They are "spiritual corpses," from them "goes forth a poisonous infection," "they have a vile odour," says Abdul Baha,[38] the preacher of brotherly love and unity. In this way they fulfill their boast of consorting with all men in "harmony and fragrance."

The minority seem to have the best of the argument,[39] but Abbas has established himself as Supreme Pontiff. His most honoured agents call him by titles which imply his divinity. American pilgrims worship him as "Christ, the Master."[40] Sprague[41] declares him to be "the third of the great Trinity of Revelators."

---

[36] *S. W.*, July, 1912. See Chapter X.

[37] See "Sacred Mysteries," p. 100.

[38] *S. W.*, Sept. 8, 1913, pp. 170-174.

[39] See "Facts for Behaists."

[40] Dr. H. H. Jessup in N. Y. *Outlook*, June, 1901.

[41] "A Year in India and Burmah," p. 10. Compare the Trinities of the Nusaireyah, as given in "The Asian Mystery," p. 111. The first is Abel, Adam and Gabriel: after others,

M. Abul Karim[42] writes: "God appeared in the Bab as the Holy Ghost, in Baha as the Father, in Abbas as His Son." Mrs. Grundy[43] says: "Within Abdul Baha is the inexhaustible fountain of knowledge." Remey[44] says: "Through Abdul Baha and through him only can believers receive the spiritual power and sustenance necessary for their growth." Among Abbas's titles are the "Greatest Branch of God," the "Mystery of God."[45]

These are a few of the salient points of the "new revelation."

III. Another claim of Bahaism is that of superiority to former religions.

(*a*) Its founder is declared to be superior in his personality, in his divine knowledge, in his power of revealing. In what has already been quoted, this is evident. The great cycle which began in Adam is said to have reached its culmination in Baha Ullah. "The Manifestations are ended by the appearance of this, which is the greatest of all Manifestations," which "manifests itself only once in 500,000 years." "He is exalted above all those who are upon earth and in the heaven." Abdul Baha[46] says: "Consider the time of Jesus. This is greater than that for as much as it is the calling of the Lord of Hosts." "All the great prophets were perfect mirrors of God—manifestations of the 'Primal Will' of God—and sinless, but in Baha[47] in some sense the Divine Essence is manifested." Phelps[48] says: "He is greater than his predecessors." "Baha," says Kheiralla,[49] "is the Everlasting Father, who spoke in Abraham, Moses, and Jesus Christ, who were His ministers, and at these latter days He came Himself in the flesh to judge the quick and the dead." Abbas said to Mrs. Grundy: "Baha is the consummation of all degrees. He is the Revelation of all truth and light." "Christ is the vine, Baha is the husbandman—the Lord of the vineyard." A poem says of Baha:

> By His life-fostering lip live a hundred such as Jesus;
> By the Sinai of His aspect sit a thousand such as Moses;
> Thou, on the night of ascent, didst entertain the prophet as Thy guest.

Refrain:—

> The Temple of God's glory is none other than Baha;
> If one seeks God, let him seek Him in Baha.
> Thou art the King of the Realm of the everlasting,
> Thou art the Manifestation of the essence of the Lord of Glory,

---

comes Simon Peter, Jesus and Rozabah; Ali, Mohammed and Salman the Persian. The first of each group, for example Peter and Ali, is the supreme manifestation, the *maana*, meaning or essence of God; the second of each group, Mohammed and Jesus represent the *ism-azim*, the Greatest Name: while the third, that is, Salman is termed the Bab. Baha is the Greatest Name. The place of Peter remains for Abbas.

[42] "Facts for Behaists."
[43] "Ten Days in the Light of Acca," p. 105.
[44] *S. W.,* Nov. 23, 1913, p. 242.
[45] See Chapter IV.
[46] "Tablets of Abdul Baha," Vol. I, p. 10.
[47] "Some Answered Questions," pp. 129-131.
[48] *Ibid.,* p. 148.
[49] "Beha' Ullah," by Kheiralla.

The Creator of Creation.

Such are some of the "great swelling words" with which his followers exalt Baha. Yet when we examine his life we find nothing to justify such extravagance. He was simply a man of like passions as others. It may seem invidious to refer to scandalous stories of Baha's youth in Teheran. But does not truth demand that it be stated that his reputation in Persia is sullied by definite accusations of vice and immorality? I have heard such narratives with statements of the time, place, and associates who were partakers of his guilt. His family in riper years exhibits no higher example than a bigamous household. According to the narrative of Abdul Baha in the "Traveller's Narrative,"[50] he planned in duplicity to reach the headship of the Babis; for while purposing all the while to set forth a claim for himself, he put forward his half-brother, Subh-i-Azal, as the successor of the Bab—to protect himself and to insure his own safety during times of danger. He outwardly supported Azal for many years, while secretly planning to supplant him. While acting as Azal's trusted minister, he was drawing the people to himself. We pass over the attempts of these brothers to poison each other. Each accuses[51] the other, and, as the Persians say, "God knows" whether both speak the truth. We pass over, at present, the definite accusations against the Bahais of assassinating the Azalis.[52] In the notorious case where Azalis were foully murdered[53] by Bahais at Acca, and the latter were brought to trial before the Turkish authorities, they were defended and kept in favour by Baha. He had near Subh-i-Azal a spy named Maskin Kalam,[54] who by guile and deceit kept away any who wished to visit Azal. He received this disciple to his intimate circle after years of such active deception. Azal, who is called by Bahais "the point of Satan," and is likened to Cain and Judas, has a character gentler, more lovable, and more sincere than Baha as the two are depicted in the writings of Professor Browne; albeit, Baha is abler, more astute, more a leader of men. Professor Browne, in his interviews at Famagusta and at Acca, did obeisance to each of them. His bow to Azal may have been one of respect for his character or disposition; his bow to Baha must rather have been out of regard for his influence and leadership. But after all we need not wonder so much at the delusion of the Bahais in exalting Baha, for we are familiar with Dowie and Zion City, and with Joseph Smith and the Mormons. And we are surely led to expect the appearance of such a deceiver who "as God sitteth in the temple of God, showing himself that he is God." Bahais certainly, in the words of the Apostle,[55] "have strong delusion, that they should believe a lie."

(*b*) The Bahais claim superiority for the books and writings of Baha Ullah.

(1) As to the rapidity of their composition, their style, and their quantity. One of the proofs of the Bab was the rapidity with which he composed verses,[56] "with amazing rapidity, without any reflection." Sayid Yahya of Darab, one of his first

[50] "Trav.'s Narr.," pp. xlv, 62-63.
[51] "Trav.'s Narr.," pp. 359, 368-369.
[52] See *Ibid.*, Index word "Assassination"; "New Hist.," pp. xxiii.-iv.
[53] *Ibid.*, pp. 82, 278; "Trav.'s Narr.," pp. 361, 371.
[54] *Jour. Roy. As. Soc.*, 1889, p. 516; 1892, pp. 994-995.
[55] 2 Thess. ii. 4 and 11.
[56] "Bahai Proofs," by Abul Fazl, p. 42.

converts,[57] was gained by such a "sign," implying, as was supposed, divine inspiration. He propounded certain questions. The messenger brought the answer, of which he says: "I beheld a marvel a hundred thousandfold beyond what I sought for. Over two thousand verses and illustrations of eloquence and beauty of style revealed and written down during five or six hours." So also in Ispahan, in answer to the Imam-Juma[58]: "The Bab began to write, and in three hours wrote 1,000 verses. Then the Imam-Juma was convinced that such power was from God, being beyond the capacity of man." In his trial at Tabriz[59] the Bab cited as a proof of his divine mission: "I can write in one day 2,000 verses. Who else can do this?"

In like manner the claim was made for Baha Ullah that he could compose with miraculous rapidity. "The maximum speed of Baha's revelation is said to be 1,500 verses in one hour." These were "written without premeditation or reflection,"[60] and often dictated to his amanuensis. To Baha is attributed the marvellous feat of composing and writing the "Ikan" in a single night. This book in its English translation consists of 184 printed pages. The translator, Mirza Ali Kuli Khan, Persian Chargé des Affaires at Washington, a zealous Bahai, says in his preface:[61] "According to the prevailing opinion of Bahais, the 'Ikan' was written in one night by the supreme pen." He argues (faint-heartedly apparently) for the truth of the statement, and cites Abul Fazl as corroborating the tradition. It is altogether probable that Baha prepared the "Ikan" during his retirement for two years to Kurdistan, in the region of Suleimaniyeh. It is curious to note how the Bahais have outdone Mohammed. He made his verses (ayat = signs), and their eloquence and beauty the signs of his mission. But Babis and Bahais add rapidity of composition as an additional sign or miracle.

The quantity of the writings is also emphasized as proving their divine source and power. It was a matter of boasting that the Bab's writings were from 100,000 to 500,000 verses, and he was executed at twenty-five years of age. Of Baha's Abdul Baha says: "The Books of his Holiness number more than 100; each one sufficient for mankind." Abul Fazl[62] writes: "His Holy Tablets exceed in quantity the Heavenly Books and Divine Writings possessed by all the different nations of the earth." The number of these tablets is stated to be over 1,000. By way of contrast, Christ's teachings are said by Abdul Baha to consist of only a dozen pages scattered in the Gospels.

When they speak of the style, the eloquence, the enlightening power of Baha's writings, it is with similar superlative adjectives of high-flown Persian rhetoric.

It is hardly necessary to call attention to the fact that this so-called proof is simply a matter of assertion and opinion. As to rapidity, we could wish Baha had taken more time and made such books as the "Kitab-ul-Akdas" more systematic, for, as we have pointed out, it is sadly lacking in plan. The veriest tyro could im-

---

[57] "New Hist.," p. 112.

[58] *Ibid.*, p. 209.

[59] "Trav.'s Narr.," p. 289.

[60] "Bahai Proofs," pp. 67-68, 72.

[61] "Ighan," Chicago Edition, pp. vii-viii.

[62] "Proofs," pp. 258-259.

prove on it by rewriting.

If quantity were an argument, the product of Baha's pen has been exceeded by many Christian and Moslem divines. Besides, what advantage is it for a religion to be set forth in 100 volumes? Will God be heard for His much speaking any more than man would be? The story of redemption and God's revelation through 4,000 years makes but one goodly volume.

As to style, the Persians would scorn to have the beauty of their great poets or of such writings as the "Masnavi" put into comparison with the "Ikan" or "Akdas." The Bab's writings were not even grammatical. Baha's are more intelligible than the Bab's, but lack his originality and depth. Baha's style is rhetorical, verbose, prolix, but with a certain strength. But Mirza Abul Fazl holds a more forceful and sagacious pen. In some things Baha's writings remind one of the Church Fathers in contrast to the Gospel narratives. The quantity of his writings, his system of quotations from former Holy Books, his allegorical interpretations, recall Irenæus or Origen.

As to "verses" in general, and their rhetorical quality as a proof of divine inspiration and revelation, it would be well for Bahais to remember that the Bab recognized divine quality in the verses of Subh-i-Azal, which the Bahais reject with disdain. When the "verses" of Azal came to the Bab, he "rejoiced exceedingly,"[63] nominated him as his successor, and left to him the completion of the "Bayan." Was he mistaken in so important a matter? However that may be, the Bahais contradict him and pronounce the "verses" of Azal good for nothing. M. Ahmad Zohrab,[64] the interpreter of Abdul Baha, avers that "the writings of Azal are most childish. They are jumbled, confused, meaningless composition." Another Bahai, Nabil the poet, at one time wrote "revealed verses," and Azal approved of them and sealed their inspiration. Afterwards Nabil repudiated his own "divinity." Evidently, then, the "proof from verses" is a very uncertain and unreliable one.

(2) They claim superiority for the contents of the Revelation. In describing the substance and variety of it, their "great swelling words" know no bounds. Abdul Baha says: "They are universal, covering every subject. He has revealed scientific explanations ranging throughout all the realms of human inquiry—astronomy, biology, medicine, etc. He wrote lengthy tablets upon civilization, sociology, and government." "One book of the Blessed Perfection is more comprehensive than fifty volumes of the world's greatest wisdom." Empty boasting!

Professor Browne[65] says: "The countless tablets are for the most part rhapsodies interspersed with ethical maxims." Let us give a few of Baha's "revelations" on morals, philosophy, and science. His ethics permit bigamy and *tagiya*, dissimulation regarding one's faith; his Law punishes habitual theft by branding, and arson by burning, and compounds adultery with a small fine; his philosophy affirms the eternity of matter and the emanation theory of divine Manifestations; his science decides the purity of water by three points—"colour, taste, and smell"—but knows nothing of analysis, and affirms that "the food of the future will be

[63] "New Hist.," p. 381; "Trav.'s Narr.," pp. 353-354.
[64] *S. W.,* Nov. 4, 1913, p. 224.
[65] "Life of Abbas," by Phelps, p. xxii.

fruits and grains"; it abolished the weeks and months and substitutes nineteen months of nineteen days each, and a system of nineteen units for the decimal or metric system; it creates a new alphabet to bother childhood; its ritual for prayer, fasting, and pilgrimage somewhat resembles the Moslem, with times and places changed. These are samples of its new and superior (?) laws and precepts, which are mingled with a mass of ordinary moral teaching. There is far too much of it for a religious system, but it is entirely inadequate as a judicial and criminal code. Abul Fazl[66] grossly exaggerates when he writes that "Baha has enacted laws and regulations concerning every point or subject."

As a system Bahaism is not superlative. "It is," says Professor Browne,[67] "at most a new synthesis of old ideas; ideas with which the Eastern mind has for centuries been familiar, and which have ere now been more clearly and more logically systematized by older schools of thought, though perhaps they were without a certain tincture of modern Western terminology which is perceptible in Bahaism." "Of the doctrines of the Bab"—and the same is true of Bahaism—"taken separately, there was hardly one of which he could claim to be the author, and not many which did not remount to a remote antiquity."[68] "The theories of symbolism,[69] incarnation, and other doctrines differ in no essential particular from those held by the Ismielis." If desirable, the doctrines and laws could be traced severally, as has been done by Doctor Tisdall in his "Yanab-ul-Islam" regarding the Koran, and the source of each shown. Borrowing so much from the Shiah sects, its fundamental basis in philosophic thought is inferior even to Islam. But because it borrows so much from the enlightened principles and practices of advanced Christian peoples, its moral system is an advance on Islam. Christianity may boldly assert its unique superiority to this "half-cooked" system, to use a Persian idiom. Professor Browne[70] vetoes its claim to superiority, saying: "I do not admit that the Bahai or any other religion can supply a rule of life higher than that which Christ has given us." Discussing with the Bahais in Shiraz,[71] he said: "The religion of Mohammed was certainly not a higher development of the religion of Christ. It is impossible for any one who has understood the teachings of Christ to prefer the teachings of Mohammed. As you say each Manifestation must be fuller, completer, and more perfect than the last, you must prove that the doctrines taught by Baha are superior to those of Christ—a thing that I confess seems to be almost impossible, for I cannot imagine a doctrine purer and more elevated than that of Christ."

IV. Bahaism claims to be the Universal Religion. Dreyfus called his book on Bahaism "The Universal Religion." Remey[72] says: "The Universal Religion is what the Bahai movement offers to the world." Phelps[73] says: "It is divinely inspired world-religion in its first youth. Baha Ullah is a world-teacher in a broader

<hr>

[66] "Bahai Proofs," p. 93.
[67] Phelps, p. xvii.
[68] "New Hist.," p. xiii.
[69] *Ibid.*
[70] Phelps, p. xviii.
[71] "A Year Among the Persians," p. 307.
[72] "Bahai Movement," p. 1.
[73] "Life of Abbas," p. 148.

sense than they"—*i. e.*, the founders of other religions. This claim is not only that it is intended "for all people, under all conditions," and is adapted to all, but that it is so all-inclusive and latitudinarian that it can[74] "unite all those now following many systems into one universal faith," and that "each religious sect[75] will hear in the words of Baha its own oft-repeated message, which has been dulled and distorted."

The latter phase of this claim we may dismiss in a word. It is simply a gloss. It is an imagination of enthusiastic Bahais. Neither Christians, Moslems, nor others will be thus included, except some few before they understand Bahaism. The only inclusion it offers is by accepting the divine character and mission of Baha and Abbas;[76] in other words, by becoming Bahais. When they address the Hindu, saying, "We are one with you," "We teach the original Hinduism of your fathers," it is simply to add: "Baha is the fulfillment of your books, follow him." When they allow the Jewish Bahai of Hamadan still to consort with the Jews as a Jew, and to be baptized and pass as a Christian at the same time, it is an inclusiveness which is unjustifiable and deceitful. It is teaching *tagiya* or religious dissimulation to other races after the manner of the Persian Shiahs. It is, at most, merely a temporary subterfuge.

Let such double-faced Bahais read Remey's article in the *Star of the West*,[77] entitled "Let the New follow the New," and they will see how untenable is their position. He says: "The Bahai Cause is not merely one of many phases of universal truth (as some say), but is the only living truth to-day; the only source of divine knowledge to mankind. The revelation of Jesus was for His own dispensation— that of 'the Son.' Now it is no longer the point of guidance to the world. We are in total darkness if we are refusing the revelation of the present dispensation. Bahais must be severed from all and everything that is past—things both good and bad—everything. Now all is changed. All the teachings of the past are past. Abdul Baha is now supplying all the world." We read this, with amazement at such pretensions, such groundless assumptions, yet are pleased with the ring of sincerity. We, too, say, "Let a Bahai stand for Bahaism." Even so, let a Christian stand for Christianity, and not stultify his intellect by professing to hold to both religions. But such teachings as Remey's absolutely negative the claim of Bahaism to be able to include the professors of all religions. In conclusion, Bahaism aims at being universal just as every other "ism," even as Mormonism, by persuading the world to forsake its old faiths and adopt its new dogmas. Baha[78] states in a tablet: "Blessed is the brave one, who, with a firm step, walks out of the corridors of intimacy [the old religious restrictions] and takes a place in the ranks."

Is Bahaism fitted to be a universal religion? It has copied much from Christianity and Islam; it would not be strange if it has caught something of the same impetus towards universality. This is specially to be looked for in Bahaism, since it is historically a revision of Babism—revised with an aim to broadening

[74] Remey, *Ibid.*, p. 39.

[75] Phelps' "Abbas," p. 254.

[76] *Ibid.*, p. xxi.

[77] December 13, 1913.

[78] *S. W.*, Jan. 10, 1914, p. 282.

it. Babism was notoriously unfitted to be universal. Dreyfus[79] confesses: "Looking at the Bab's work, we cannot fail to notice in it a certain sectarian particularism which would have confined to Shiah Islam its benefits." Similarly Professor Browne pronounced it[80] "utterly unfitted for the bulk of mankind," and refers to[81] "the useless, impractical, and irksome regulations and restrictions" which Baha abolished in order to make it more capable of becoming what he intended it to be—"a universal system suitable to all mankind." The question arises, Where was the Bab's power of supernatural revelation if he promulgated a system and regulations of such inferiority and destined to be superseded in less than a score of years? Among these regulations[82] were the prohibition of the learning of foreign languages, logic, philosophy, and jurisprudence, discouraging foreign travel, enjoining the expulsion of all unbelievers from the five chief provinces of Persia, together with the confiscation of their property, the destruction of all books more than 202 years old, etc.

Baha, like a tailor trying to change a misfitting garment, ripped up the seams, cut a piece out here and there, added some patches imported from Christian civilization, until he had a coat of many colours, which he advertised as the latest style of religion, fitted to humanity in general. But he should have heeded the precept not to put new cloth on an old garment. No wonder they have never yet published the "Kitab-ul-Akdas" in English. It would tax their ingenuity to adapt all its regulations and laws to the world-life.

Again I return to the question, "Is Bahaism specially adapted to be universal?" By no means. It is unfitted in the most essential particular. It is a religion of laws, not of principles. Mirza Abul Fazl, in "The Brilliant Proof,"[83] emphasizes the fact that Bahaism enjoins, commands, has imperative ordinances, laws, and enactments. But the Gospels enunciate principles. These principles of the New Testament are conscience-educating and life-directing. They are applicable to all conditions the world over, and to every stage of human development. Christianity implants in the heart great ruling motives. Its laws and regulations are few. Hence it does not find itself butting against a wall of unforeseen circumstances. Bahaism, on the contrary, is full of the "beggarly elements." It has regulations, as we have noticed, in regard to personal habits, hygiene, sociology, languages, the calendar, civil government, penology, etc. It is like an omnibus with its top overloaded with all sorts of baggage, which will delay and finally wreck the vehicle. It has made itself a "judge and divider of inheritances."[84] It gives directions as to the barber and the undertaker; how you must bathe and wash your face, and what prayers you shall say during each process. It directs as to the use of knives and forks, of chairs, of perfumes. It graciously permits one to shave his beard, but "the hair must not be allowed to grow below the level of the ear." It tells us that "the nails are to be cut at least once a week," that "every one should wash his feet daily in summer,

---

[79] "The Universal Religion," p. 43.
[80] "New Hist.," p. xiii.
[81] *Ibid.*, p. xxv.
[82] *Ibid.*, p. xxvi.
[83] Pages 31-32.
[84] Luke xii. 14.

and at least every three days in winter." And alas! for antique furniture and old Persian rugs! For house furnishings must be changed every nineteen years. In obedience to this command my old teacher in Persia got rid of his rugs, whose sheen was polished and colours were mellowed with age, and refurnished his house with gaudy modern rugs. In prescribing the Moslem fast and namaz (prayer-rite), with some modifications, Bahaism limits the spirit of liberty, which is the essence of universality.

Copying from the Bab, Baha has seen fit to regulate the calendar. Following the Zoroastrian custom, Baha ordains that the year begin at the vernal equinox—March 21—because that is the spring-time, the time of the renewal of vegetable life. Good! But in Australia it is the time of death—of the approach of winter. The reason assigned is not universal, and is not adapted to all climes. As has been said above, the months are ordained to be nineteen of nineteen days each, with four or five intercalary days in March. The week is abolished, that primitive division of time which has such a definite place in nature, in the phases of the moon, and is established in the three great monotheistic religions with their weekly Sabbaths. Instead of the latter is substituted the nineteenth day Unity feast. How do such changes aid universality or unification? Coinage, fines, taxes, and tithes are arranged on the number 19. Remey's book has nineteen chapters, as the "Bayan" has. *The Star of the West*, a magazine of the American Bahais, is published every nineteen days, and bears the Bahai calendar on its editorial page. Instances might be indefinitely extended. But later the number nine, the number of Baha, has come more into use. Abbas has set apart the ninth day of the month as well as the nineteenth for certain religious purposes. The Bahai era is sometimes dated from the declaration of the Bab in 1844, and sometimes from the birth of Baha in 1817. Are these innovations more an aid to universality than adherence to the established calendar and era, or than the decimal system or the metric system which the civilized world has been striving to extend? Professor Browne says: "What could be more impractical than the adoption of the number nineteen as the basis of measures or calculations?" It bears the mark of Oriental fancy rather than of divine revelation.

Another illustration of this point—namely, that Bahaism enjoins and regulates specifically, and does not, like Christianity, inculcate guiding principles, is seen in the law regarding civil government. In "Glad Tidings"[85] Baha teaches, as from God, that "although a republican form of government profits, yet the majesty of kingship is one of the signs of God. We do not wish that the countries of the world should be deprived thereof." "Statesmen should combine the two," and[86] "At present the form of government followed by the British nation seems good, for that nation is illuminated both with the light of kingship and consultation—*i. e.*, parliament." "In the principal Laws [of Bahaism] affairs have been placed in the hands of just kings and chiefs, and the House of Justice." As a matter of opinion, I can join with Baha in expressing my admiration for the British Constitution, but prescribing it as a law of revelation is a different matter. A "universal religion" should be adapted to all conditions. It is a fact of history that when the tablet "Glad

[85] Section 15, p. 91, Chicago Edition.
[86] "Tablet of the World," p. 33.

Tidings" was sent to Russia, section 15 was omitted. The Bahais suppressed this portion from expediency, and it appears thus mutilated in Baron Rosen's translation.[87] Is not this a high-handed way to deal with God's Word, as they profess to regard it? Is it not also conceivable that republics might take offense against Bahaism because it maintains monarchy, even as autocracies because it approves of parliamentary government? Had not a "universal religion" better let politics alone? Christianity could adapt itself even to the government of a Nero.

Another institution of Bahaism, ill-adapted to all races and conditions, and certain to bring the very conflict and strife against which it is supposed to guard, is the House of Justice. This is a religious court, with civil and political functions, to be set up in every town and country. It is to be composed of nine or more Bahai men. "They are divine agents, representatives of God." Much is said of this House of Justice in the Books of Revelation.[88] Dreyfus devotes a chapter to it.[89] It is to have legislative, judicial, and administrative functions. It will regulate estates, taxes, tithes, fines, capital and labour, marriage, divorce, inheritances, minors, servants, charities, reforms, houses of correction, schools, besides all matters of religion and morals. They will rule "absolutely," and be "infallible," "guided by God." It is the old dream of theocratic rule. I must leave it to the imagination of the student of history to picture the dire confusion which would ensue if this politico-religious hierarchy should begin its sway. Those who are familiar with the perpetual conflict between the urfi and the shari, the civil and the religious law in Persia, know how this proposed organization would work confusion worse confounded.

Similar to these invasions of the province of science and Cæsar is the attempt to improve philology by "revelation." Following the Bab again, Baha Ullah promulgated a new alphabet. The Babi alphabet, unlike the Arabic and Persian, was written from left to right. "Each letter consists of thick, oblique straight lines, parallel and equidistant from each other, running down to the left, to which thin hooks and curves are appended to make separate letters." It is called the Khatti-Badi. There were nineteen kinds of it; one kind was called the Khatti-Baha. It was intended for the time when Babism would be prevalent. It appears that Bahais have a new alphabet, different from that of the Babis.

In the Akdas and in the sixth Ishrak[90] it is commanded that the "House of Justice" must select one tongue out of the present languages, or a new language, to teach the children in the schools of the world. Let us suppose they decide on Persian or Arabic. The Anglo-Saxon children must all begin to learn Arabic. Suppose they decide on English. Then Germans, French, and Russians will have an additional reason for opposing the religion. Suppose that Abdul Baha decides on Esperanto, as he seems inclined to do, then will it be heresy for some one to invent a language as much superior to Esperanto as it is to Volapuk? Had not a "universal religion" better let linguistics alone? The spirit of Christianity gives a free field to

[87] "New Hist.," p. xxv.

[88] See "Glad Tidings," pp. 39, 90; "Words of Paradise," p. 53; "Tablet of the World," p. 33; "Israket," p. 37; and "Kitab-ul-Akdas."

[89] "Universal Religion," pp. 131-144.

[90] "Ishrakat," p. 36.

all tongues—this is the essence of liberty, of universality. After this brief review of some of the provisions of the "New Revelation," we can deny the claim that "its statutes meet the necessity of every land," and that they can serve the world well for 1,000 years.

III

ITS SPECIFIC CLAIMS

Unification of Mankind—Divisions in Persia—Of Bahais—Compulsory uniformity—One Language—Peace Movement—History of—Abdul Baha on war—Bahaism dogmatic and boastful.

> Bahaism is a Persian delusion, whose headman Baha Ullah in Acre claimed to be an incarnation of God. Abbas Effendi succeeded him and is running the "incarnation" fraud for all it is worth, and it is worth a good deal, as pilgrims constantly come from Persia and bring their offerings in money with great liberality. Such men ... as the Babites of Persia turn up now and then in the East, "go up like a rocket and down like a stick."—*H. H. Jessup, "Fifty-three Tears in Syria," p. 637.*

> I cannot understand how a Christian can possibly exchange the clear consistent plan of salvation through Christ for the misty and mystical platitudes of Bahaism.—*Ibid., p. 687.*

BAHAISM makes various claims of a practical nature. Some of these will require detailed treatment. Several of them I will group in this chapter. Additional light is thrown on the question of their validity by facts subsequently brought forward, for many facts have a bearing on several subjects.

Among the specific claims put forth by Bahaism is that of being *specially adapted to promote the unification of mankind,* and of accomplishing that end. Bahaism reiterates the Christian ideas that God hath made of one blood all nations and that all shall be united in God's spiritual kingdom. It repeats as a slogan, "the brotherhood of man." C. M. Remey[91] says: "The Bahai cause stands for the unity of all religions, political unity of nations, the social unity of all classes, peoples and races." "Its aim," says Harold Johnson, "is to knit all the faiths and all the peoples into one."[92] "The essential principle of the teachings of Bahaism is the unification of the religious systems of the world," says MacNutt.[93] This is a high ideal, which interpreted in their several ways is the aim of Christianity, Islam, Socialism, etc. And Bahai writers mean what all the other systems have meant, namely, unity by all

---

[91] "The Bahai Movement," p. 73.
[92] *Contemporary Review*, March, 1912.
[93] In "Unity Through Love."

accepting their beliefs, for Remey[94] says: "Baha Ullah's mission is to unite those now following many systems into one brotherhood and one universal faith.... May God speed the day when all of us may become true *Bahais*."

But the claim of Bahaism is presented in another form. It asserts that it is actually bringing about this unification. "Abdul Baha is harmonizing Christians, Jews, Mohammedans, Zoroastrians, Buddhists, Hindus in the one and true faith."[95] Dreyfus says: "It is uniting all men in the great universal religion of the future." At Oakland, Cal.,[96] Abdul Baha said, "The revelation of Baha Ullah is the cause of the oneness of the world of humanity. It is a unity which welds together all the races." In illustration of this alleged result, the pilgrims to Acca express their gratification and amazement that at Acca several races meet together in love and unity. So in Rangoon, says Mr. Sprague,[97] "I attended a Bahai meeting at which six of the great world religions were represented united in the wonderful bond of friendship and unity." In like manner Mr. Harold Johnson says, "What Christianity has failed to accomplish, Bahaism has accomplished in uniting men of different races and religions." If these assertions mean external association, it may be said that Christians have had their Parliaments of Religions and Congresses of all faiths, examples of polite toleration and laboratories of the science of religion. If it means that Christianity refuses to put itself on a level with other religions and consort with them as equals, this is true, for Christianity is an exclusive religion. It has entered the world, as it entered the Roman empire, to displace all others. It refuses to have Christ occupy a niche in the Pantheon. But Bahai writers mean rather that Bahaism is to be the bond of unity by all races and religions accepting Baha. In this sense their claim is based on very meagre premises. A few thousand only, outside of Persia, have embraced Bahaism. Harold Johnson says: "The Non-Mohammedans do not number probably very many thousands." But do we not see myriads gathering into the Christian brotherhood out of every race and religion of Asia, including even thousands from Islam. Thirty thousand Moslems have become Christians in Malayasia in Abdul Baha's lifetime. In Asia how many races and religions, forgetting their former antagonisms, are united in the faith and baptism of the Lord Jesus Christ. As an example of the living power of the Christian faith to unite the races of men, take the Conference of the International Christian Students' Federation, held at Lake Mohonk, N. Y. There Hindus and British, Japanese and Koreans, Russians and Chinese, Greeks and Armenians, French and Germans, Canadians and Brazilians, Americans and Mexicans represented the wide world. Mutual esteem, love and spiritual fellowship united members of the various Protestant Churches with representatives of the Oriental Churches. The unity in Bahai Assemblies is on so small a scale as to be not worthy of mention. How little Abdul Baha knows of or appreciates the reality and power of Christian spiritual fellowship is shown in his remarks at West Englewood, N. Y.[98] "This gathering (of Bahais) has no peer or likeness upon the surface of the earth, for all other gatherings and assemblages

---

[94] "The Bahai Movement," p. 39.

[95] *Ibid.*, p. 27.

[96] *S. W.*, Oct. 1912, p. 190.

[97] "Story of the Bahai Movement," p. 4.

[98] June 29, 1912.

are due to some physical basis or material interests. Bahai meetings are mirrors of the kingdom." When Abdul Baha speaks about the results of Bahaism in bringing about unification in Persia, his claims seem utterly extravagant. To one who knows that country from long residence they are explicable only on the supposition that he has been misinformed or deceived by his own followers, for it must be borne in mind that Abdul Baha left Persia when a child of six or eight and has never returned. Hear these words which Abdul Baha addressed to Rev. J. T. Bixley, who was writing on the Sect in the *North American Review*: "The fundamental question is the unification of religious belief. In Persia, during the last fifty years[99] ... the various religionists have united in the utmost love and fellowship. No traces of discord or difference remain: the utmost love, kindness and unity are apparent. They live together like a single family in harmony and accord. Discord and strife have passed away. Love and fellowship now prevail instead. Whether they be Moslems, Jews, Christians, Zoroastrians, Buddhists, Nestorians, Shiites, Sunnis or others—no discord exists among them." In an address at New York,[100] he said:

"In the Orient different races were at constant warfare until about sixty years ago Baha Ullah appeared and caused love and unity to exist among these various peoples. Their former animosities have passed away entirely. It was a dark world, it became radiant.... You now see the same people who were formerly at enmity and strife in far-off Persia, people of various religions and denominations living in the utmost peace." "His Highness, Baha Ullah, established such unity and peace between the various communities." What does such language mean? At their face value these words are erroneous in a high degree. All know indeed that in Persia bigotry and religious and racial hatred have been modified. In bringing this result about, Bahaism has had a share along with Western civilization and education, the Nationalist movement, medical missions, and even Pan-Islamism, for the latter has tended to bring Shiahs and Sunnis nearer to each other. But it is notorious how great the enmity and hatred is yet; how the Kurds have raided the Shiahs and massacred or plundered the Nestorians and the Armenians: how the Moslems oppress the Armenians in Karadagh: how Sheikhis have suffered from Mutasharis; and Ali Allahis continued the practice of tagiya for fear of them both. If Parsees enjoy more ease, it is through the efforts of their co-religionists in India; if Christians are safer, it is through the favour of the Shahs and the power of Christian governments: in neither case is it due to Bahaism. The union with the Bahais of possibly a dozen Armenians, a few score Zoroastrians and several hundred Jews cannot be the basis for such extravagance of language: neither can the rejection by Baha of the Shiah notion that other religions are "unclean," for Sunnis all along held the "peoples of the Book" to be "clean" and Christians of old learned to "call no man common or unclean."

As to unification, how is it? Babis were divided off from Sheikhis, and Baha-is from Babis, and Behais from Bahais and the flames of hate and vindictiveness burn hotter between them than between the older sects and races, while the Shiahs curse and at times persecute Babis and Bahais. Instead of unity the Babi-Bahais have brought a greater division of sects: instead of love renewed fires of animosity

[99] *S. W.*, Sept. 27, 1912.
[100] *S. W.*, Sept. 8, 1912.

and fanatical hate. In view of these conditions, how unreasonable for Abdul Baha to say that "through the power of Baha Ullah, such affection and love is produced among the various religions of Persia that they now associate[101] with each other in the utmost love and concord."

Passing now to another phase of this subject, let us inquire what means are prescribed for religious unification. The chief means seems to be the forbidding of the right of private interpretation or opinion. Abdul Baha writes[102] that he is "the Interpreter of all the works and books of the Blessed Perfection. Were this not the case, every one would give an interpretation according to his own inclination—this would lead to great differences." This point is more plainly stated by M. Abul Fazl:[103] "One of the explicit commands of Baha Ullah is the ordinance abrogating differences which separate men.... If those having two points of view, engage in strife in expressing their views, both will be delivered to the fire.... Bahai law prohibits the interpretation of God's word and exposition of personal opinion ... lest different sects arise." "You must ask him (Abdul Baha) regarding the meaning of the texts of the verses. Whatsoever he says is correct. Without his will, not a word shall any one utter."[104] Baha Ullah "made provision against all kinds of differences, so that no man shall be able to create a new sect ... indicating the Interpreter so that no man should be able to say that he explains a certain teaching in this way and thus create a new sect."[105] After Abdul Baha whenever the House of Justice is organized, it will ward off differences. But though the right of private judgment was denied, yet a new sect arose and bitter disunion occurred over the question of the Infallible Interpreter.

Another Bahai scheme to promote unity is the adoption of one language to be a universal language; another is the amalgamation of all the races by the marriage of blacks and whites, and all indiscriminately; another is the discouragement of patriotism or any special love for one's country or people, teaching an internationalism in the words, "Let not him glory who loves his country, but let him glory who loves his kind." These points need not detain us, nor need we stop to enlarge on the fact that the new calendar, feasts, rites, laws, weights and measures, etc., tend to disunion.

The claims of Bahaism in regard to its relation to the movement for peace and arbitration require consideration. Abdul Baha at Boston[106] said: "Baha Ullah spread the teaching of Universal Peace sixty years ago, when it was *not even thought of* by the people. He sent tablets to kings advising this." He wrote to Mr. Smiley of

---

[101] Professor Browne, in the Ency. of Ethics and Religion, article "Bab," writes: "The Bahais are strongly antagonistic alike to the Sufis and the Mohammedans, but for quite different reasons. In the case of the Sufis they object to their latitudinarianism, their Pantheism, their individualism and their doctrine of the inner light. With the Mohammedan they resent the persecutions they have suffered. The Bahais detest the Azalis, the followers of Abbas Effendi dislike and despise the followers of his brother Mehemet Ali."

[102] *S. W.,* Aug. 20, 1914.
[103] "Brilliant Proof," pp. 26-28.
[104] *S. W.,* Nov. 23, 1913, p. 238.
[105] *S. W.,* April 9, 1914.
[106] *S. W,,* July 13, 1913, p. 122.

Lake Mohonk, "The matter of International Peace was instituted by His Highness, Baha Ullah, sixty years ago in Persia." Dreyfus[107] says: "Long before these ideas, i. e., peace, brotherhood and arbitration, had taken form among us, at a time when the Bab himself had sometimes excused the use of arms for the propagation of religion, Baha Ullah had made these high principles the one basis of his religion." Remey[108] states this claim yet more strongly, saying: "Peace, arbitration, in fact universal civilization *were unthought of*, when over half a century ago these teachers (Baha Ullah and Abdul Baha) announced their message." Again, "Christ states that His dispensation is to be a militant one, which would be followed by another of peace. Baha Ullah has now brought that peace to the world. He is the Prince of Peace who has established the foundations of peace on earth."[109]

Now as to the facts. Bahaism certainly does advocate peace and arbitration, in common with Tolstoism, socialism and many schools of thought. Baha said to Professor Browne at Acca, in 1886: "This fruitless strife, these ruinous wars shall pass away and the Most Great Peace shall come. These strifes and this bloodshed and discord must cease and all men be as one kindred and one family." In accordance with this, Abdul Baha declares[110] universal peace and an international Court of Arbitration to be fundamental principles of Bahaism. The Court will be called the House of Justice and will be composed entirely of Bahais. "Disputes will find a final sentence of absolute justice ... before the Bahai House of Justice. War will be suppressed."[111]

It is good to have such a programme approved by one raised in a Moslem environment. Yet it is evident that the claim to priority and originality regarding it, constitute a grave anachronism and betray ignorance of or perversion of history. Both the ideals and the programme were in existence and in partial operation long before the time of Baha Ullah. In the first place, Bahai teachings on peace are but an echo of Christian hopes and doctrines of "peace on earth: good will to men." Baha has but thrown on the screen again the vision of the seers of Israel who foretold the age when "men shall learn war no more." The hopes of the prophets, the longings of saints, the anthems of the worshipping church found voice through the Christian centuries, with a faith never dimmed, a desire never quenched, anticipating that

> "Then shall wars and tumults cease,
> Then be banished grief and pain,
> Righteousness and joy and peace
> Undisturbed shall ever reign."

Baha's teaching, though growing up in Islam, is transplanted from Christian soil. He repudiates the teaching of Mohammed regarding "holy wars." "The first Glad Tidings is the abolition of religious warfare from the Book," *i. e.*, the Koran.

---

[107] "The Universal Religion."

[108] "Bahai Movement," p. 75.

[109] Page 54. In Dealy's "Dawn of Knowledge," the chapter on Baha Ullah is entitled "Prince of Peace."

[110] *S. W.*, Vol. IV, pp. 6, 8 and 254.

[111] "Answered Questions," p. 74; "Tablet of the World," p. 28.

What Bahais would do in case of provocation, accompanied by reasonable opportunity of success, is not evident. The Babis were fierce warriors (1848-1850) and the Bab expected that wars would continue. In the "Bayan" he makes provision for the distribution of the spoils.[112] Baha, together with Azal, started for and tried to join the army at Tabarsi,[113] and was absent from participation in its sanguinary conflict, solely because his arrest by the Persian authorities at Amul prevented him from reaching the fort. After his release he fell under suspicion because[114] he "not improbably harboured designs of setting up a standard of revolt on his own account." He was, therefore, rearrested and sent to the capital. But during his exile in Turkey, he tried to be reconciled to the Shah of Persia. Following this change of policy, he was able to claim later[115] that "for nigh upon thirty-five years no action opposed to the government or prejudicial to the nation has emanated from this sect." The Bahais did not join in the effort to establish constitutional government in 1908-1911.[116] They have never had an even chance to fight for their own cause and it remains to be seen what they would do in such a case. There is no assurance that they would act like Quakers or Dukhobors, for even Abdul Baha at times identifies himself and his cause with the fighting Babis and appropriates their martial glory. He said to Mr. Anton Hadad:[117] "When in Persia we were very few but owing to animosity we stood before our numerous enemies, fought and defeated them and gained the victory." He wrote a prayer on behalf of the American army for the use of Bahais: "O God! Strengthen its soldiers and its flag."[118] In his teachings, he leaves several prts for the prosecution of war. He says:[119] "War is sometimes the foundation of peace. If, for example, a sovereign should wage war against a threatening foe or for the unification of the people, this war may be attuned to peace: this fury is kindness; this war is a source of reconciliation." In his scheme for arbitration, one is reminded of the old saw, "we must have peace even if we have to fight for it." For he says: "If any nation dares to refuse to abide by the decision of the international court, all the other nations must arise and put down this rebellion, ... they must rise up and *destroy it*, ... band together and *exterminate it*."[120]

As to the claim that Baha *originated* the movement for universal peace and international arbitration, it only deserves consideration because it is apparently put forth in sincerity. It absolutely contradicts history. In fact the movement for "peace on earth" has long been an active one in Christian lands, and arbitration has long been recognized and employed as a method for promoting peace." "Under the influence of religious and feudal ideas," says Professor Moore,[121] "arbitrations were very frequent in the Middle Ages, which offered the remarkable spectacle of conciliation and peace making way." Treaties were made which provided for

[112] "Trav.'s Narr.," p. 287.
[113] "New Hist.," pp. 378, 379.
[114] *Ibid.*, p. 380.
[115] "Trav.'s Narr.," pp. 65-67.
[116] See Chapter VI.
[117] "A Message from Acca," p. 9.
[118] Tablet "9," p. 8, published by the New York Bahai Council.
[119] "Principles of the Bahai Movement," pp. 43, 47, Washington, 1912.
[120] *Ibid.*, pp. 43, 45.
[121] "International Arbitrations," pp. 4826-4833.

arbitration. In Italy there were one hundred arbitrations in the thirteenth century. In the following centuries they were frequent in Europe. Sometimes a king acted as arbitrator between kings or between king and people. At other times a city, as for example the Republic of Hamburg, or a great juristconsult or a Professor of a University acted in this capacity. More often "the predominance of the popes constituted them natural judges of international cases." Projects for universal peace were put forward. One of the most celebrated was formed by Sully, the minister of Henry IV. The Abbe de St. Pierre in 1713 published a scheme for the federation of Christian States, with a central council to decide all disputes. Grotius strongly advocated arbitration as a means of avoiding war and the placing of nations under obligations to settle disputes peaceably. Bentham in the eighteenth century proposed a plan for a common tribunal to maintain universal and permanent peace.[122] Fox, Penn and the Quakers, from Christian principles, strenuously opposed war. There were nine principal arbitrations between the United States and Great Britain, France and Spain from 1794 to 1863.

In 1815, before Baha's day, the Massachusetts Peace Society was formed and in the following year the American Peace Society "to promote universal permanent peace through arbitration and disarmament."[123] For this purpose World Congresses were held at London 1843, Brussels 1848, Paris 1849, Frankfort 1850, London 1851, etc., and with great enthusiasm. Men like Elihu Burritt, Victor Hugo, Richard Cobden, John Bright and Charles Sumner led in advocacy of the cause. Tennyson, too, saw the vision of peace,

> "In the Parliament of men, the Federation of the World,"

and the Scottish bard declared,

> "It's coming yet for a' that
> When man to man, the world o'er,
> Shall brothers be and a' that."

We can easily conceive how these ideas would penetrate the Near East and how Baha Ullah in Turkey caught an echo of them and was happily influenced to become himself an advocate of peace.

But what becomes of the claims of Abdul Baha and other Bahais, mentioned above, that Baha, in 1863-1867, "*instituted* the movement for peace and arbitration" that he advised it to kings "when it had not even been thought of," "before the attention of Western thinkers had to any degree been directed towards universal peace." They are like so many claims made by Bahaists, utterly groundless. Such statements, when made by Abdul Baha, we may attribute to ignorance of the history of the Occident, but this does not excuse American advocates of Bahaism for endorsing such errors.

I need not discuss the assertion of Bahais that the Millennium began in 1844[124] or at latest in 1892, nor the announcement that the Most Great Peace will be inaugurated in 1917, which they declare to be the end of the 1335 days of Dan. xii.

[122] New International Ency., Art. "Arbitration," p. 713.
[123] *Atlantic Monthly*, Vol. XCIV, p. 358.
[124] *S. W.*, March 21, 1914, p. 8.

12.[125]

Another claim made for Bahaism is that it is a rational and undogmatic religion. Remey[126] says: "It does not put forth doctrine or dogma.... It is a religion free from dogma." It is "logical and reasonable." Dreyfus denounces "dogmatic religions," and claims that Bahaism has paved the way for the harmony of religion with free thought."[127] With these accord the words of Abdul Baha to Pastor Monnier in Paris.[128] "Our aim is to free religion from dogmas. Dogmas are the cause of strife. We must give up dogmas." Now it is evident that Bahaism has not a fixed body of doctrines: that it has not a definite and clear system of theology. But it is very dogmatic in the common usages of that word. Webster defines it as (1) positive, authoritative, and (2) as asserting or disposed to assert with authority or with overbearing and arrogance. Is not Bahaism a mass of assertions? For example, Baha declares that "the universe hath neither beginning nor ending." Abdul Baha adds the comment:[129] "*By this simple statement* he has set aside elaborate theories and exhaustive labours of scientists and philosophers." Similarly he is said to have settled by a single word all discussions about divine sovereignty and free agency. Abdul Baha might be called the Lord of dogmas, for from his dicta none must vary by a hair's breadth. Remey himself dogmatizes as follows: "The religion of Baha is the cause of God, outside of which there is no truth in the world." Much in Bahaism must be taken on faith, without logical proof. Professor Browne[130] puts it mildly when he says: "The system appears to me to contain enough of the mysterious and the transcendental to make its intellectual acceptance at least as difficult as the theology of most Christian churches to the sceptic." Elsewhere he says:[131] "It must be clearly understood that Babism (or Bahaism) is in no sense latitudinarian or eclectic, and stands therefore in the sharpest antagonism to Sufism. However vague Babi doctrine may be on certain points, it is essentially *dogmatic*, and every utterance or command uttered by the Manifestation of the Period, *i. e.*, Bab or Baha Ullah or Abbas Effendi must be accepted without reserve."[132] Similarly Dr. G. W. Holmes[133] writes: "Baha's appeal is only to his own word and to his own arbitrary and forced interpretation of the Word of God, which interpretations, as he states, find their sanction solely in his own authority."

There are other claims of Bahaism of a specific nature which might be considered. They would be found equally assertive and equally groundless. Bahaism reminds me of a horse which was offered for sale in Persia. It appeared like a fat and well fed animal. But the would-be purchaser was warned that its skin had been puffed up with air which would soon leak out, and he would have on his hands a lean, lank, bony *yabi* scrub. Bahaism does not even stop short of claiming that

[125] Dealy's "Dawn of Knowledge," p. 44; Kheiralla's "Beha Ullah," pp. 480, 483.

[126] Tract "Peace," pp. 8 and 14; "Bahai Movement," p. 89.

[127] "The Universal Religion," pp. 21, 44.

[128] *S. W.*, April 28, 1913, p. 55.

[129] *S. W.*, June 5, 1913, p. 90.

[130] Phelps, p. xviii.

[131] Ency. of Religion and Ethics, Art. "Bab."

[132] See also his "Literary History of Persia," p. 422.

[133] "Missions and Modern History," by Robert E. Speer, p. 171.

the civilization of the nineteenth and twentieth centuries is due to it. Its braggart attitude may be fittingly symbolized by Rostand's "Chanticler," standing in the barnyard, flapping its wings in vain exultation, imagining that it, by its crowing, has caused the sun to rise.

IV

BAHAISM AND CHRISTIANITY

Antagonistic—Makes Christianity one among many—Abrogates it—
Dethrones Christ—Presumes to be Christ's Second Coming—And
the fulfillment of prophecy—Bahai meeting in Chicago—Method
of interpretation—The "Ikan"—Dishonours and belittles the historic Christ.

The whole Bahai movement is in fact, whatever it may have
been in the mind of its originator the Bab, a counterfeit of the
Messiahship of Christ. At least this is the side of it that is turned
towards both Christians and Jews. All that relates to the second
coming of Christ in the Old Testament or the New is bodily appropriated by Baha to himself and everything in them relating to
God is boldly applied to himself.... It will bring a few of the Persians nearer to Christ. By far the greater number of its adherents
will be brought into more active antagonism to Christianity than
before.—*G. W. Holmes, M. D., in Speer's "Missions and Modern History," Vol. I, p. 169.*

Can Bahaism make good its claim to be the fulfillment of and
substitute for Christianity? It has no place for Christ except as one
of a series, one, moreover, whose brief day of authority closed
when Mohammed began to preach in Mecca.... If the claim be admitted that Bahaism is a republication of Christianity, the whole
interpretation of the death of Christ contained in the Epistles must
first be rejected.—*W. A. Shedd, in "Miss. Rev. of World," 1911.*

ABDUL BAHA says: "Some say Abdul Baha is Antichrist. They are not informed of Bahai principles. Baha Ullah[134] established Christ in the East. He has
praised Christ, honoured Christ, exalted Him, called Him the Word of God, the
Spirit of God, and spread His mention."[135] These words could be written with the
name Mohammed substituted for Baha Ullah. But in the case of both of them it
is the kiss of betrayal. Judas also made known Jesus. Both Mohammed and Baha

[134] In an interview with Rev. J. T. Bixby, who wrote on Bahaism in the *North American
Review*, June, 1912, Abdul Baha says: "Baha Ullah has upraised the standard of Christ in
the East in countries and among peoples where there was formerly no mention of Christ's
name." Not true. Christ was known in Moslem lands, in India and Burmah.

[135] *S. W.*, Sept. 8, 1913, p. 176.

write "ex" before His title "King of Kings." To accept Baha and Abdul Baha is to deny and forsake Christ.

I hear some Christian say: "Of course. What you say is self-evident. Bahaism is a new religion whose aim is to supplant Christianity." This is true. Yet *the claim* is put forth by Bahais, and, more strangely, it is accepted by some Christians, *that the two religions are not antagonistic, and may be held at one time by the same person.* To an esteemed Christian lady I expressed my regret that a certain doctor, forsaking Christ, had gone as a Bahai missionary to Persia. The reply startled me: "Doctor— —is very much a Christian." Yet why was I startled? It was simply hearing an idea with which I was familiar in the writings of the Bahais. Sydney Sprague says: "The true Bahai is also the truest Christian."[136] Charles M. Remey says: "To be a real Christian in spirit is to be a Bahai, and to be a real Bahai is to be a Christian," for "Bahai teaching is only the perfection of Christianity."[137] A report of an interview of Rev. R. J. Campbell, of City Temple, London, with Abdul Baha, states the claim of Bahaism as follows: "It does not seek to proselyte. One can be a Bahai without ceasing to be a Christian, a Jew, or a Mohammedan."[138] In accordance with this idea, Thornton Chase and some Bahais in America continued to worship and teach in Christian churches, and to have their dead buried by pastors. Some in London, in connection with the City Temple and St. John's Church (Canon Wilberforce's), profess both Christianity and Bahaism. Of Southern India, Dr. A. L. Wylie said: "It is said that there are thirty-five Bahais in our city [Ratnagiri]. Some of these are Christian converts. They continue to be Christians, saying that they can remain such and are instructed to do so." Such an erroneous idea, when not due to the misrepresentations of the leaders and Oriental *tagiya* ("dissimulation"), must arise from ignorance of or dislike to true Christianity or ignorance of what Bahaism is.

I. Bahaism assigns Christianity a place as but one among the true religions. Bahaism indorses and accepts in the same category with Judaism and Christianity, as true and divinely revealed religions, Zoroastrianism, Confucianism, Brahmanism, Buddhism, Mohammedanism, Babism, and Bahaism. Abdul Baha says: "The reality of the religions is one, the difference is one of imitation."[139] Remey says: "Bahais consider all religions to be, from a spiritual standpoint, one religion."[140] "Every religion has had its birth in the advent of its divine founder."[141] "The founders of the world religions have been seers as well as channels of truth to the people."[142] It tries to build on all the other religions by professing to be the fulfillment of each one. "The Bahai propaganda in India," says Sprague, "has not the difficulty that besets a Christian missionary, that of pulling down: his duty is only to build on what is already there. He sees the Hindu, Buddhist, and Mohammedan with the same eye, acknowledges their truth and shows that a further revelation has

<hr>

[136] Sprague, "Story of the Bahai Movement," p. 21.
[137] Remey, "The Bahai Movement," p. 45.
[138] *The Christian Commonwealth* (London), Sept. 13, 1911, p. 850.
[139] "Wisdom Talks," p. 21.
[140] Remey, "The Bahai Movement," p. 54.
[141] *Ibid.*, p. 39.
[142] *Ibid.*, p. 2.

come through Baha Ullah."[143] It says to each one, Baha fulfills your traditions and prophecies.[144]

But this liberality is only apparent. Only original Buddhism, Christianity, etc., was God-given and true. Now all are corrupted. "The key-note of Bahai teaching is identical with the Christian, but in Christianity it was so forgotten that it came almost as a fresh, new illumination from Baha."[145]

Christianity refuses to be classed with the ethnic religions. In its nature it is exclusive. It admits that there is a measure of truth in all religions, but Christ's gospel is the truth "once for all" delivered to men.

II. Bahaism claims to abrogate and supersede Christianity. Bahaism in its origin is a Mohammedan sect. It declares that Islam is from God. Christianity was a divine revelation, but Islam was a better one. In the "Ikan," Baha maintains the validity of Islam, testifies to its truth, defends Mohammed's prophetic mission as the fulfillment of the New Testament prophecies, and the Koran as the Book of God.[146] Abdul Baha exalts Mohammed, and declares that he "gave more spiritual education than any of the others,"[147] *i. e.*, than Moses or Jesus. He justifies Mohammed's life and conduct, and defends his laws and doctrines."[148] He declares that "whatever European and American historians have written regarding His Highness Mohammed, the Messenger of God, is mostly falsehood.... The narrators are either ignorant or antagonistic."[149] Christians have therefore been in the wrong for thirteen centuries. They have sinned against God, and were a stiff-necked and perverse people in rejecting Mohammed, as the Jews were in rejecting Jesus the Christ. "If those who have accepted a revelation refuse to believe a subsequent revelation, their faith becomes null and void."

Similarly Babism abrogated Islam. At the Badasht (Shahrud) Conference (1848) the law of the Koran was formally declared to be annulled. Baha abrogated Babism in the Rizwan at Bagdad in 1864. Bahaism is the New Covenant, "which confirms and completes all religious teaching which has gone before."[150]

Christianity is, according to this, a system of the distant past. It was effective in its day, for "the Christian teaching *was* illumined by the Sun of Truth: the Christian civilization *was* the best,"[151] concedes Abdul Baha. But now, says Remey, "Bahaism is not one of many phases of Universal Truth, but *the Truth*, the only Living Truth to-day, ... the only source of Divine Knowledge to mankind.... Abdul Baha's word is the Truth.... There are those who will say, 'Have we not Jesus? We want no other.' The Revelation of Jesus is no longer the Point of Guidance to the world. We are in total blindness if we refuse this new Revelation which is the end of the

---

[143] "The Story of the Bahai Movement," p. 17.
[144] So of Persia, *S. W.*, April 28, 1914, p. 42.
[145] C. E. Maud, *Fortnightly Review*, April, 1912.
[146] Pages 68-158.
[147] "Table Talks with Abdul Baha," Dec. 2, 1900.
[148] "Answered Questions," pp. 22-29.
[149] *S. W.*, Dec. 12, 1911, p. 7.
[150] Remey, "Tract on the Bahai Movement," p. 8.
[151] "Talks in Paris," p. 20.

Revelations of the past.... All the teachings of the past are past.... Only that which is revealed by the Supreme Pen, Baha Ullah, and that which issues from the Centre of the Covenant, Abdul Baha, is spiritual food."[152] Bahaism in proclaiming thus the abrogation of Christianity is emphatically antichristian.

III. Bahaism casts Christ from His throne as the unique manifestation of God. Bahaism recognizes two classes of prophets: (1) The independent prophets, who were lawgivers and founders of new cycles. Of this class were Abraham, Moses, Christ, Mohammed, the Bab, and Baha. (2) The others are dependent prophets, who are as "branches." Such were Isaiah and Daniel. All the greater prophets, of the first class, were Manifestations of God.[153] So Bahaism continues to honour Christ as the Incarnate Word, the Spirit of God, God manifest in the flesh. At the same time it exalts Baha to supreme and unique dignity and glory above Christ and all prophets. In order to understand this essential, fundamental doctrine of Bahaism, we must know its doctrine concerning God and His Manifestation.

The teaching of Bahaism regarding God is hard to grasp, because it oscillates between Theism and Pantheism. Myron Phelps' exposition of it is certainly pantheistic.[154] Baha Ullah in many places bears out his interpretation, as, for example, "God alone is the one Power which animates and dominates all things, which are but manifestations of its energy."[155] In subsequent expositions, as in "Answered Questions," Abdul Baha repudiates Pantheism, and so does M. Abul Fazl in "The Brilliant Proof." Kheiralla, while maintaining that Baha taught Theism, accused Abdul Baha of Pantheism. In "The Epistle to the Shah" Baha simulates a monotheism almost as rigid as Islam: "We bear witness that there is no God but Him. He is independent of the worlds. No one hath known Him.... God singly and alone abideth in His own place which is holy, above space or time, mention and utterance, sign, description, definition, height and depth.... The way is closed and seeking is forbidden." A favourite text is that of the Koran, in which God says: "I was a hid treasure, I desired to be known, therefore I created the world." In this process "the first thing which emanated from God [eternally] was that universal reality which the ancient philosophers termed the 'First Mind,' and which the people of Baha call the 'Primal Will.' This is without beginning or end, essentially but not temporally contingent, and without power to become an associate with God."[156] The Primal Will, Holy Essence, Word, Spirit, is manifested in perfect men, who are the Great Prophets. They are supreme, holy, sinless souls, godlike in their attributes. They show the perfections of God.[157] This reality does not change, but the garment in which it is clothed is different. One day it is the garment of Abraham,

---

[152] Remey, *S. W.*, Dec. 31, 1913, pp. 267-271.

[153] In thus regarding the prophets as divine, Bahais are not setters forth of strange doctrine in Persia, for the Ali Allahis (Nusaireyeh), who number, possibly, twice as many as the Bahais in Persia, have the same doctrine, and, in addition, regard the Imam Ali and others as divine incarnations.

[154] Phelps, "Life of Abbas Effendi."

[155] Baha's "Words of Wisdom," p. 61. Notwithstanding these repudiations of Pantheism, nearly every investigator finds it at the basis of Bahai teaching.

[156] "Answered Questions," p. 23.

[157] Abdul Baha in Mrs. Grundy's "Ten Days in Acca."

who is Zoroaster, then Moses, Buddha, Krishna, Christ, Mohammed, the Bab, and Baha Ullah.[158] Abul Fazl says: "All the prophets are respectively the Manifestations of the single Reality and one Essence."[159] The "Ikan" says: "All are one, as the sun of yesterday and to-day are one. The sun is one, the dawning-points of the sun are numerous. One light, many lanterns."[160] "Baha is the same light in a new lamp."[161] Yet there are differences in degree. Of the Bab, Baha says: "His rank is greater than all the prophets, and His Mission loftier and higher."[162] But he is merely as a forerunner in comparison with Baha. Baha is superior to all, greater, more glorious.[163] He is infallible, absolute, universal. "All the prophets were perfect mirrors of God, but *in Baha, in some sense, the Divine Essence is manifested.*"[164] "All preceding ones are inferior to him: all subsequent ones are to be under his shadow."[165] But even the latter are not to come for a "thousand or thousands of years," and perhaps not then, for the "Kitab-ul-Akdas" says: "O Pen, write and inform mankind that the Manifestations are ended by this luminous and effulgent Theophany."

The Manifestation has two stations: "One is the station of oneness and the rank of absolute Deity, the second station is one of temporal conditions and servitude. If the manifestation says, 'Verily I am only a man like you,' or 'Verily, I am God,' each is true and without doubt." The "Tajallayat" quotes the Bab as saying concerning "Him whom God shall manifest"; "Verily he shall utter, 'I am God. There is no God but Me, the Lord of all things, and all besides is created by Me! O ye, my creatures, ye are to worship Me.'"[166] In Bahai literature such words as the following are not uncommon: "Baha Ullah is the Lord of Hosts, the Heavenly Father, the Prince of Peace, the Glory of God."[167] "He is the framer of the whole

---

[158] *Ibid.*, p. 61: "The Blessed Perfection said in His Tablets that once He was Abraham, once Moses, once Jesus, once Mohammed and once the Bab. Baha Ullah is all the prophets, no matter by what name he chooses to call himself."

[159] "Bahai Proofs," p. 209.

[160] Pages 14-15.

[161] "Answered Questions," pp. 199-201. Mr. Sprague says: "The Bahai Faith teaches that the Universal Spirit, which is God, has manifested itself to every race at some time or other, and that it comes again and again, like the spring, to make all things new" ("A Year in India," p. viii).

[162] "Ikan," p. 175.

[163] "Bahai Proofs," pp. 156-160. At the time of Azal there was a whole "galaxy" of Manifestations. Baha wishes to stop the claimants, so he declares that none is to be expected "for a thousand or thousands of years." Persia has had numerous incarnations, so-called. They were found among the Ismielis, Assassins, Ali-Allahis and all the *Ghulat*. The veiled Prophet Mukanna, Babak and many pretenders have proclaimed themselves God. In truth Persia never lacks for an incarnation or two. One of these, of the Ali-Allahi sect, arrived in Tabriz some years ago, and made an appointment to visit me at three o'clock P. M. My somavar was set to boiling and I awaited his arrival. But he failed to keep his engagement because the Governor-General, the Amir-i-Nizam, heard of his presence in the city, and this God fled, forgetting to send me word not to expect him.

[164] "Answered Questions," pp. 129-131, 199-201.

[165] *Ibid.*, p. 184.

[166] "Ikan," pp. 123-127.

[167] Asad Ullah, "The School of the Prophets," p. 109.

Universe, the Cause of the life of the world, and of the unity and harmony of the creatures."[168] "No one of the Manifestations had such great power of influence as was with El-Baha."[169] In passing, it may be noticed how little ground for such boasting they have. How great in comparison was the influence of Moses as leader of Israel, emancipator, lawgiver, and prophet! How great even was Mohammed's success and influence, compared with what Baha has accomplished! How evidently antichristian is Bahaism in denying that Christ's name and glory are above all, and that to Him every knee should bow!

IV. Bahaism wrongly assumes that its leader is Christ come again. There is confusion about this claim, for some Bahais represent Baha to be Christ, and others make Abdul Baha Abbas to be Christ come the second time. Confusion also arises from the fact that Baha is set forth as the Manifestation of all the "promised ones." He is set forth as the Messiah for the Jews, God the Father, the Word, and the Spirit for the Christians, Aurora or Shah Bahram for the Zoroastrians, the fifth Buddha for Buddhists, reincarnated Krishna for Brahmans, the Mahdi or the twelfth Imam or Husain for the Moslems.[170] "All are realized in the coming of Baha Ullah."[171] In accord with this, Baha declared in his "Epistle to the Pope": "Consider those who turned away from the Spirit [Christ] when He came to them. Verily He hath come from heaven as He came the first time. Beware lest ye oppose Him as the Pharisees opposed Him. Verily the Spirit of Truth has come to guide you into all truth. He hath come from the Heaven of Preëxistence." "Baha," says the editor of the *Star of the West*, "is the fulfillment of the promise of the 'second coming' *with a new name* (Rev. iii. 11-13)."[172]

It must be remembered that Bahaism, chameleon-like, takes on a different aspect according to the environment of its adherents. In Persia its creed is different from that of America in regard to the "return." For the most part American Bahais regard Baha as God the Father, and Abdul Baha Abbas as the Son of God, Jesus Christ. After the quarrel and schism following the death of Baha (1892), Abbas became very wary of assuming titles and dignities, lest he give a handle to his opponents to accuse him of claiming to be a "Manifestation." So he assumed the title Abd-ul-Baha, the "servant of Baha," which his followers translate "Servant of God." He also calls himself the "Centre of the Covenant." Baha had entitled him the "Greatest Branch of God" (Zech. vi. 12) and the "Mystery of God" (1 Tim. iii. 16). He was commonly called "Agha," an equivalent in Persia of Effendi or Mister, but his followers translate it "Master," and put into it the full New Testament significance. Undoubtedly Western Bahais worship Abdul Baha as Jesus Christ the Master come again. In spite of all disavowals and beclouding by words, their faith is plain. Getsinger, a leader and missionary, says: "Abbas is heir and Master of the

[168] Mrs. Brittingham, "The Revelation of Baha Ullah," p. 32.

[169] *S. W.*, Jan. 19, 1914, p. 283.

[170] "The Revelation of Baha Ullah," p. 24. Similarly Gulam Ahmad Quadiani of India claimed to be Christ come again as well as Mohammed and the Mahdi and also, for the Hindus, a new avatar or incarnation.

[171] C. M. Remey's tract, "The Covenant," pp. 14-15; Kheiralla's "Baha Ullah," p. 533, and "Lawh-ul-Akdas," translated in *S. W.*, Vol. IV, p. 15.

[172] *S. W.*, March 21, 1913, p. 13.

Kingdom: he was on earth 1,900 years ago as the Nazarene." Mrs. Corinne True says: "If this is not the resurrection of the pure Spirit of the Nazarene of 1,900 years ago, then we need not look elsewhere."[173] Mr. Anton Hadad says: "The Master, Abbas Effendi, the Lord of the Kingdom, is the one who was to renew and drink the cup with his disciples in the Kingdom of the Father, the one who taught the world to pray, 'Thy kingdom come,'" *i. e.,* Jesus Christ.[174] Chase says: "He has come again in the Kingdom of his Father."[175] Mrs. Brittingham, on pilgrimage to Acca, writes: "I have seen the King in his beauty, the Master is here and we need not look for another. This is the return of the Lion of the tribe of Judah, of the Lamb that once was slain;—the Glory of God and the Glory of the Lamb."[176]

Emphasizing the side of his divinity, we have such declarations as these: M. Haydar Ali taught Mrs. Goodall, "God is not realized except through His Manifestations. Now you have recognized Him and have come to see Him,"[177] *i. e.,* Abdul Baha (1908). M. Asad Ullah gave instructions (1914): "This world has an owner, and Abdul Baha owns the world and all that is in it."[178] "He is the Son of God"[179]—the only Door, "the Lord of Mankind."[180] A supplication from Persia, given out for publication, says: "O! Abdul Baha! Forgiver of sins, merciful, bountiful, compassionate! How can a sinner like me reach Thee? Thou art through all the Forgiver of Sins."[181]

But there is an interpretation to all this for "those of understanding." Bahais reject metempsychosis, but they have a doctrine of "Return," which must be borne in mind. This principle is expressed by Phelps as follows: "When a character with which we are familiar as possessed by some individual of the past, reappears in another individual of the present, we say that the former has returned."[182] Baha states it thus: "In every succeeding Manifestation those souls who exceed all in faith, assurance, and self-denial can be declared to be the return of the former persons who attained to these states in the preceding Manifestation. For that which appeared from the former servants became manifest in the subsequent ones."[183] Their classic illustration of this is John the Baptist. Abdul Baha says: "Christ said that John the Baptist was Elijah. The same perfections which were in Elijah existed in John, and were exactly realized in him. Not the essence but the qualities are regarded. As the flower of last year has returned, so this person, John, was a manifestation of the bounty, perfections, the character, the qualities, and the virtues of Elias. John said, 'I am not Elias'—not his substance and individuality."[184] <u>Remey clearly st</u>ates the idea: "The return of a prophet does not refer to the return

[173] "Notes at Acca," p. 24.
[174] "A Message from Acca."
[175] "Before Abraham was, I am," p. 46.
[176] "The Revelation," etc., p. 25.
[177] "Daily Lessons," p. 61.
[178] "Flowers from Rose Garden," p. 5; also, Dealy, "Dawn of Knowledge," Chap. IV.
[179] Asad Ullah, "Sacred Mysteries," pp. 74, 85.
[180] "Bahai Proofs," p. 121; *S. W.,* Jan. 19, 1914, p. 288.
[181] "A Heavenly Vista," p. 12.
[182] "Life of Abbas Effendi," p. 197.
[183] "Ikan," p. 113.
[184] "Answered Questions," p. 152.

to this world of a personality. It refers to the return in another personality of the impersonal Spirit, the Word or Spirit of God, which spoke through the prophets in the past.... People are mistakenly looking for the personal *individual* return of their own special prophet."[185] In accordance with this theory of the "Return," Abdul Baha wrote to the Bahai Council of New York: "I am not Christ; I am not eternal."[186] To Mrs. Grundy he said: "Some call me Christ; it is imagination."[187] Yet the final word of his missionary, Mr. Remey, is: "The same Christ which was in Jesus is again manifest in the Bahai Revelation. The real Christians are those who recognize the New Covenant to be the return of the same Christ,—the Word of God."[188] In like manner this usurper of Christ's name is proclaimed to be "the expected one," the "desire of all nations" under other names to the various religions.

V. Bahaism deals with the prophecies of the Bible in a manner derogatory to the glory of the Lord Jesus Christ and His Kingdom. Bahaism asserts that "the promises and prophecies given in the Holy Scriptures have been fulfilled by the appearance of the Prince of the Universe, the great Baha Ullah and of Abdul Baha."[189] A volume would be necessary to review their treatment of the prophecies. They quote a multitude of verses without proof that their applications are valid. The "messenger" and "Elijah" of the Book of Malachi are declared to be the Bab.[190] He is also the Angel with the sound of the trumpet (Rev. iv. 1) and his cycle is the "First Resurrection." Baha is declared to be the fulfillment of Isaiah's prophecies. Of chapter ix. 1-6, "unto us a child is born, ... the Prince of Peace." Dealy says: "Many misguided people have referred this to Jesus Christ."[191] In verse 1, "Galilee of the nations," land of Zebulun and Naphtali, is made to mean Acca (Acre in Syria) where Baha lived in exile, and not the region of Christ's ministry, contradicting Matthew iv. 13-16. By a great stretch of imagination Acca[192] becomes Jerusalem, "the city of the great king" (Ps. xlviii. 12), and Mount Carmel becomes Mount Zion, and Isaiah ii. 3 refers to them, "for out of Zion shall go forth the law and the word of the Lord from Jerusalem." Even "the root out of Jesse"[193] and the millennial peace are only partially referred to Christ. They find the real fulfillment in Baha Ullah, whom they imagine to be descended from Abraham, through an imaginary descendant of his named Jesse.[194] The new covenant and the law written on the heart is again the Bahai dispensation, contrary to Hebrews viii. 8, 10, 16. When Baha as a prisoner in chains rode into Acca seated on an ass, he fulfilled

---

[185] "The Bahai Movement," p. 39.

[186] Phelps, p. 99.

[187] "Ten Days in the Light of Acca."

[188] *S. W.*, Dec. 31, 1913, p. 269.

[189] M. Asad Ullah in M. H. Dreyfus's "Universal Religion," p. 63.

[190] Mal. iii. 1; iv. 5-6. See Dealy, "The Dawn of Knowledge," pp. 13-15.

[191] *Ibid.*, pp. 25, 30.

[192] Dealy says: "To quote all the passages of Scripture referring to Acca would necessitate reading a great portion of the Bible. They identify Accho with Acca (Acre). Even if this were so, Accho was not in the land of Naphtali and Zebulun, but in Asher. Napoleon's siege of Acre is called 'the abomination of desolation, standing in the holy place'" (p. 40).

[193] Isa. xi. 1-10.

[194] "Answered Questions," pp. 72-75.

Zechariah ix. 9.[195]

I attended a Bahai meeting in the Masonic Temple in Chicago. The leader read the following verses as all fulfilled in Bahaism.[196] The "son of man" (Dan. vii.) was Abdul Baha, and the "Ancient of Days," Baha. The question of Proverbs xxx. 3, "What is his name and what his son's name?" was answered, Baha and Abdul Baha; similarly in Psalms lxxii. and ii., "The King" and the "King's Son." The "Branch" (Zech. vi. 12-13) who shall build the temple was again Abdul Baha, and the latter is specially urgent that the Bahai Temple in Chicago should be built in his day, so that the prophecy may appear to be fulfilled. The dates in Daniel are juggled with. For example, Abdul Baha explains Daniel viii. by taking the *solar* year. He calculates[197] that the 2,300 days were completed at the Bab's manifestation in 1844. In Daniel xii. 6 the *lunar*[198] year is resorted to, and the forty-two months (1,260 years) are dated from the hegira of Mohammed, but Daniel xii. 11 does not come exactly right, so the *terminus a quo* is made to be the proclamation of the prophethood of Mohammed, three years after his mission, which was ten years before the hegira. By this means the date of Baha's manifestation (1863) is reached. In connection with Daniel xii. and Revelation xi. we have the startling information, so contradictory to history, that "in the beginning of the seventh century after Christ, when Jerusalem was conquered, the Holy of Holies was outwardly preserved, that is to say, the house which Solomon built. The Holy of Holies was preserved, guarded, and respected."[199] On this alleged fact Abdul Baha founds an argument.[200] Prophecies referring to the glory of God or of the Father are applied to Baha, because his title means "glory of God." The Bab, according to the custom in Persia, gave many high-sounding titles. Baha's rival was called "The Dawn of the Eternal." Voliva, the successor of Dowie, might assume some fitting title and claim to fulfill the prophecies. He has a good foundation for interpretation, he does really live in Zion City (Illinois). Our Bahais further tell us that the "New Jerusalem," the new heaven and the new earth, mean the new dispensation, the new laws of Baha. This is now "the day of God," "the day of judgment," "the kingdom of God," "the second resurrection."[201] The parable of the vineyard is a favourite proof text. It says that the Lord of the vineyard will come *himself* and will utterly destroy the wicked husbandmen. This, they say, is a real coming of the Father, even as the Son came. In that case the destroying must be real, and we should expect that Baha would have destroyed the religious leaders of Mecca or Kerbela, Jerusalem or Rome. "No," says the Bahai, "the destroying is figurative, and means simply the abrogation of their authority." Well, if he escapes to a figurative interpretation, we too can interpret the coming of the Lord of the Vineyard as his

[195] Kheiralla, p. 419.

[196] Dealy, pp. 31-32, 44.

[197] "Answered Questions," pp. 50-52.

[198] Kheiralla (pp. 412, 480-483) also skips from lunar to solar year and back, to make the dates tally.

[199] "Answered Questions," pp. 54-55. See Milman's "Gibbon," Vol. II, p. 433. "The Emperor Hadrian's plowshare levelled the temple area."

[200] "Answered Questions," pp. 54-55.

[201] "Bahai Proofs," p. 140. "All in their graves arose spiritually at his call, for service in his cause."

visitation on Jerusalem in the time of Titus.

Baha Ullah's method of interpretation and adaptation of prophecies is best seen in his "Ikan." In it he interprets at length Matthew xxiv.[202] In brief it is as follows: "After the tribulation of those days" means times of difficulty in understanding God's word and attaining divine knowledge; "the sun shall be darkened and the moon cease to give light," that is the teachings and the ordinances of the preceding dispensation shall lose their influence and efficiency. "The stars shall fall," etc., means the divines shall fall from the knowledge of religion, and the powers of science and religion shall be shaken. Because of the absence of the Son of Divine Beauty, the moon of knowledge, and the stars of intuitive wisdom, "all the tribes of the earth shall mourn." "They shall see the Son of Man coming in the clouds of heaven," that is Baha Ullah shall appear from the heaven of the Supreme Will, outwardly from his mother's womb. "In the clouds" means in doubts which are caused by the human limitations of the Manifestation, eating, drinking, marrying, etc. "And he shall send his angels," the spiritual believers sent as preachers of Baha. The separation of the sheep from the goats, as we learn subsequently, means the schism at the death of Baha, when the violators, the brothers of Abdul Baha and their adherents, were exscinded.[203] Even granting an allegorical interpretation of Christ's words, only a stretch of imagination can find any reference to Baha.

It should be borne in mind that Oriental Bahai writers have read Keith on Prophecy in Persian and the publications of the Mission Press at Beirut. Abdul Baha said to Dr. H. H. Jessup, "I am familiar with the books of your press."[204] M. Abul Fazl refers to and quotes them. Writers in English (as Kheiralla, Remey, Dealy, and Brittingham) refer to Miller, Cummings, Seiss, Guinness, and others. Yet with all their familiarity with apocalyptic literature, they make an exceedingly weak presentation. Their claims are so baseless as to require no refutation. They are a mass of unfounded assertions and assumptions,—vain, bold, and brazen. We may admit the declarations of Baha and Abul Fazl, which are but trite principles of hermeneutics, that figurative and allegorical language abounds in the Scriptures, that many meanings are "sealed" till after their fulfillment, that the prophecies of the Old Testament were only partially fulfilled at Christ's first coming. But their inference does not follow. There is nothing to prove the assertions that the prophecies were fulfilled in the Bab and Baha. They furnish no scintilla of evidence. For example, "the government shall be upon his shoulders." Was this fulfilled in Baha? He came and went; the nations and their rulers from 1817 to 1892 were neither literally nor figuratively under his sway. He did not nor does he rule over the nations. He did not reign in Mount Zion nor in Jerusalem. Jerusalem did not cease to be trodden down of the Gentiles. Abundance of peace did not attend him, but

---

[202] Pages 17-67.

[203] Doctor Potter of Teheran says ("Missions and Modern Hist.," by R. E. Speer, p. 162): "Their fanciful interpretations of plain Scripture declarations renders it difficult to make any impression on them with proof texts from the Bible. They reply, 'Yes, but we must break open the word and extract its meaning.'" This, says Doctor Holmes, "is often directly at variance with its apparent meaning, but this only displays more clearly the divine insight of their teacher, that he is able to recognize words no one else can understand."

[204] *The Outlook* (New York), 1901, June, p. 451.

great wars. The signs of Christ's Second Advent have not been fulfilled in Baha, either actually or metaphorically.[205] As well may Ahmad Quadiani or Dowie assert their pretensions. Baha's claim is antichristian. The day of Christ's power through the Holy Spirit has not passed. It is still His day. The knowledge of Christ is yet more covering the earth. Men of diverse races and religions in Asia, Africa, and the isles of the seas are being joined in the common faith and fellowship of Jesus Christ as Saviour of Men. There are more Christians in Korea than Bahais in Persia. More Jews have become Christian since Baha was born than have become Bahais from all races and religions outside of Persia. Christ still goes forth conquering and to conquer.

VI. Bahaism, in its treatment of Jesus Christ as a man in His earthly life, belittles Him by both its denials and its affirmations. Of His temptation it says, "the devil signifies the human nature of Christ, through which He was tempted." His miracles of healing are denied.[206] Baha and Abul Fazl admit the possibility of miracles, but deny their evidential value,[207] but Abdul Baha denies their reality. He says: "The miracles of Christ were spiritual teachings, not literal deeds."[208] The raising of the dead means that the dead (in sin) are blessed with spiritual life.[209] By blindness (John ix.) is meant ignorance and error; by sight, knowledge and guidance.[210] The spittle coming from Christ was the meaning of His words, the clay was the expression He used in accordance with their understanding.[211] At the crucifixion darkness did not prevail, nor the earthquake, nor was the vail of the temple rent in twain.[212] The crucifixion was not an atoning sacrifice; Christ quaffed the cup of martyrdom "to cultivate and educate us."[213] The washing away of sins by Christ was not by His blood, but was by the practice of His teachings."[214] Christ did not rise from the dead. "Resurrection of the body is an unintelligible matter contrary to natural laws."[215] The body, which signifies His word, arose when faith in His cause revived in the minds of the disciples after three days.[216] Christ's real resurrection was the coming of Mohammed. "Christ by saying that He would be three days in the heart of the earth meant that He would appear in the third cycle. The Christian was one, the Mohammedan the second, and that of Baha the third." "The ascension of Christ with an elemental body is contrary to science." He ascended in the same sense as Baha ascended, viz., departed to the other world. Thus Bahaism

---

[205] In one particular, no doubt, Baha has fulfilled prophecy. At least the Azalis say that he came "as a thief" and stole the succession from Azal.

[206] "New Hist.," p. 321.

[207] "Bahai Proofs," pp. 190, 204-207.

[208] Mrs. Grundy, p. 13.

[209] "Answered Questions," pp. 115-118.

[210] "Bahai Proofs," p. 232.

[211] M. L. Lucas, "My Visit to Acca," p. 20.

[212] "Answered Questions," p. 45.

[213] *S. W.,* April 9, 1913, p. 40.

[214] Ibn Abhar. Thornton Chase says: "Christianity stands condemned because it refuses to reject miracles and the blood atonement and will not confine itself to the precepts of Jesus" ("Bahai Revelation," p. 158).

[215] "Bahai Proofs," p. 155.

[216] "Tablets of Abdul Baha," Vol. I, p. 192; "Answered Questions," pp. 120-121.

denies the miracles,[217] atonement, resurrection, and ascension of Christ.

A section of the "Tarikh-i-Jadid"[218] is devoted to the denial and refutation of miracles. A blind man in Teheran sent to Baha praying that his eyes might be opened. He received answer that it was for the glory of God that he remain blind. The Bab, at his examination in Tabriz, was asked to restore the sick Mohammed Shah to health. He replied: "It is not in my power, but I can write two thousand verses a day. Who else can do that?" He thus appealed not simply to the quality of his poetry but to its quantity as a proof of his manifestation. In like manner, Manes, in old times, painted pictures in his "revelations" and appealed to them as proof of his inspiration. While denying miracles, Bahais lay much stress, as we have seen, on minute fulfillments of prophecies.

Bahaism belittles the life and work of Jesus in instituting comparisons between Christ and Baha derogatory to the former. Baha says: "It is not meet ... to repeat the error of seeking help of ... the Son Jesus. Let thy satisfaction be in myself." Abdul Baha says: "The difference between Baha and Christ is that between the sun and moon. The light of the sun [Baha] subsists in itself while the moon gets light from the Sun." "All the teachings of Christ will not exceed ten pages.[219] Those of the Blessed Perfection exceed sixty or seventy volumes. Christ's instructions refer to individuals. Those of the Blessed Perfection are for all nations, although they apply as well to all individuals. The instructions of Christ were heard by but few persons; there were eleven who believed, although Christians say there were one hundred and twenty. The teachings of the Blessed Perfection were spread throughout the world during his lifetime. The reputation of Christ did not extend from Nazareth to Acca [22 miles]; the reputation of the Blessed Perfection extended throughout the world. Jesus Christ did not send a letter even to a village chief; the Blessed Perfection sent letters to all the kings of the earth."[220] Notice how he repeats *ad nauseam* the title for Baha, but uses no title for the Lord Jesus Christ, though the Moslems invariably do use a title in speaking of the latter.

There is an evident effort on the part of Kheiralla and Abul Fazl to minimize the proofs regarding Christ from prophecy, miracles, and history, with the idea thereby of magnifying the proof for Baha in contrast. For example, "The Gospels contain only a few pages of the true Words of God. Christ's teachings were not written in the original language nor written in His day, His power was slow in proving effective, and many even denied His existence."[221] "Even Peter denied Him, but Baha Ullah has educated thousands of souls, faithful under the menace of the sword."[222] In explaining the progress of Bahaism among the Jews and Zoroastrians, Abul Fazl says: "Christians could not convert even one Jew or Zoroastrian except by force or compulsion." He ignores the fact that millions of Persians had been converted to Christ from Zoroaster before the sword of Islam smote Persia.

[217] Yet Baha informs us that "copper in seventy years becomes gold in its mine if it be protected from a superabundance of moisture" ("Ikan," p. 111).

[218] "New Hist."

[219] "Winterburn's Table Talks," pp. 19-20.

[220] "Bahai Proofs," p. 231.

[221] "Answered Questions," p. 42.

[222] "Bahai Proofs," p. 265.

This belittling of Christ—His life and work and influence—shows that a spirit antagonistic to Christ really animates the Bahai leaders, in spite of their professions to the contrary.

V

BAHAISM AND CHRISTIANITY (CONTINUED)

Immortality and sin—Faith in Baha—Bahai Scriptures—Its worship—
Hierarchy—Substitutes for Baptism and Lord's Supper—Christ's
words   imitated—Rites—Ablution—Fast—Prayer—Pilgrimage—Acca Shrines—Festivals—Era—Propaganda anti-Christian.

Mrs. Goodall:—"Is it necessary to arise to say the midnight prayers and to make ablution before them?"

Abdul Baha:—"Ablution is only for obligatory prayers three times a day."—*"Daily Lessons,"* p. 74.

Abdul Baha restores man to his state a little lower than the angels.... On this occasion we newcomers were presented with a Bahai stone marked with Baha Ullah's name. Such objects contain a spiritual influence ... actually retain and set free something of the holy man's personality.... At my request, Abdul Baha graciously took back the stone I had received and returned it with a blessing for my baby girl, who thus, as it were, accompanied us on our pilgrimage and received its benefit.—*Horace Holley at Thonon. His "The Modern Social Religion,"* p. 216.

VII. BAHAISM teaches another way of salvation. Man's origin and destiny were formerly points of doubt in Bahai teaching, but the muddy mixture has settled enough to give us a clearer view, at least as regards Western Bahaism, though pantheistic notions still prevail. Abdul Baha teaches that matter is eternal, self-existent, and fills all space.[223] "God always had a creation; the universe has neither beginning nor end."[224] "Creation out of nothing is unthinkable. Separate entities come into being through the operation of God—are the perceptible manifestations of Him." "There are four degrees of spirit concerned with evolutionary growth: The mineral spirit, the vegetable, the animal, and the human. The mineral spirit contains the latent principle of life."[225] Yet man's origin is not from the animals.[226] "Species is fixed; man was developed gradually as a distinct species."[227] The spirit

---

[223] Phelps' "Life of Abbas Effendi," p. 69.
[224] "Answered Questions," pp. 209, 238, 317; *S. W.,* June 5, 1913, p. 90.
[225] Phelps, p. 116.
[226] "Answered Questions," p. 209.
[227] *Ibid.,* p. 213.

of man emanates from God as an action from an actor, a writing from a writer—a manifestation of the Divine but not a division from it. Sin arises from the physical qualities, from the physical nature which we derive from Adam. Evil is really non-existent; it is simply lack of good qualities. There is no Satan.[228] The "Genii" (jins) of the Koran are evil passions in man; demons are the spirits of bad men.

As to the doctrine of personal immortality, there has been much confusion of thought. Some have understood the doctrine of "rijat" or "Return" as teaching transmigration of souls. Others have understood their allegorizing about heaven as a rejection of the future life. Others, as Phelps,[229] affirm the absorption of the soul in the Infinite. My language teacher in Persia, a fervent Behai, said: "We believe in a future state so unthinkably ecstatic that if its joys were now revealed to men, they would commit suicide to hasten their entrance into it." Baha Ullah wrote a "Tablet of the Spiritual World," of which it is said:[230] "All who read it are filled with an anxious desire to leave this world and enter the next condition, so wonderful are the glories of the spiritual kingdom. In Persia one man who read the tablet killed himself. He could not wait for the happiness it promised him. Another, a youth of Ispahan, could not stand it and lost his reason."

Mrs. Grundy[231] and Mr. Phelps[232] understood Abdul Baha to teach the annihilation of the wicked, but he denied this[233] and affirms their conscious existence.[234] Heaven and hell are affirmed in some places, denied in others.

Sin is little dwelt upon in Bahai literature, and the word repentance is seldom used. In the "New History" and "Traveller's Narrative" sin, transgression, forgiveness, expiation and such words find no place in the indexes. The Moslem appeal for mercy is rarely made. In the chapter on prayer, in the "Sacred Mysteries," there are no directions for the confession of sins, no petition like, "forgive us our trespasses," no cry of the prodigal—"Father, I have sinned." There is no atonement. The daily sacrifice of the Book of Numbers is explained to mean "Divine bounty." "The blood of Christ cleanses us" is interpreted "His spiritual teaching and love which saved His disciples from the ruin of ignorance and heedlessness." The stages of travel to God, the "Seven Valleys," are (1) research, (2) love, (3) knowledge, (4) union, (5) content, (6) perplexity or astonishment, (7) poverty and annihilation. There is no mention of hatred of sin, turning from it and apprehending the mercy of God. The plan of salvation has neither the Christian idea of atonement by a mediator, nor the Mohammedan one of expiation by works of merit or an equivalent. Its plan of salvation is simple, viz., to believe in and follow Mirza Husain Ali, Baha Ullah, as the supreme and final manifestation in this universal cycle which began in Adam and culminated in Baha Ullah, who was God the Father in the flesh. Later Bahais put Abdul Baha in the place of Christ as Son of God and Divine Mediator.

---

[228] Phelps, p. 137.
[229] Page 173.
[230] Mrs. Grundy, p. 6.
[231] "Ten Days in the Light of Acca," p. 23.
[232] Pages 121-127, 173.
[233] "Tablets of Abdul Baha," Vol. I, p. iv.
[234] *S. W.*, March 2, 1914, p. 321.

Remey's chapter on Eternal Life[235] is orthodoxy with Baha as "Word of God." The doctrines of faith, regeneration, and sanctification are Christian with the historic Christ eliminated. Error has clothed itself as in garments of light. Antichrist would steal the livery of Heaven and lead Christians to forget that there is no other name under Heaven given among men, whereby we must be saved (Acts iv. 12), and that if Abdul Baha or an angel from Heaven pervert the Gospel of Christ or preach any other Gospel, he is to be rejected (Gal. i. 7-9).

VIII. Bahaism abrogates the New Testament.

It is indeed honoured, but as the Revelation of a past dispensation. Abdul Baha wrote in the Bible in the City Temple, London: "This book is the Holy Book of God, of celestial inspiration. It is the Bible of salvation, the noble Gospel. It is the mystery of the Kingdom of God and its light. It is the Divine bounty, sign of the guidance of God." But Harold Johnson, a friend of Bahaism, wrote, with true discernment:[236] "In the same spirit he would have written the same words upon the *Koran* or the *Vedas*." Baha certifies the *Koran* times without number in the "Ikan." He wrote:[237] "Whoso hath not acknowledged the *Koran* hath not in reality accepted the books which preceded it." By the same reasoning, whoso does not acknowledge Baha's writings as "revealed" rejects the former books also.

Bahais, even Persian Bahais, are familiar with the Bible. They quote largely from the prophets, the Gospels, and the Book of Revelation. They use them for apologetic purposes, to dispute with Christians and to find proofs for their perverted teachings. As the real Scriptures for the present age, they present the writings of Baha Ullah and Abdul Baha. These are read at their meetings and in their devotions and are chanted at their shrines. These *only* are to be read in the *Mashrak-ul-Azhar*, the Bahai Temples.[238] The authority of all other Scriptures is abrogated, even the "Bayan" of the Bab.[239] The "Kitab-ul-Akdas," the Most Holy Book, consists of laws, exhortations, and warnings. The "Ikan," written by Baha before he set up his own claim, is an attempt to show from previous books the truth of the Bab's claims. The "Hidden Words," "Surat al Haykal" (The human temple), the "Seven Valleys," the "Effulgences," the "Glad Tidings," etc., contain principles, precepts, and rhapsodies. There are also the Epistles to the Kings and numerous tablets (letters) to individual believers. Besides all these, the discourses and letters of Abdul Baha, containing interpretations and commands, are regarded as revealed and inspired Words of God. These are collected in "Tablets of Abdul Baha," "Addresses in Paris," "Addresses in London," "Some Answered Questions," and in the *Star of the West*, newspaper.

IX. Bahaism abolishes the Christian institutions—the Church, its sacraments, and its polity.

The Church must soon cease to have any meaning for those who look for grace and strength to another than "the head, even Christ" (Eph. iv. 15). Bahais in Amer-

[235] "The Bahai Movement," p. 80.
[236] *Contemporary Review*, March, 1912.
[237] Page 145, Chicago Edition.
[238] Goodall, "Daily Lessons," p. 17.
[239] Dreyfus, "The Bahai Revelation," p. 59.

ica have already organized separate meetings for worship in all places where they have a score or more members. In Chicago, which is the chief seat of the sect in America, they have 150 or more members. I attended their regular Sunday service, in a room which they have rented in the Masonic Temple. About sixty were present, one-half of whom were visitors like myself. The service was modelled somewhat after the Protestant week-day meeting, but without any prayer. Several hymns were sung in praise and worship of Baha, from a book specially written for his adoration. The leader, a woman, read selections from the "Tablets of Abdul Baha" and gave an exposition of Bahai teachings and an invitation to faith in Baha and Abdul Baha, as specially the fulfillment of the prophecies of the Bible. Another woman read from the "Hidden Words." The editor of the *Star*, one of six Bahai men present, gave the announcements and said that the meetings during the summer would be on the ground, at Wilmette, where they expect to build the temple (*Mashrak-ul-Azkar*). This temple is a darling project of Abdul Baha. He dedicated the ground when he was in America and urges all believers to build it quickly. He says: "The temple is the greatest matter today for the upbuilding of the cause."[240] It will fulfill prophecy!

The government of Bahaism is to be by "Houses of Justice." Each will be composed of nine or more Bahai men elected by the people. Bahaism will be the state religion. Kings will exist, but the politico-religious hierarchy will perform many of the functions of the state, even to settling international disputes. Churches, assemblies, and conferences, bishops and popes—all will be dispensed with. The Bahai "houses" will conduct and control religion for the world. The first universal vicegerent of God is Abdul Baha. After him the supreme power will be vested in the "house." Already signs of Bahai tyranny are manifest. Abdul Baha declared that no believer "must vary one hair's breadth from his word." No Bahai may publish anything on religion without first submitting it to him for censorship. Such a command is made applicable to all Bahais.[241] In the good time coming there will be a graduated hierarchy—local, national, universal—who will bring "all secular affairs under spiritual guidance."

With the Church and its ministry the "new revelation" abolishes also the sacraments. Baptism is no longer necessary, for "baptism by water," says Abdul Baha, "was a symbol of repentance and of seeking forgiveness of sins. In the cycle of Baha there is no longer need of this symbol, for its reality, which is to be baptized with the Spirit and love of God, is established."[242] Yet a substitute is at hand:[243] "Thou hast asked regarding the naming of children. Prepare a meeting, chant verses, supplicate guidance for the babe; then give the name and enjoy beverages and sweetmeats. This is spiritual baptism." So Remey did. "I will make mention of a Bahai christening [?] in Ferouzay [Persia]. We were asked to name the baby. On the fifth day after the child's birth a feast was spread. The baby was brought out. Mr. Sprague gave the name Ruhullah; prayers, tablets, and a hymn in praise

---

[240] "Table Talks," by True, p. 21; "Tablets of Abdul Baha," Vol. I, p. 17.
[241] *Star*, July 13, 1913, p. 121; "Tablets of Abdul Baha," Vol. I, pp. 118, 124.
[242] "Answered Questions," p. 106.
[243] "Tablets of Abdul Baha," Vol. I, pp. 149, 150.

of Baha Ullah were chanted."[244] Such is the substitute for baptism in the name of the Father, Son, and Holy Spirit.

The Lord's Supper as a remembrance of the sacrifice of Christ is abolished. Instead of it there is introduced an imitation, called the Unity Feast, with traces of the Lord's Supper and of the *Agape*. Of it Abdul Baha[245] says: "It must be inaugurated in such a way as to resurrect the feast of the ancients, namely, the Lord's Supper." We have descriptions of it as celebrated by Abdul Baha in America and at Acca.[246] Sprague says: "The Master [at Acca] did not sit down with us, but served us, going from one to another, heaping rice on our plates, bringing home to us the words: 'Let him that is greatest among you be your servant.' The Orientals could hardly bear that their Master should wait on them. They felt as Peter did when Christ washed his feet. After the supper a tablet of Baha was chanted in Persian. The supper was truly the Lord's Supper in all its spiritual significance." Abdul Baha said that the prophecy was fulfilled which said, "They shall come from the east and the west and sit down in the kingdom of God." In America Abdul Baha celebrated the supper with each group of his followers. In his absence a vacant seat is left at the head of the table for the "master" and passages from the "Hidden Words" are read as food is passed.

Other imitations of Christ's works and words are repeated to keep up the pretense that He is the Saviour. In Chicago and other places "the children were on hand to receive the spiritual blessing of Abdul Baha. He called each child to him and took him in his lap. He blessed them all, laying his hand in blessing on each little head." At a Unity Feast he said: "Abdul Baha is standing and waiting upon you." What is this but a copying of the words: "I am among you as one that doth serve." Palpable imitations of Christ's words abound in the so-called Revelations. In the "Lawh-ul-Akdas "there is a series of beatitudes as: "Blessed is the lowly one who holds to the rope of my might. Blessed is the hungry one who hastens away from desire. Blessed is the thirsty one who seeks the nectar of my benediction. Blessed is the spirit who was stirred by my breath. Blessed is he who has suffered tribulation for my name's sake," etc. Baha Ullah doubles the number of Christ's Beatitudes! In the "Kitab-ul-Akdas," written many years before his death, Baha imitates the parting words of Christ:

Christ in the Gospel says:	Baha Ullah says:
"Let not your hearts be troubled."	"Be not troubled"
"Let not your heart be troubled; neither let it be afraid."	"Let not your trouble take possession of you."
"I am with you always."	"We are with you under all conditions."
"If any man love me, he will keep my words."	"Whoso knoweth me, will rise up to serve me."

[244] "Observations of a Bahai Traveller," p. 40.

[245] "Tablets," p. 149.

[246] "Daily Lessons," Goodall, p. 18; Sprague's "A Year Among Bahais," p. 8; *Star*, 1913, pp. 121, 159, 203.

"It is expedient for you that I go away."   "Verily there is in my occulation a reason."

"I will see you again."   "We shall see you."

What palpable imitations of words so dear to the Christian heart! Words which were in the mouth of Christ Jesus the expression of deep and sincere emotion are used for effect!

X. Bahaism is antichristian in its rites and ceremonies.

These regulations are, for the most part, copied from the Moslem law and are prescribed in the "Kitab-ul-Akdas." Ablution is commanded as a religious rite, to be followed by sitting with one's face towards the *Kibla* (Acca) and repeating *Alla hu Abha* ninety-five times (5×19). As a Fast, Bahaism substitutes the last month of their year, named Ala for Ramazan. As Christians have Carnival week before Lent, followed by Easter rejoicings, and as Moslems have the Oruj Bayram, so Bahais have five days of feasting before the Fast. This extends through a Bahai month of nineteen days, March 2-20, and is followed by the Noruz or Vernal Equinox. Noruz is consecrated and its ceremonies prescribed with religious sanctions as among the Nusaireyah. The ordinance of fasting says: "Thus ordaineth the Lord of men; abstain from eating and drinking from dawn to sundown." This abstinence includes smoking as among Moslems. The same exceptions are made as in the Koran—that the traveller, the sick, and pregnant and nursing women are excused. Fasting is obligatory after the age of fifteen. The Bab put the age limit at forty-two, but Baha enjoined it as long as strength permits.[247] The question naturally arises if obligatory fasting is good, why reduce the time from thirty to nineteen days: if reform is the watchword, why not have the liberty of the Gospel?

As in fasting, so in prayer Bahaism follows the Moslem ceremonial law. Baha laid down a ritual on the same lines. There are modifications, but no essential difference, from Islam. In Islam devotion is a strong point, formalism is its weakness. Bahaism lessens the amount of devotion, without getting rid of the prescribed formalism. Ablutions are a necessary preliminary to the obligatory prayers, at least three times a day, but if one wishes to make other prayers at night, he need not get out of bed to perform the ablutions.[248] "He who doth not find water, must say five times, 'In the name of God,'" etc. ("Akdas"). During the ablutions certain petitions are prescribed as "while washing the hands, say," etc.; "while washing the face, say," etc. Then the worshipper must "stand facing the Holy Place" (Acca) and say a portion of the prayers; then "bowing down with hands on knees," say another portion; then "standing with hands outstretched forward and upward," another; then "sitting down," another portion. Each prayer has three prostrations (*rika*). Prayer times are morning, afternoon, and evening. Congregational prayer or at funerals was abolished by Baha, but Abdul Baha permits it for Americans.[249] Prayer is directed to Baha Ullah. When the terms "God," "Lord," "Thy Greatest

---

[247] *Star*, Feb. 7, 1914, p. 306.
[248] "Daily Lessons," Goodall, p. 74.
[249] "Tablets," Vol. I, p. 15.

Name" are used, Mirza Husain Ali is intended: "He, Baha," says Abdul Baha[250] "is the dawning place of Divinity and the manifestation of Divinity. He is the ultimate goal, the adored one of all, and the worshipped one of all." The editors add (the capitals are theirs): "*Further than this* MAN HAS NO OTHER POINT FOR CONCENTRATION. HE (BAHA) IS GOD, *the worshipped one of all*." Prayer, therefore, is no longer to be in the name nor for the sake of Jesus Christ but in the "Greatest Name," *i. e.*, Baha Ullah's, "at the mention of which the people before the Houris fall down," "the Name of Him who is Ruler over what was and is."[251] This name is graven on the breastpins of Bahais, and as a monogram on rings, with two stars alongside it, one of which represents the Bab and the other Abdul Baha. This charm is to be buried with the body. A rosary of ninety-five beads is used daily by the worshipper in saying the "Greatest name" 5×19 times. Allahu Abha is also to be said at the beginning of a meal or of any business, or as a greeting, just as the Moslems say, "Bism ullah" (In the name of God) or "Peace be to you." The figure 9, the sum of the letters of Baha, is also a talisman.

Pilgrimage is considered meritorious and has been popular among American as well as Persian Bahais, though Baha says:[252] "Visiting the tombs of the dead is not necessary, it is better to give the money to the House of Justice." The chief shrine is the tomb of Baha Ullah and of the Bab[253] at Acca. There have been published accounts of a score of American women and of some men who have obtained permission and entered, as it were, through "the gate of heaven" and "paid their vows unto the Most High." But not the least attraction was Abdul Baha, "the king in his beauty." The pilgrim first does obeisance to him. This is an ecstatic, hysteric event. Mrs. True, "perfectly intoxicated with the realization," kissed his hand.[254] Another lady sat at his feet with her head on his knee. Another, when she entered his presence, held out her arms, crying: "My Lord, my Lord,"[255] and

[250] *Star*, Feb. 7, 1914, p. 304.

[251] *Star*, Feb. 7, 1914, p. 298.

[252] "Glad Tidings," Tablets, p. 90.

[253] The Bab's body, at the time of his martyrdom at Tabriz, was thrown to the dogs. It was rescued, taken to Teheran and interred. After many years it was secretly transferred to Acca. The Bab's house in Shiraz was first of all a shrine, and pilgrimage to it is enjoined in the "Akdas." Another is the mausoleum over the grave of the martyrs at Teheran. Similarly at Ispahan ("A Year Among the Persians," p. 13). Abdul Baha seems to desire to increase reverence for shrines and inculcates such honour for the martyrs as will soon develop into superstition. In the "Visiting Tablets for Martyrs," he says (pp. 9-12): "Blessed is the one who attains to visit thy grave. Blessed is the forehead that is set against thy tomb. Blessed is the person who lights a lamp at thy resting-place." "I beg God to make thy sepulchre a mine of mercy, a depository of gifts, and to encompass it with manifold signs." A chant for the pilgrim begins: "O peerless martyr! Verily I salute thy pure dust and thy holy blessed tomb. The everlasting abode is for such as visit thy tomb."

[254] "Table Talks," pp. 13, 17.

[255] Rev. H. H. Jessup, D. D., refers to this incident as published in the *Literary Digest* (*Outlook, Ibid.*, and "Fifty-three Years in Syria," p. 687). He said to Abbas Effendi, "An American woman has stated that she came to Haifa and when she entered your room she felt that she was in the presence of the very Son of God, the Christ, and that she held out her arms, crying, 'My Lord, my Lord,' and rushed to you, kneeling at your blessed feet sobbing like a child. Can this be right to accept worship?" "I left Abbas Effendi with the painful feeling

rushing forward, fell on her knees, sobbing.[256] Another narrative says[257] that Abbas greeted them, "clasped each one in a loving embrace," anointed each one with the attar of roses. "Some of the believers kissed his hand." Of her good-bye this lady says, "I held his hand a long time." Even Mr. Horace Holley, author of "The Modern Social Religion," writes,[258] "This was he. My whole body underwent a shock. My heart leaped, my knees weakened, a thrill of acute receptive feeling flowed from head to foot.... From sheer happiness I wanted to cry." Another man, L. G. Gregory, a negro, writes: "My knee bent reverently before him." When Abdul Baha says: "I am glad to see you," the pilgrims thrill at such wondrous words! "His heavenly smile" gives them happiness! His trite platitudes are written down beside the midnight lamp, for the delectation of similar dupes.

Next the pilgrims visit the Palace of Bahja and the beautiful pleasure grounds where Baha resided during most of his confinement at Acca, enjoying much freedom and even luxury as a "prisoner." The tomb of the Bab draws them, but more sacred do they deem the tomb of Baha Ullah, "the culmination of our pilgrimage." This shrine is in the Garden of Bahja. Its outer court is adorned with beautiful rugs, vases, chandeliers, and flowers. Here they chant verses from the Tablets. Each pilgrim, taking off his shoes, enters the "holy precincts" alone. In this "holy of holies," "the heavenly silence of that centre of peace," he "kneels and prays at the throne of grace for pardon and help," "remembering the friends far away before the presence." He counts it a "glorious experience at once solemn and joyful." Coming out he is "served with tea and given some beautiful roses which are carefully preserved." Mrs. Grundy says that "they remained all night at the tomb, chanting and praying without intermission, and standing throughout the ceremonies ... communing with the glorified spirit of Baha Ullah." Under the arbour was a chair where Baha Ullah used to sit. No one sits in it any longer. She knelt at the foot of the chair whilst one of the daughters of Baha chanted a prayer.[259]

A shrine, deemed even more sacred, yet remains. The pilgrims are conducted to it in an inner room of the residence of Abdul Baha. Here are the images "of the Glorious Ones of God." "We were all impelled to remove our shoes before crossing the threshold. Approaching in reverent awe, we were anointed with a fragrant perfume, and as we knelt before the majestic likeness[260] of the Blessed Perfection,

---

that he was accepting divine honour from simple-minded women from America and receiving their gifts of gold without protest or rebuke."

[256] New York *Outlook*, June, 1901, pp. 45, 46.

[257] Mrs. Grundy, *Ibid.*, p. 73.

[258] Page 212.

[259] See "Ten Days in the Light at Acca," pp. 71-73; "My Visit to Acca," p. 21; "In Galilee," p. 69; "Heavenly Vista," p. 22; "Daily Lessons," p. 80; "Flowers from Acca," p. 36; "Table Talks," p. 14.

[260] Baha, in the "Akdas," forbids women from going on pilgrimage, the adoration of pictures and the kissing of hands. Why does Abdul Baha encourage them? Ignorant devotion has so soon degenerated into superstition and iconolatry. Others are trading on the superstitious. Abdul Baha writes: "I have received news that some one in Persia has imitated the picture of the Manifestation and sold it for $200 to a believer. The real picture is not in the possession of any one but me."

Baha Ullah and that of the Bab, we were unable to speak."[261] "Here is seen the expression of gentleness, meekness, wisdom, light, love, majesty, power, holiness, in short, every attribute of God."[262]

How far from the Christian position the Bahais have wandered is seen in the narratives of these pilgrims who take little interest

> In those holy fields,
> Over whose acres walked those blessed feet
> Which, nineteen hundred years ago, were nail'd
> For our advantage to the blessed cross.

To them not Jerusalem but Acca is the Holy City. Not Nazareth and the Sea of Galilee, but Haifa and its bay, not the Garden of Gethsemane but the Rizwan, not Calvary but the Turkish prison barracks, not Mount Olivet but Mount Carmel, attract their interest and engage their love.

XI. Bahaism in its festivals abandons the Christian year. In the "Akdas," besides *Noruz*, New Year, there are two sacred days: (1) The anniversary of the declaration of the Bab, May 23, 1844; and (2) the birthday of Baha Ullah, November 12, 1817. To these have been added: (3) The feast of *Rizwan*, April 21-May 2, commemorating the declaration of Baha Ullah in Bagdad; (4) the death of Baha Ullah, May 28, 1892, at Acca; and still later (5) the birthday of Abdul Baha, May 24, 1844; and (6) his appointment as "Centre of the Covenant," November 26. The four or five intercalary days, February 26-March 2, corresponding in a measure to Carnival, are a feasting time before the annual fast.

The weekly holy days of the three monotheistic religions are abolished. Instead of a Sabbath, every nineteenth day, the first of each month, is a sacred day; even the week is abolished. The ninth day of each month has been made sacred by Abdul Baha.

The era is also changed. The world and its events are to be reckoned from the Bahai cycle. Just what this is seems to be doubtful, for some date from the Declaration of the Bab and write 1914 as the year 70. The *Star of the West* is so dated. Some date from the birth of Baha Ullah and count this as the year 97, as on the title page of "The Bahai Movement," by Remey. Even the year of Abdul Baha's accession (1892) is used as a date.[263] Thus Bahaism has no Christian era, no Christian Sabbath, no Easter, no Christmas, no Trinitarian formula in benediction, doxology, or sacrament, no symbol of the cross, no hymns to Christ, no Apostles' Creed, no Lord's Prayer. Yet it claims to be Christian!

XII. In conclusion, Bahaism is antichristian in its aim and propaganda. Whenever it comes in contact with Christian missions, in Persia, Syria, Egypt, India, or Burmah, it is the opposer of the messenger of Christ and His Gospel. A hope cherished thirty years ago, by some missionaries and others, that it might be a stepping stone for Moslems to Christ has not been fulfilled; albeit some of the best

---

[261] "Flowers from Acca," p. 34.
[262] "A Heavenly Vista," p. 22; and above references.
[263] *Star*, March 2,1914, p. 321.

converts from Islam have first sought the broken cisterns of Bahaism.[264] Bahaism is plainly antichristian. It is a new and a different, an inferior and a false religion. Its claims are contradictory to the claims of Christ. It would draw men's allegiance to another person, to other Scriptures, to a system of doctrine and way of salvation inconsistent with the Gospel, to forms of worship, ceremonies, and festivals at variance with those of Christianity. It declares that Christianity is abrogated and superseded. Its erroneous dictum is that "the revelation of Jesus is no longer the point of guidance for the world." Why cannot Christian people see that its claims annul faith and loyalty to Christ? Surely giving Bahaism countenance, assistance, and encouragement or opportunity for its propaganda is to wound Christ in the house of His friends.

---

[264] Doctor Jessup, *Outlook, Ibid.*, says, "An old Persian Sheikh, in 1897, came to the American Press in Beirut, with a large sheet of paste board on which was written the motto 'Ya Baha ul Abha' and wished to have a map mounted on the face of it. In reply to inquiry why he thus would use it, he said: 'I have had it hanging on my wall for twelve years and prayed to it, and found it to be vanity and worthless. I now prefer to read the Bible.'"

VI

BAHAISM AND THE STATE

Babism political Mahdiism—Hostile to Shah—Insurrections—Bahaism opportunism—Sought reconciliation—Tolerated—Indifferent to Constitutional struggle—Aided reactionary Shah—Reward-
ed by him Its political scheme—Houses of Justice—Dangerous to
liberty

Bahaism certainly does contemplate an earthly dominion
which shall eventually subvert all existing governments.—*Doctor
Holmes in Speer's "Missions and Modern History," Vol. I, p. 129.*

The supreme manifestation of social morality is always government and in formulating a politic, Baha Ullah most clearly
earned our reverence as the prophet of modern society.... Democ-
racy alone tends to vulgarize personal values, as the United States
proves. By uniting the aristocratic spirit with the democratic form
of Government, he insured a politic at once equable and effective.—*H. Holley, "The Modern Social Religion" p. 203.*

In calling Babi-Bahaism a worse cult than Mormonism, I do
so deliberately.—*S. K. Vatralsky in "Amer. Jour. of Theology," 1902,
p. 73.*

There can be little doubt from the intolerance they show to
those who recant, that should they gain power enough they would
be as ready to persecute Christians as was Mohammed to put to
death the Jews of Medina.—*Dr. G. W. Holmes in Speer's ibid., p. 130.*

BAHAISM, as a new religion bidding for popular favour, should be considered in its relation to the State, for this is an important factor in forming our judgment of it. As it historically sprang from Babism, it is well to review, first of all, the
political relations of Babism.

I. Babism in Persia was a form of Mahdiism. Mirza Ali Mohammed, the Bab,
claimed to be the Mahdi, the Kaim, the twelfth Imam returned. According to Shiah
doctrine, the rulership of the State by divine law belongs to the Imam. The Kajar
Shahs had the right to kingship only in the absence of the Imam. Their authority
would cease with his appearance. This is so universally recognized that the constitution of Persia drawn up by the Parliament in 1906-1907 contains in the preamble

the provision that it shall continue only till the manifestation of the Imam.

In accordance with this principle the Babis looked upon Mohammed Shah and Nasr-ud-Din Shah as no longer the rightful rulers. They were, *ipso facto*, supplanted by the Bab, the Sahib-i-Zaman or Lord of the Age. The Kajars were called by them "unlawful kings." Hazrat-Kuddus says,[265] "We are the rightful rulers; know that Nasr-ud-Din is no true king and that such as support him shall be tormented in hell-fire." Disloyalty was an essential corollary of Babism and not a consequence of the repression and persecution which it met. The measures of the Persian Government were caused by this knowledge. The rebellions of the Babis were justified in their eyes by self-preservation as well as by the desire to remove, if possible, the Shah and make way for the reign of the Bab. Professor Browne's opinion on these points is conclusive. He says:[266]—

"The Babis looked for their immediate triumph over all existing powers, culminating in the universal establishment of the true faith and the reign of God's saints on earth.... They intended to inherit the earth; they held those who rejected the Bab as unclean and worthy of death, and they held the Kajar Shahs in a detestation which they were at no pains to hide.... They did not make any profession of loyalty to or love for the reigning dynasty.... Unbelievers were flouted with scorn because they supposed that the Promised Deliverer would confirm the authority of the Shahs."

The "Bayan," the chief book of the Bab, anticipates the time when the Shah's government shall be superseded by a Babi state, which shall prevail in Persia. It gives the laws for this Babi state as well as regulations for the distribution of the spoils of war and for the Jahad,[267] showing that the Bab anticipated religious wars. The kings of the Bayanic dispensation are directed what they should do. In the five chief provinces of Persia, no unbelievers are to be allowed to live, except some foreign Christian merchants. They are not to be killed, but to be driven out and their property confiscated.[268] Directions are given as to the use of their property. The strongly intolerant doctrine is set forth[269] that "unbelievers have no right to anything, not even to a believing wife. All that thou seest in the hands of unbelievers is not theirs by right. If the manifestation has power, he would even forbid their breathing."

Babism, therefore, was a political as well as a religious movement. As such it fought and with some prospect of success, for, as Browne says, "it seemed at one time to menace the supremacy alike of the Kajar dynasty and of the Mohammedan faith in Persia."[270]

The Bab was executed in 1850. The Babi insurrections were suppressed. Terrible reprisals followed the attempt on the life of Nasr-ud-Din Shah. The leaders fled into exile to Turkey. Babism, repressed and forced into concealment, entered upon

[265] "New Hist.," p. 362.
[266] *Ibid.*, p. xvi.
[267] "Trav.'s Narr.," p. 287.
[268] "Bayan," VI, 4.
[269] "Beyan Persan," Vol. IV, p. 118.
[270] Browne, "New Hist.," p. vii.

a new phase. It emerged somewhat changed as Bahaism (1867).

II. Bahaism should be considered in its political aspects in relation to the Government of Persia.

(a) In Persia, the issue of the sword had declared against the Babis. Baha Ul-lah adopted a policy aptly called "political opportunism."[271] He proclaimed the loyalty of himself and his followers to the Shah, denounced the attempted assassinations, wrote prayers to be said for the Shah,[272] and pleaded for the toleration of the sect as one without political aspirations. Bahai apologists condemned the Bab and the conduct of the Babis, declaring it contrary to the principles of the Bab.[273] Mirza Abul Fazl, on trial before the Persian Government, repudiated the Babis, denounced their actions as unseemly and bad,[274] and declared with emphasis that Bahaism was an entirely different religion. He pronounced the Shah free from blame regarding the death of the Bab[275] and the persecutions of the Babis, casting the responsibility and reproach on the mullahs and the Ministers of State.[276] He even made a show of blaming the attendants for the death of Badi, the messenger who bore Baha's epistle to the Shah, and made as though the Shah regretted it. The "New History" and the "Traveller's Narrative" are both tendency writings, following out the same purpose, glossing over the facts as given in the contemporary narrative of Mirza Jani, putting the odium on the mullahs and asserting "that no particular blame attaches to His Most Sacred Majesty the Shah";[277] though other writings of Baha show a spirit of hostility to the Shah.[278] Following the policy of conciliation the Bahais made petition to the Shah stating that[279] "this sect has no worldly object nor any concern with political matters, it has nothing to do with affairs of Government neither has it any concern with the powers of the throne." They stated that[280] "they have made no disturbance, or rebellions, or any sign of sedition." So Baha[281] enjoined that "in every country they must behave towards the Government with faithfulness, trustfulness, and truthfulness." The Persian Government responded to this policy and ceased to persecute as before. During the past fifty years the Bahais have not been much molested. Their persecutions have been few and generally due to local causes. The number of Bahais who have lost their lives in the course of their history (after they cease to be Babis) is probably not more than 300, more than half of whom were killed in riots at Ispahan and Yezd in 1903. The Bahai historian[282] states that "on rare occasions certain Ulema, for their own personal and private advantage, molest one or two individuals of the

[271] Browne, "New Hist.," p. vii.

[272] *Ibid.*, p. 316.

[273] "Trav.'s Narr.," p. 65.

[274] "Bahai Proofs," pp. 51, 63, 77.

[275] *Ibid.*, p. 38.

[276] "New Hist.," pp. 172, 180.

[277] "Trav.'s Narr.," p. 189.

[278] See "Surat-ul-Muluk," and *S. W.*, Sept. 27, 1913, pp. 9, 10. See Chap. VIII, p. 186, 191.

[279] "Trav.'s Narr.," p. 156.

[280] *Ibid.*, p. 160.

[281] "Words of Paradise."

[282] "Trav.'s Narr.," p. 166.

sect." But the Shah's Government has tolerated them.[283] Not counting the present Holy War against the Christians, more have been killed in Persia in the half century than Bahais.[284] The Government has shown liberality towards Bahais by allowing them to occupy positions in the civil service, as clerks in the post, telegraph, customs, courts, and consulates, and has not discriminated against them.

(*b*) Coming to the period of the agitation for a constitution and the revolution, it is plain that the Bahais had little to do with the struggle. Neither they nor their teachings were the cause of it. The causes were the same, in general, as those which influenced Turkey and China towards constitutional reform. The occasions in local circumstances and politics had nothing to do with Bahaism. The leaders were enlightened Moslems, and even mullahs of the Shiahs. They were not Bahais. These held aloof from the propaganda and the struggle for popular liberties, took little part in the elections or in parliament, and joined neither the army of the constitutionalists nor that of the reactionaries. They displayed no love of country by striving for the cause of the people, nor any real love or loyalty to the autocratic Shah. Yet the influence of Abdul-Baha Abbas was thrown in favour of Mohammed Ali Shah, and after he had scattered parliament at the cannon's mouth and annulled the constitution, Bahais were granted appointments in the civil service and rejoiced in the reactionary régime. A tablet of Abdul Baha was circulated prophesying a long and prosperous reign for Mohammed Ali Shah, who before many months was driven from his throne into exile.

My personal knowledge of these circumstances is supported by abundant printed evidence. First of all there is Abdul Baha's own statement. He said in America,[285] "In Persia the Bahais have no part in the movements which have terminated in corruption. They must have nothing to do with seditious movements." Excerpts from his letters[286] show that they were constantly enjoined "from the very beginning of the revolution to stand aside from the struggle and war." To the same effect are the words of the Bahai Remey,[287] "The Bahais had remained neutral in the struggle for constitutional liberty and the renewal of Persia." So Dreyfus, another Bahai,[288] "He (Abdul Baha) dissuaded them from mixing themselves up in the political struggle. This explains the apparently passive rôle played by the Bahais in contemporary events in Persia." Because of this attitude, Professor Browne accuses them of lack of patriotism and laments their inaction. But this attitude of neutrality was only maintained by them as far as taking up arms and public action were concerned. Their secret influence was on the side of the reactionary party. It is plain that the constitutionalists regarded the Bahais as their opponents, and Mohammed Ali Shah counted them as his supporters. Abdul Baha said in

---

[283] Browne, "A Year Among the Persians," p. 101. M. A. Ford in "The Oriental Rose," p. 74, says, "For many years before the death of Baha Ullah, there was no persecution of the friends."

[284] See "Missions and Modern History," R. E. Speer, p. 130, Note 2.

[285] *S. W.*, July 13, 1913.

[286] Browne's "Persian Revolution," pp. 424-429.

[287] "Observations of a Bahai Traveller," p. 53.

[288] *Ibid.*, p. 172.

New York,[289] "The Bahais have taken no part whatever in political questions and disturbances. Their clamorous persecutors were the revolutionists. These discontents wanted constitutional rights and privileges. They were politicians, not religionists." Certainly the hostile animus of these words is unmistakable. There is indubitable proof, too, that Abdul Baha carried on correspondence with Mohammed Ali Shah. M. H. Ford, a Bahai writer,[290] states the fact in detail. Its purport was such that, when the Constitutionalists knew it, Abdul Baha feared violence. This was commonly reported in Persia. In Chicago the first Bahai missionary to America confirmed this fact which he had heard from Acca. He said, "The authorities intercepted Abbas's letter intriguing with Mohammed Ali Shah, and therefore the revolutionists threatened him." Remey shows the affiliation of the Bahais with the Shah, and his satisfaction with them. He arrived at Teheran just when the Shah had scattered the parliament and hanged the editors. He says, "We found the Bahais in the utmost peace and happiness. They were in good esteem and respect of the [reactionary] Government, and were now enjoying *unusual* privileges.... Several of the Bahais had been appointed to high governmental positions." In accord with all these facts is the statement of J. D. Frame, M. D., of Resht:

"The political influence of the Bahais has been grossly exaggerated. They were forbidden to accept seats in the first parliament and professed to maintain strict neutrality, but in the spring of 1908 a 'tablet' was circulated among them, promising that Mohammed Ali Shah would rule for the remainder of his life; and the writer possesses a copy of another 'tablet' promising him speedy peace and prosperity. The subsequent forced abdication of the king cost the Bahais considerable prestige and some followers."[291]

We thus see a double failure on the part of this movement. As Babism it failed in 1848-1852 in its rebellion and wars against the Kajars; as Bahaism it failed to enter into and assist the modern movement, which, aiming at reform and progress, inaugurated a constitution. The cause of the latter is not far to seek; Bahaism has a political scheme of its own. We will now consider it.

III. Bahaism has set forth a system of civil government. Claiming to be a revelation from God, it has enunciated the laws and regulations of the future State. It approves of constitutional monarchy as the best form of government, and permits republics.[292] But this monarchy will be limited not so much by its constitution as by the law of Bahaism and its hierarchy. Baha, in the "Kitab-ul-Akdas," the Book of Laws, directs that Bet-Adl, houses of justice, be established in every place, with nine or more members, all Bahai men, who shall be Trustees of the Merciful, Administrators for God. In the thirteenth of the "Glad Tidings"[293] he says:

"The affairs of the people are placed in charge of the men of the House of Justice. They are daysprings of command (divine agents, representatives of God). They may execute what they deem advisable. It is incumbent upon all to obey

---

[289] *S. W.*, August 1, 1912.
[290] "The Oriental Rose," pp. 185-186, 197.
[291] *The Moslem World*, 1912, p. 238.
[292] "Glad Tidings," p. 91.
[293] Chicago Edition, p. 89.

them. Their souls will be inspired with divine aspiration. God will inspire them with what He willeth."

With them will lie the interpretation of points of doctrine. They must decree and judge according to Bahai revelation. "They must gaze day and night towards that which hath been revealed from the horizon of the Supreme Pen." They shall rule by divine right. Their authority shall be absolute. Abdul Baha restates the words of Baha:[294] "The House of Justice must be obeyed in all things." "It is the centre of true government." "The Law of God will be invested in them, and they will render decisions." "All judgment will be from the standpoint of God's laws." "Its decisions and commands will be guarded from mistake. It will have conferred upon it infallibility." The House of Justice will have local councils, national ones, and an international one.[295] Of the latter, Abdul Baha said in an address in New York:

"A universal or world House of Justice shall be organized. That which it orders shall be the Truth in explaining the commands of Baha Ullah and shall be obeyed by all. *All men shall be under its supervision.*"[296]

Its functions are not confined to matters of faith, for Abdul Baha continues: "The House of Justice is endowed with a political as well as a religious aspect. It embodies both aspects, and is protected by the preserving power of Baha Ullah himself." *In the political aspect it will be supreme.* "The separation of the Religion and the State can only be temporary," says Dreyfus,[297] "a momentary stage. For the present the two spheres are separate. When Bahaism triumphs they will be united." "The House of Justice[298] will have under its control almost the whole administration, and naturally will take the place of our municipal councils. Such has been Baha Ullah's intention. Further he clearly aims not only at a municipal House of Justice, but also at a legislative one, sitting as a national parliament and as an international tribunal." Remember that all the members are to be Bahais. So Remey says, "There will be a union of Religion and the State—the governments of the nations. The material laws of men will be founded and enforced according to Bahaism."[299] In this politico-religious régime, the political will be subject to the religious. "The kings and rulers of the world," says Abdul Baha,[300] "will find their true authority under the rulings of the House of Justice. It will decide between kings and kings." Baha addressed letters[301] to kings with arrogant assumption of authority to control the civil powers.

The Houses of Justice will have *large financial powers.* They shall inherit all property of those dying without heirs, and one-third of that of those dying child-

[294] Grundy's "Ten Days in Acca."

[295] "Answered Questions," by Abdul Baha, Barney, pp. 198-199.

[296] *S. W.,* Dec. 12, 1913; April 9, 1914, p. 21.

[297] "The Bahai Revelation," p. 123.

[298] *Ibid.,* p. 144.

[299] "Bahai Movement," p. 69.

[300] Grundy, *Ibid.*

[301] Mohammed wrote to the rulers of Constantinople, Persia, Egypt, and Syria. That which was a bold and striking act on the part of Mohammed is a weak imitation on the part of Baha.

less.[302] One-third of all fines for crimes shall go to them. For example, in case of murder, two-thirds of the blood money shall go to the family of the murdered and one-third to the House of Justice. A tithe of nineteen-hundredths shall be given into their hands. They shall act as trustees for minors and incapables, and as a Poor Board.

They shall have *civil* jurisdiction, "to settle material difficulties between believers,"[303] for the protection of men, for the preservation of human honour.[304] "If any man refuses to educate his children, the House of Justice shall do it at his expense," and "shall order all the negligent to pay" and use police powers to enforce it.

They must also interpret and administer *criminal* law, for Baha has "revealed" a code of laws and regulations concerning material as well as spiritual things.[305] Abdul Baha says, "The revelations of Baha Ullah contain all the great laws of social government." "The laws cover all points and questions of national administration."[306] For example, in the "Kitab-ul-Akdas," the punishment for theft is prescribed: for the first offense, exile; for the second, imprisonment; for the third, branding "thief" on the forehead, "lest other countries accept him." For adultery a fine is to be paid to the House of Justice, and for the second offense, double of the fine. Arson is made punishable by burning, etc. This fiat legislation of Baha Ullah is to be imposed upon the parliaments of all nations. "All legislative and administrative functions," says Dreyfus,[307] "shall assume a sacred character" under the control of the Bahai House of Justice.

In brief, Bahaism would set up in each town, in every country, ruling councils, and a central one universal in its sway, composed entirely of Bahais, clothed with supreme authority, because God-given, over kings, parliaments, and peoples; councils infallible and absolute, superior to appeal or protest; deciding and exacting obedience in every department of the life of humanity—religious, domestic, social, educational, financial, judicial, and political. It would be not an *imperium in imperio*, but an Empire over all. It would be a priestcraft[308] such as the world has not yet seen—a religious-political régime in which kings and presidents will go not to Canossa but to Acca, and alike hold the stirrups of Bahai justices, and laws of parliaments will be subject to revision and veto by the Bahai House. In it is the certainty of priestly oppression when fallible men set up their judgment as God's. The Bahais claim to have no priests and no *hierarchy*. It is a question of names. Their system and laws contain the real thing, full-fledged, men mediating God's will. We may call it a *bahaiarchy*, if they prefer.

---

[302] They become what they accused the Shiah Mullahs of being; "Dead men's heirs, consumers of endowments, and collectors of tithes and 'thirds.'"

[303] Dreyfus, p. 131.

[304] "Ishrakat," p. 33.

[305] Remey, p. 61.

[306] Kheiralla, p. 433.

[307] "The Bahai Revelation," p. 32.

[308] The word "priest" is used loosely for an officer of religion. Bahais use no special term. Abdul Baha says ("Universal Principles," p. 38): "The making of specific laws is apportioned to the House of Justice. The members will not form laws and statutes according to their own opinions and thoughts, but by the power of inspiration."

Abdul Baha, recognizing the objections that will be made to the political functions of the Bahai justices, and foreseeing difficulty with Governments, has, for the time being, directed that in America and Europe the name "House of Spirituality" or "House of Consultation" be used.[309] But change of name does not alter the reality or change the "revelation" of Baha. The House of Justice (central) is to be set up when Abdul Baha dies, and it will assume its functions gradually as opportunity and expediency demand. Already orders have gone forth prohibiting the interpretation of the words of Baha or personal expositions of them.[310] Already the fiat has interdicted the publication, by a Bahai, of a tract, book, or translation on the Bahai religion without submitting it to the censor at Acca.[311]

The effect of the working of the Bahai system may be realized by imagining it as set up in Persia. Suppose, for example, that the small minority of Bahais now in Persia should become a majority, with a Bahai Shah, Bahaism would become the established religion. "Houses of Justice" would come into operation. What of those who remain Moslems and Christians? Fortunately Baha has abolished the law of the Bab that required their expulsion from the chief provinces of Persia and the confiscation of their property. But either the other religions must be judged by Bahai courts, or separate courts must be set up for them. This would perpetuate the double system of courts, the *urfi* or civil and the *shari* or religio-civil courts. The latter would be entirely Bahai and either lording it over or in conflict with the civil administration. This would be a continuation of the present confusion of Persian conditions, only with the Bahais in control. What might the minority expect? The oppressions and anathemas received by the old Bahais from the followers of Abdul Baha Abbas give the answer.[312] Fortunately for the world, the universal reign of Bahaism is not to be realized, neither is the prophecy of Abdul Baha to be fulfilled which says[313] "that the flag of Baha Ullah will overcome every other flag and all rulers will do homage to it."

---

[309] "Tablets," Vol. I, pp. 1 and 6.

[310] "Brilliant Proof," p. 26.

[311] *S. W.*, July 13, 1913, p. 121.

[312] Abdul Baha justified Mohammed's use of the sword, saying, "Mohammed commanded his followers to carry the religion of God by the sword. It is right to inflict injury to save a man's life," therefore to save his soul by force.

[313] "Daily Lessons at Acca" (Goodall and Cooper), p. 72.

VII

BAHAISM AND WOMAN

Abdul Baha teaches equality of sexes—Baha does not—Education of girls neglected—Marriage enjoined—Bigamy allowed—And practiced—Polygamy of Baha—His family—Loose divorce—Intermarriage of races—Aims at amelioration of woman—Moslem efforts—Babi Kurrat ul Ayn—No successor to—Baha's haram—Men only to be rulers—Women secluded

Baha Ullah in a letter to one of his wives:—This writing is to the Exalted Leaf, who hath tasted My Most Holy and Wonderful Saliva. We have given thee to drink from My Sweetest Mouth, O thou blessed and sparkling leaf. We have bestowed upon thee such a station as no woman had who preceded thee.—*In Prayers, Tablets and Instructions, 1900.*

There is a touch of oriental luxury of admiration in some estimates of Kurrat-ul-Ayn, who in important moral characteristics did not rise above the level of her time and place. And in its results Babism has not exalted woman.—*R. E. Speer, "Missions and Modern History" Vol. I, p. 150.*

ABDUL BAHA while in Europe and America had much to say about the relation of man and woman. In New York City, after referring the audience to various books of the Bahai religion, he said: "Similarly all the other tablets of Baha Ullah contain *new* teachings, which have not been revealed in any books of the past Prophets. The sixth new teaching is the equality between men and women. This is peculiar to the teachings of Baha Ullah, for all other religions placed men above women."[314] In the exposition of Bahai teachings at Clifton, England, he declared: "His Highness, Baha Ullah, established certain precepts or principles."[315] "The sixth principle of Baha Ullah regards the equality of the sexes. God has created the man and the woman equal. In the animal kingdom the male and the female enjoy suffrage [laughter]; in the vegetable kingdom the plants all enjoy equal suffrage [laughter and applause]. The male and the female of the human kingdom are equal before God. Divine justice demands that men and women have equal rights."

My first thought on reading these statements was one of surprise, for they con-

---

[314] *S. W.* (Bahai), Dec. 12, 1913, p. 254.
[315] *S. W.* (Bahai), March 21, 1913, p. 5.

tradict my observations during thirty years' residence in Persia, in close touch with Bahais. I decided to make a thorough investigation of the teachings and practice of Baha Ullah bearing on the relation of the sexes, to determine definitely whether these claims of the "inspired interpreter" were valid or not. A considerable body of Bahai literature and "revelation" is accessible. Examination of the chief books, the "Kitab-ul-Akdas," the "Ikan" and the "Surat-ul-Haykal" disclose no such teaching. Neither the 155 paragraphs of the "Hidden Words," nor the "Seven Valleys" have any such delectable thoughts for Oriental women. Neither the six "Ornaments"[316] of the faith nor the four "Rays,"[317] nor the nine "Effulgences,"[318] nor the eleven "Leaves of the Words of Paradise," nor the nine precepts of the "Tablet of the World," nor the fifteen "Glad Tidings"—though they announce many blessings, from freedom to cut the beard as you please to constitutional monarchy as the best form of government—give the teaching of the equality of woman with man. Neither Mirza Abul Fazl in his "Bahai Proofs," representing the new Bahais of Abdul Baha, nor Doctor Kheiralla in his ponderous volume on Beha Ullah, representing the old Behais, in this bitter and rancorous schism; nor Myron Phelps in his "Life of Abbas Effendi," nor Professor Browne of Cambridge University in his learned and impartial investigations regarding the religion makes the statement that Baha Ullah teaches the equality of man and woman. On the contrary, investigation confirmed my previous conviction that the position of woman under Bahai laws and customs is inferior to that she holds in Western lands and that her lot is far less desirable and less blest than in Christian civilization. I reached the conclusion that this doctrine as enunciated by the "Interpreter" is a late addition to Bahaism, intended to attract the attention and tickle the ears of audiences in Europe and America.

Of the two or three thousand Americans who are following the cult of Bahaism, most are women. Concerning this Abdul Baha says in a tablet: "Today the women of the West lead the men in the service of the cause (Bahaism) and loosen their tongues in eloquent lectures."[319] The editor adds, "Nine-tenths of the active workers in the cause are women."[320] Hence it is timely to consider the teaching and practice of Baha Ullah with regard to women.

I. I will first take up the *subject of education*, for in regard to it the law of Bahaism justifies, theoretically, their boast of maintaining the equality of the sexes. In this it is, however, simply imitating the law of enlightened Christian lands, nor does their practice at all keep pace with their precepts. In the seventh Ishrak

---

[316] Tablet of Tarazat.

[317] Tablet of Tajalliyat.

[318] Ishrakat.

[319] *Bahai News*, Aug. 20, 1911.

[320] Mr. Remey writes: "In most places the work is carried on by the women almost entirely. There is an absence of many men.... Men are most in need of being reached.... Today I had a letter from a good maid-servant, saying that the only man in *her* assembly had refused to come to meetings, because he was the only man present. I mention this because it is typical of most assemblies in America.... In most places the men are doing but little." (*Bahai News*, Aug. 20, 1910, p. 3).

(Effulgence) it is "enjoined upon all to instruct and educate their children."[321] The "Kitab-ul-Akdas" decrees "that every father must educate his sons and daughters in learning and in writing" and also in the Bahai religion. Education is to be compulsory and if neglected by the parents must be attended to by the "House of Justice." But, notwithstanding this law, most Persian Bahais have allowed their girls to grow up in ignorance, while educating many of their boys. Even at Acca,[322] Syria, the headquarters of the sect, where Baha had a school for boys, no like opportunity was furnished to the girls for an education. The fact that modern schools for girls could not be opened in Persia is no adequate excuse, for private tutors could have been employed, as is the custom in many Persian Shiah families, or the fathers could at least have taught their daughters to read. Lately American Bahais have begun to stir them up. They have organized the Persian-American or Orient-Occident Educational Society. It raises funds in America for Bahai schools and hospitals. With exceeding lack of candour, it poses as simply a philanthropic enterprise and conceals its primary and ulterior object, which is the propagation of Bahaism. Its missionaries make their reports of their work in the *Bahai News* or *Star of the West*, of Chicago. They have one or more schools for girls in Persia and several scores of girls in attendance. The American Bahai missionaries are residing in Teheran and Tabriz,[323] directing the propaganda and working for the elevation of the girls and women through the Bahai religion.

II. I pass to the consideration of *the civil and domestic rights of woman under Bahaism*, and will review the customs and regulations regarding marriage—so fundamental in the constitution of human society.

(*a*) Marriage seems to be obligatory, according to the "Kitab-ul-Akdas." It says: "A solitary life does not meet God's approval; adhere unto what the trustworthy Counsellor commands. Deprive not yourselves of that which is created for you."[324] Monks and nuns are called upon to marry that they may have children "to celebrate the praise of God." A tablet says: "Nor must they refrain from marriage which causes procreation and multiplication of the servants of God."[325] Mirza Abul Fazl, the learned philosopher of the dispensation, interprets the law to mean: "He has enjoined upon the people of Baha abstinence from monkhood as well as from ascetic discipline. He has commanded them to marry."[326] Professor Browne says: "Marriage is enjoined upon all." In like manner the "Bayan" of the Bab previously made marriage obligatory, but unlawful with an unbeliever.

(*b*) Marriage is declared to be conditioned on the consent of both parties and of the parents. But in practice the matter of consent is still one-sided. Take, for example, an incident in the life of Abbas Effendi.[327] The mother and sister were very desirous that he should marry and looked about and found a girl of whom they approved. The sister narrates that "without consulting my brother, I invited

[321] "Tablet of Ishrakat," p. 36.
[322] Phelps, pp. 110, 229.
[323] Afterwards withdrawn from Tabriz.
[324] "Principles of the Bahai Movement," p. 16.
[325] Mirza Abul Fazl's "Bahai Proofs," p. 105.
[326] *Ibid.*, pp. 95-96.
[327] Phelps, *Ibid.*, pp. 86-87.

the girl to visit us. After a wearisome journey, she and her brother reached Haifa. We commenced quietly to make preparations for the marriage without making known to my brother the arrival of the girl. My brother saw that there was something unusual afoot, so he demanded of us with considerable energy, 'What is this? What are all the people smiling about? Are you again planning to get me a wife? If you are, give it up; I will not marry.' We pleaded and reasoned with him. At length we said, 'She has come, what shall we do?' He hesitated and finally said: 'Well, since you have brought her here, she belongs to me, and I will give her in marriage to some one else.' At length my brother brought about her marriage to a husband of his own selection." The "consent" of the girl in this case seems to have been considered about as much as in ordinary Oriental usage.

(c) Baha Ullah advised against child-marriages, yet, strange to say, seems to have tolerated child-betrothals. Among Persians it is a common custom to betroth children. Abbas was after this manner betrothed to his cousin in infancy. When the household of Baha thought the time had come for the marriage, Abbas thought differently and refused to agree to it. This incident[328] occurred before the one narrated above and is concerning a different girl. Curiously it was a girl named Moneera, who had been betrothed to another in infancy who finally became the wife of Abbas Effendi. She had been promised to her cousin Mohammed Tagi, and after she had reached the age of maturity, the youth urged on the marriage. The wedding was celebrated and the bride brought to the groom's house. Then, so the story goes, the husband refused to see his bride and continued in stubborn neglect and denial of marital rights till his death—six months afterwards. Later Baha Ullah persuaded Abbas to take the "sweet and amiable" virgin-widow for his wife and he is said to have attained to "a warm affection and regard" for the woman he was asked to marry.[329] Did I wish to assume the rôle of higher critic, I might suggest that the latter incident, like that in "When Knighthood was in Flower," is apocryphal, and intended to create a legend of her virginity up to the time she became the "leaf" of the "Greatest Branch of God."

Another account I have gathered from a Syrian disciple of Baha. He reports that Abbas Effendi would not marry the girl his parents had betrothed him to, because he had a love affair with Moneera, the wife of Mohammed Tagi. The speedy demise of the husband was attributed to poison administered by his wife, who thereupon became the wife of Abbas Effendi. Her title among Bahais is "Holy Mother."

(d) Another part of the marriage law gives directions as to the number of wives a man may take. The "Kitab-ul-Akdas" says: "God hath decreed you to marry. Beware of marrying more than two, and whosoever is content with one, attaineth peace for himself and her."[330]

Mr. Phelps[331] calls attention to this fact that the Book of Laws permits of taking two wives. This limitation of the man to bigamy is deemed an improvement on

[328] Phelps, *Ibid.*, p. 85.

[329] *Ibid.*, pp. 88-90.

[330] See also Professor Browne in the *Jour. Roy. As. Soc.*, 1892.

[331] "Life of Abbas Effendi," p. 139.

the law of Islam allowing polygamy.

But Bahai law does not permit a wife to have two husbands. This absolutely invalidates the claim and declaration of Bahaism concerning the equality of the sexes. It proclaims the woman the inferior, not the equal. No equality can exist in a household under such a license. Where is the boast of progress and superiority, when the most essential unit of human society is nullified? "Twain shall be one," says the Gospel of Christ. Can we believe that the "Incarnated Father of all" has revealed a new "Most Holy Book" in which bigamy is permitted? *Akstag fur Allah!* God forbid!

I will now give some details from the history of the Babi and Bahai "Manifestations" to show their practice in regard to marriage.

After the execution of the Bab, 1850, the rival claimants to prophethood were Mirza Yahya, surnamed Subh-i-Azal, and Mirza Husain Ali, surnamed Baha Ullah. They were sons of Mirza Abbas of Nur,[332] called Mirza Buzurk. He had a wife and a concubine. Yahya was the son of the wife and Husain Ali of the concubine. This was under the law of Islam. The subsequent enmity of the half-brothers exhibits one of the evil results of polygamy.

Subh-i-Azal was the "Lord of two wives," whose names and condition are recorded in the pension records[333] of the Turkish and British Governments in Cyprus. The first was named Fatima and her companion wife was Rukayya. They had fourteen children. Besides the two, who were with Azal in Cyprus, it seems there were two others. Of the third wife he says[334] in his personal narrative: "My wife, who was taken captive and was released, has now grown old in Persia without an interview being possible." The fourth quarrelled with her lord and accompanied the Bahais to Acca.[335] After several of the Azalis, with whom she was living, were murdered by the Bahais,[336] she was sent on to Constantinople with a surviving Azali.[337]

Baha Ullah, like Mohammed, surpassed his own law. He had three wives, or two wives and a concubine. Bahai writers generally omit this information in describing his life and character. Kheiralla has a chapter on his household and gives the names and titles of his children, twelve in all, but fails to mention the fact that he had two wives, though he says: "Like Abraham, by establishing his household, Baha Ullah perfected the laws of man, and fulfilled the prophecies of scripture."[338] C. M. Remey passes over the subject with the remark: "As a man he lived a life in harmony with his Oriental environment."[339] Abbas Effendi in his "Traveller's Narrative," Abul Fazl, Dreyfus, Sprague, Thornton and others fail to inform their

[332] "New Hist.," pp. 374-375.

[333] "Trav.'s Narr.," p. 384.

[334] "New Hist.," p. 415.

[335] Phelps, p. 73.

[336] "New Hist.," p. xxiii; "Trav.'s Narr.," p. 361. Compare "A Year Among the Persians."

[337] Phelps, p. 79.

[338] "Baha Ullah," by Kheiralla, pp. 491-492.

[339] "The Bahai Movement," by C. M. Remey, p. 24.

readers of the truth and this omission is evidently with definite purpose. Phelps is more candid. He says that "Baha Ullah had two wives; that the Book of Laws permits it."[340] Professor Browne refers to the three, giving the honorary titles conferred upon two of them. He makes a quotation[341] from Hasht Behasht which reads: "Among the titles conferred by Baha Ullah are the following:—on his wives, Madh-i-Ulya, 'the Supreme Cradle,' and Varaka-i-Ulya, 'the Supreme Leaf.'" And in the "New History," he says: "The title of Varaka-i-Ulya was conferred by Baha Ullah on one of his wives."[342] The name of the first wife was Aseyeh or Nowab. She was the mother of Abbas Effendi and six other children.[343] According to Subh-i-Azal's narrative[344] she was a niece of the Shah's vizier. She survived Baha and suffered much from the children of the other wife, according to Abbas Effendi.[345] The first marriage was in Teheran in 1835. He took a "companion for her" in 1850. Her title was Madh-Ulya. She was the mother of Mirza Mohammed Ali, Mirza Badi Ullah and other sons and daughters. The manuscript, "Life of Baha Ullah," continues: "In the last year at Bagdad (1867-68) before the exiling of our Lord to Constantinople, the sister of Mirza Mahdi of Kashan was honoured to be His wife." It appears that she was sent by a rich believer from Persia to be a maid-servant in Baha's household. The Persian Consul in Bagdad, Mirza Buzurk Khan Kasvini[346] desired to take her as his wife or concubine. Baha himself took her as a concubine. Because he was thwarted, the Consul showed special enmity to Baha and his followers. The only child of this wife, a girl, was born at Acca in 1873. The three wives survived Baha. After his death one of them suffered gross indignities at the hands of Abbas Effendi, being furiously attacked by him in his own house, so that she fled precipitately. This, at least, is the report of Khadim Ullah, the lifelong amanuensis of Baha Ullah.[347]

It should be noted that all of Baha's wives[348] had children, and that the first wife had a living son (Abbas) when he took the second wife, so that the usual excuses cannot be pleaded in palliation. For it is common for Bahais in Persia to quote their law, in speaking to a Christian, as meaning that a man may take an

---

[340] Phelps, p. 139.
[341] "Trav.'s Narr.," p. 361.
[342] "New Hist.," p. 273, Note 2.
[343] "Tablets of Abdul Baha," Vol. I, pp. 209, 218.
[344] "New Hist.," p. 415 and Note 1.
[345] "Tablets," Vol. I, p. 107.
[346] "Trav.'s Narr.," p. 84.
[347] "Facts for Behaists," p. 59.
[348] *The Family of Baha Ullah (1817-1892)*

First wife, named Nawab, or Aseyeh, entitled Veraka-ulya, "the Supreme Leaf," married at Teheran, 1251 A. H., *i. e.*, 1835 A. D.

Her children,   (1) Aga Mirza Sadik, born at Teheran, died at 4 years.

(2) Abbas Effendi, born at Teheran, 1841.

(3) Bahiah Khanum, born at Teheran, 1844.
N. B.: Some reverse the order of (2) and (3).

(4) Ali Mohammed, born at Teheran, died at 7 years.

additional wife if the first one is childless. Mr. Phelps pleads[349] in extenuation for Baha Ullah that "his second marriage occurred early in his life and under peculiar circumstances, the exact nature of which I do not know." Such an excuse might be accepted for a man like Mullah Mohammed Ali, the Babi leader of the Zenjan insurrection, for, as far as is known, he entered upon his polygamous life while he was a Mohammedan. Two of his wives[350] were shot by a cannon ball and were buried with him in a room of his house, while his third wife, with children, escaped and lived at Shiraz. But for Baha Ullah the excuse of Mr. Phelps is inadmissible, for he was no longer a Moslem when he took the second wife, and was thirty-three years old, and he was fifty when he took the third wife in Bagdad, having been born in 1817. At that time Baha had been for many years a leader in the Babi religion, had written the "Ikan," and announced his mission. Nor was this polygamous union a passing phase of his life, but one continued through thirty or forty years. It would have concerned us little to know the private life of Baha Ullah so long as the religion presented itself merely as aiming at a reformation of Islam, for it may readily be admitted that it is somewhat less of an evil to have two wives and one concubine than the four wives and unlimited concubines that the Koran allows, or the nine to thirteen wives that Mohammed took, and that if Bahaism should cut off the temporary concubines, which disgrace Islam, it would be doing a good thing—so far forth—but when the "Interpreter, the centre of the Covenant," Abdul Baha, comes and stands in Christian churches in London and New York and proclaims Bahaism as a new and superior gospel, it is expedient that Baha's real life should be made known to the women of Christian lands.

It is well to note the sentiment of Oriental Bahais with regard to plural marriage. The opinion of those at Acca can be understood from Mr. Phelps' narrative.[351] Abbas Effendi (Abdul Baha) had two sons and six daughters. The sons died. After this, as his sister Behiah Khanum narrates, "Many influences and those

---

(5) Aga Mahdi, born at Teheran, died at Acca, 1871.

(6) Ali Mohammed, born at Bagdad, died at 2 years.

Companion wife, Ayesha, title Mahd Ulya, "the Supreme Cradle," married A. H. 1266, 1850 A. D.

Her children,   (1) Mohammed Ali, born at Bagdad, 1854.

(2) Samadiah, Bagdad, 1857, died Acca, 1904.

(3) Ali Mohammed, Bagdad, died at 2 years.

(4) Saz-Habbieh, Bagdad, died Constantinople.

(5) Zia Ullah, Adrianople, 1867, Haifa, 1898.

(6) Badi Ullah, Adrianople.

Concubine, a sister of Mirza Mahdi Kashani, taken at Bagdad.

Her child,   (1) One daughter, born 1873, at Acca, name Shuruk.

The wives and concubine of Baha Ullah all survived him.

[349] Phelps, p. 139.
[350] "New Hist.," pp. 160-162, 164.
[351] "Life of Abbas Effendi," p. 92.

of the very strongest character have been brought to induce my brother (Abdul Baha) to take another wife. Believers have urged it strongly for several reasons. *Very many of them wish to take a second wife* themselves. Then there is a general wish that the Master might have a son to succeed him. The pressure brought to bear upon him has been very great, greater than you can imagine." Baha desired that Abbas should take a second wife, but he refused to do so unless Baha should command it. There is deep pathos in the words of Abbas[352] welling from his sorrow-stricken heart. "If it had been God's will that I should have a son, the two that were born to me would not have been taken away." Albeit he was forgetful of his theology which proclaims Baha as "God the Father incarnate." Why did not Baha preserve alive one of the sons rather than wish him to marry a companion-wife in order to have another? Mr. Phelps[353] attributes Abbas Effendi's refusal to adopt polygamy, notwithstanding these "very powerful influences which have urged him to do so" to "his appreciation of the sufferings and discontent which it causes among women."[354] Certainly the animosity and bitter quarrellings between the wives of Baha and their respective children, resulting in a permanent split in the family and a schism[355] in the Bahai community, were sufficient to impress Abbas and his followers with the evil effects of plural marriage. The narrative shows, however, that public sentiment among the believers at Acca strongly favoured taking more than one wife. They evidently had no desire to give up the license granted to them by the "Kitab-ul-Akdas." They inclined to follow it and the example of Baha Ullah rather than the example of Abdul Baha.

In conclusion, it is evident that the law and example of Baha Ullah both sanction polygamy. By this the social *inequality* of the sexes is fixed. Any claim that Bahaism teaches and establishes equal rights for man and woman is vain and groundless boasting.

III. *The regulation of divorce* is another matter that vitally affects the relation of man and woman. The divorce law of Baha, as prescribed in the "Kitab-ul-Akdas," is a loose one. I again quote from Professor Browne's translation.[356] It will be noticed that the conditions of the law are set forth from the standpoint of the man. "If quarrels arise between a man and his wife, he may put her away. He may not give her absolute divorce at once, but must wait a year that perhaps he may become reconciled to her. At the end of this period, if he still wishes to put her away, he is at liberty to do so. Even after this he may take her back at the end of any month so long as she has not become the wife of another man." "The practice of requiring a divorced woman to cohabit with another man before her former husband can take her back is prohibited." (This abolishes one of the vile laws of Mohammedanism.) "If a man is travelling with his wife and they quarrel, he must give her a sufficient

---

[352] Phelps, p. 94.

[353] Phelps, p. 105.

[354] A Chicago Bahai told me that Baha took several wives, that his experience of the evils of polygamy, the quarrels of his wives and children might be a warning to us not to follow his example!

[355] See Professor Browne's Introduction to Mirza Jani's "History." Also Abul Fazl's "Bahai Proofs," pp. 113-119, and Kheiralla's "Facts for Behaists."

[356] *Jour. Roy. As. Soc.,* 1892.

sum of money to take her back to the place they started from and send her with a trustworthy escort." From these quotations it is evident that the wife is dependent on the good pleasure and whim[357] of the man. He may put away; he may take back. The law says nothing of her right to divorce him. It does not appear that she has the right to divorce her husband even in case he is guilty of adultery. The penalty for adultery is slight. A fine of nineteen miscals of gold, equal to fifty to sixty dollars, is imposed for the first offense and this is doubled for the second offense. The fines are to be paid to the "House of Justice." According to the "Bayan" of the Bab the husband must pay the divorced wife a dowry of ninety-five miscals of gold ($300) if they are city folks, and ninety-five miscals of silver ($10) if they are villagers. These are paltry sums even on the basis of Persian poverty. I may say, in passing, that the Laws of Inheritance give to the father a greater portion than to a mother, to a brother greater than to a sister, and gives the family residence to a male heir.

Freedom from the marriage bond is made easy by desertion. "Married men who travel must fix a definite time for their return and endeavour to return at that time. If their wives have no news from them for nine months, after the fixed period, they can go to another husband. But if they are patient it is better, since God *loves those* who are patient."

How the husband who is away from his wife can act, we may judge by the example of a celebrated Bahai,[358] Maskin Kalam, who was agent for Baha to watch over and spy upon Azal and the Azalis in Cyprus. His wife was in Persia; he simply took another in Cyprus.

The ease with which desertion may be practiced under Bahai law is seen in the conduct of Doctor Kheiralla, one of the first apostles of Bahaism to America, and founder of the Chicago Assembly. Dr. H. H. Jessup wrote: "A cousin of Doctor Kheiralla, who is clerk in the American Press in Beirut, gave me the following statement: 'Doctor Kheiralla, after the death of his first wife in Egypt, in 1882, married first a Coptic widow in El Fayum, whom he abandoned, and then married a Greek girl, whom he also abandoned, and who was still living in 1897 in Cairo. He then married an English wife, who abandoned him when his matrimonial relations became known to her.'"[359]

According to the claims of Bahais these loose and imperfect divorce and marriage laws are to be accepted and administered universally under the future kingdom of Baha in its world-wide triumph!

It may be remarked in passing that Bahaism encourages the mixture of races by marriage. Already several American Bahais have married Persian women, and Persian men American women. One American Bahai woman has married a Japanese. Abdul Baha illustrates the relation of the races by a reference to animals. "Consider the kingdom of the animals. A pigeon of white plumage would not shun one of black or brown." In a tablet sent to America, he directs: "Gather to-

[357] "The wife is still in a helpless state; her fate remains entirely in the power of her husband's caprice "(Vatralsky in *Amer. Jour. of Theology*, 1902, p. 72).

[358] "Trav.'s Narr.," pp. 378-379.

[359] *Outlook*, of New York, quoted in *The Missionary Review*, October, 1901, p. 773.

gether these two races, black and white, into one assembly and put such love into their hearts that they shall even *intermarry.*[360] Again he says:[361] "The coloured people must attend all the unity meetings. There must be no distinctions. All are equal. If you have any influence to get the races to intermarry, it will be very valuable. Such unions will beget very strong and beautiful children." Mr. Gregory, an American negro, followed this advice by marrying an English woman, Miss L. A. M. Mathew.

IV. *The social position of women under Bahaism.* Professor Browne says: "Their (the Bahais) efforts to improve the social position of women have been much exaggerated."[362] It may be added that the success of their efforts has been small. It is plain that the Bab recognized the deplorable condition of women under Islam and desired to improve it. His laws gave woman some liberties. She was permitted to put off the veil. The Bab interpreted the prohibition of the Koran to mean that "only the wives of the prophet had received the order to hide the face,"[363] so "he relieved believers from the painful restraint of the veil." Women might appear in society, hold conversation with men,[364] and go to the mosques at night. Baha renewed these rules of the Bab. Still he seems to have some distrust, for the "Kitab-ul-Akdas" says that "men are forbidden to enter any man's house without his permission or in his absence." Thus Bahai precepts tend in some degree to the liberation of woman, though they fall much behind high Christian ideals and customs.

There is observable a wide-spread and influential movement among Moslems for the amelioration of the condition of woman. This movement does not have its source and inspiration in, nor is it peculiar to nor confined to Bahaism. On the contrary, an oriental writer in a review of this remarkable tendency says: "Its birth in Moslem lands undoubtedly is due to the impact of the Occident upon the Orient, the missionary influence playing a large part in it."[365] The new Moslems of India, under the leadership of Justice Sayid Ali, as well as the Young Turks, Egyptians and others, advocate freedom and education for women and have gone much beyond the Bahais in practice. The Turkish women in Constantinople, who aided in the establishment of the constitution and are aspiring to enlarged liberty under its aegis, know Bahaism, if at all, simply as a Persian heretical sect. The Persian women, described so graphically by Mr. Shuster in "The Strangling of Persia,"[366] who formed clubs and took such an active and heroic part in the constitutional agitation, were not Bahai women. The Bahai women, as well as the men, were forbidden by Abdul Baha to take part in the struggle for constitutional liberty.[367] Profes-

[360] "A Heavenly Vista," by L. G. Gregory, p. 31.

[361] Page 15.

[362] "Encyc. Britt.," article, "Babism."

[363] Dreyfus, *Ibid.,* p. 128.

[364] But if they limit themselves to twenty-eight words, it was better for them, says the "Bayan."

[365] *American Rev. of Rev.,* 1912, p. 719.

[366] Pages 191-198.

[367] "Observations of a Bahai Traveller," by Remey, pp. 53, 67; also Dreyfus, *Ibid.,* p. 172.

sor Browne laments the lack of patriotism shown in their conduct. Still the Bahais deserve some credit for the movement for the uplift of Persian womanhood. They might have done much more, notwithstanding the limitations to their liberty of action, had they followed out the first ideals of the Bab. These were exemplified in the celebrated Kurrat-ul-Ayn. This beautiful woman of genius—poet, scholar and theologian, was a pupil at Kerbela, of Haji Kazim, the chief of the Sheikhis. On his death she accepted the Bab, so that though a product of the Sheikhi sect, her fame accrues to the honour of the Babis. At Kerbela, she gave lectures on theology to the people from behind a curtain, and at times, borne away by her enthusiasm and eloquence, would allow her veil to slip off in the presence of men. Her preaching and freedom of conduct was objected to even by Babis, but the Bab answered them, commending her and giving her the title of Janab-i-Tahira, "Her Excellency the Pure," and made her one of his nineteen "Letters of the Living," or apostles. She is said to have claimed to be a remanifestation of Fatima, the daughter of Mohammed. The Turkish government at Bagdad began prosecution against her. She returned to Persia and taught Babism even from the pulpit, at Kasvin, and also by means of poetry. What were the social results of her breaking through the restrictions of Islam? Her husband was Mullah Mohammed of Kasvin, who was opposed to the Bab. On account of this she refused to live with him. "In reply to all proposals of reconciliation, she answered: 'He, in that he rejects God's religion is unclean, while I am 'Pure'; between us there can be nothing in common.' So she refused to be reconciled to her husband,"[368] and regarded herself as divorced.[369] Afterwards "she set out secretly to join herself to Hazret-i-Kuddus (Lord, the Most Holy)," that is, Mullah Mohammed Ali of Barfurush. Together they attended, with Baha Ullah also, the celebrated conference at Badasht, at which "the abrogation of the laws of the previous dispensation was announced." There a sermon was preached by Hazret-i-Kuddus, which, says Professor Browne, lends some colour to the accusation that the Babis advocated communism and community of wives."[370] This learned investigator further says: "The extraordinary proceedings at Badasht seem to have scandalized not only the Mohammedans but even a section of the Babis."[371] Mirza Jani, their first historian and a martyr, avers that not all "have understood the secret of what passed between Hazret-i-Kuddus and Kurrat-ul-Ayn at Badasht, and their real nature and what they meant."[372] The Mohammedan historians openly accuse them of immorality. The Sheikh of Kum, a Bahai, told Professor Browne, "After the Bab had declared the law of Islam abrogated and before he had promulgated new ordinances, there ensued a period of transition which we call *fitrat* (the interval), during which all things were lawful. So long as this continued, Kurrat-ul-Ayn may very possibly have consorted, for example, with Hazret-i-Kuddus, as though he had been her husband."[373]

It may be that the scandals that followed Kurrat-ul-Ayn's venture into public

---

[368] "New Hist.," pp. 274, 441.

[369] Her spirit of intolerance is condemned by Professor Browne.

[370] "New Hist.," p. 357.

[371] Mirza Jani's "History," Introduction, p. xlii.

[372] "New Hist.," p. 365.

[373] "A Year Among the Persians," p. 523.

life and her tragic death in the cruel reprisals that followed the attempt of several Babis to assassinate the Shah, gave a backset to the efforts to liberate women in Persia. Certain it is that during the sixty years succeeding she has had no imitator or successor. Bahai women have continued to wear the veil and have remained secluded from the society of men, not only in Persia but at Acca, the headquarters of Bahaism. The force of the new faith was not strong enough to free the women. Rather they have compromised with their environment. Only in the Caucasus and Trans-Caspia under Russian protection, have they partly unveiled. Not even their women of the second and third generation have been trained to act up to their precepts, but in Acca, as in Persia, they are secluded from the society of even brethren in the faith. They are more backward than some other sects and races of Moslems. I have been entertained in the households of Kurds and Ali Allahis and have dined and conversed with the host and his wife. I have, of course, conversed with the families of Christian converts from Islam, but the wife of a Bahai has never been introduced to me, even though I have known the husband intimately and visited him in his home a score of times in the course of as many years. In a few instances I have heard of Bahai women, in company of their husbands, receiving gentleman visitors, but these wives had resided in Russia. An Osmanli official, at times, receives and makes visits in company with his wife.[374] But the ladies of the household of Baha Ullah and Abdul Baha at Acca do not receive gentlemen as visitors even when they are faithful and honoured American believers. Mr. Myron Phelps, when preparing materials for his "Life of Abbas Effendi," spent a month at Acca. He wished to embody in his book the interesting narrative of Bahiah Khanum, the sister of Abbas. She, though more than half a century had passed over her head, did not grant him personal interviews.[375] Instead she told her narrative in installments day by day to Madame Canavarro, who then came out and repeated what she had heard to Mr. Phelps, who recorded it. He says: "Social custom prevented me from meeting this lady," and again, "Social custom prevented me from meeting the women."[376]

---

[374] "Mohammedan young men will no longer consent to marry girls they have not seen, but now in Beirut visit them and drive out with them on the public highways with the mothers as chaperones" (Jessup's "Fifty-three Years in Syria," p. 640).

[375] Phelps, p. xxxix.

[376] *Ibid.*, p. 109; Chase, "In Galilee," p. 63; Goodall, "Daily Lessons," p. 19. Abdul Baha did not break through oriental custom nor serve the lady guests before himself. The lady pilgrim writes, "The first day at lunch, after Baha had partaken of the honey, he passed it to us" ("Daily Lessons," p. 16). Like the ordinary Moslem he was well pleased to sit down to eat with the foreign ladies but never arranged that the American Bahai men should sit down to meals with his ladies. Mr. C. M. Remey tells, in "Observations of a Bahai Traveller," of meeting Persian Bahai women but rarely in Persia (pp. 75-76). In Kasvin, in the garden of Kurrat-ul-Ayn, one woman partly raised her veil and gave him a greeting of welcome. In Teheran a lady, unveiled, and her husband entertained the Bahais. The husband and wife received the twenty men in one room and the wife received the dozen women in another room. They were separated by a curtain, through which Sprague and Remey spoke, telling of the liberty of women in the West. The lady of the house used her best persuasion to induce the other women to mix with the men. Finally "the women arose and drawing aside their veils with one accord entered the room. The men made place for the ladies by retreating to the other side of the room, while the newcomers found seats. When the women

Now that the way is opened by the Revolution and by the Constitutionalists (who were not Bahais), liberal-minded men of all sects in Persia, Sufis, Sheikhis, Arifs, and even Mutasharis, as well as Bahais, are showing considerable zeal for the elevation of women, and for female education.

V. What does Bahaism teach as to the *political equality of man and woman*? The future Bahai State and community is to be under the administration of Boards—called Houses of Justice, local, national, and universal. These are to be "divine agents," "representatives of God." They are to have absolute authority and to be infallible in their decisions. They will adjudicate questions of property, tithes, inheritance, divorce, and of war and peace. They will have charge of schools and of wives, children and servants as well as of religion. The number of members in each Board is to be at least nine, "according to the number of Baha."[377] The members are to be all *men*. No women are to be admitted to these Boards or "Houses of Justice." This law evidently did not suit the notion of some of the American Bahai sisters, so they made bold to inquire about it. The "Infallible Interpreter," Abdul Baha, laid down the law plainly—which cannot be altered for 1,000 years at least. "From a *spiritual* point of view, there is no difference between women and men. The House of Justice, however, according to the positive commandments of the Doctrine of God, has been specialized to the *men* for a specific reason or exercise of wisdom on the part of God."[378] "As to you other maid-servants, give up your will and choose that of God." "The maid-servants of the merciful should not interfere with the affairs which have regard to the Board of Consultation, or House of Justice."[379]

To sum up, it has been demonstrated that Bahaism does not, by its laws, give woman equality with the man, either in the family or the state, either as to domestic rights or political rights; that in the matter of education it has not tried to give equal opportunities to girls; that it conforms to the social life of its environment without transforming it; that the claims of Abdul Baha before his audiences in Europe and America were without foundation, disproved both by the teaching and by the practice by Baha Ullah.

---

had arisen to the situation, they were quite equal to it. Then it was the men who were ill at ease. In fact their embarrassment was contagious, for even I began to be uneasy and scarcely dared to take a look at the faces opposite. Sherbets and other refreshments were served and chanting continued. Bit by bit the men gained their ease, but, as their embarrassment passed, the women seemed to lose courage. Little by little the veils were drawn over their faces. Then one moved as if to leave, where upon all arose and like a flock of affrighted birds fluttered from the room." This incident shows how little change has been affected in the social habits of Bahai women in sixty years after Kurrat-ul-Ayn.

[377] B = 2, a = 1, h = 5, a = 1, total 9 in Persian Abjad counting.
[378] "Tablets of Abdul Baha," Vol. I, p. 50.
[379] *Ibid.*, p. 27.

VIII

ITS RECORD AS TO MORALS

Claim superior conduct—Falsification of religious history—Suppression of facts—Changing sacred Writings—Surat ul Maluk—Lawh i Basharat—Forging quotations—Perversion of political history—Of Shahs—Of plot to assassinate—False claim to Martyrs—Double view of Abdul Hamid—Fact about imprisonment of Baha—Tagiya—Dissimulation—Orient Occident Unity—Pretense regarding Azal's succession—Maskin Kalam

The Bahais are ignorant of the dogmas of Babism and of its history and its book. The "Traveller's Narrative," a work of Abbas Effendi, is a bad romance, composed solely for the purpose of proving that the Bab is simply a precursor and announcer of Baha Ullah. With extreme bias, he misconceives in every instance the true history, and the author has not even searched, as I have, in the immense works of the Bab for the autobiographical notes which are so plentiful. He is satisfied with the legends which fall in best with the end he is pursuing. It is regrettable that a man like Abbas Effendi should show himself ignorant of the life of the Bab.—*"Beyan Persan," A. L. M. Nicolas, Vol. I, p. xvi.*

To represent him (the Bab) as simply the forerunner of Baha is an historic falsehood. It is another to pretend that the religion of the Bab was universalized by Baha Ullah.—*Ibid., Vol. III, p. v.*

The Bab did not consider himself as the herald or forerunner of another dispensation, as a John the Baptist to Christ. This is devoid of historic foundation. In his own eyes as in those of his followers, M. Ali Mohammed inaugurated a new prophetic cycle and brought a new revelation which abrogated the Koran. He declared that he is not the last Manifestation. There would be a greater, whom he calls "Him whom God would manifest," but the Bab expected that the next manifestation would be separated from his own by an interval such as had separated previous dispensations. Possibly the "Bayan" indicates 1511 or 2001 years as the interval.—*Professor Browne, "Introduction to Mirza Jani's History."*

THE moral conduct of the founders of a religion, especially one that requires trust in the person of its author, is a necessary subject of investigation. The conduct of the immediate followers is not to the same degree a subject of criticism. From one point of view it is no argument against the truth of Bahaism that Bahais fail to live up to its precepts and principles, for this can be said of all religions. But the claims of Bahai writers make it necessary to consider their conduct. They boast of superior exemplary character and make this a proof of Bahaism. Hence it is necessary to show the groundlessness of their assertions. In the following review, which covers several chapters, the conduct of Baha, Abdul Baha and their early followers is treated together. The claim made for the founders is nothing short of blessed perfection. For the disciples, it is one of superlative excellence. Myron Phelps says:[380] "This faith does not expend itself on beautiful and unfruitful theories, but has a vital and effective power to mould life towards the very highest ideals of human character—as exemplified in the life of Abbas and the salient characteristics of his followers." The Bahai historians say:[381] "They are remarkable only for their charity, kindliness, purity, godliness, rectitude, sincerity, integrity, generosity, chastity and strict avoidance of all forbidden things." "In their conduct, action, morality and demeanour was no place for objection.... People have confidence in their trustworthiness, faithfulness and godliness." Abul Fazl[382] speaks of the supernatural character and morals of the followers of Baha, who became universally celebrated for their just characters, good conduct and excellent morals. So Remey:[383] "The effect of this cause upon the lives of the peoples of every race and religion leaves no doubt as to the divine source of its teachings." Mirza Jani, speaking of the proofs the Babis gave to the Moslems, says:[384] "We say, 'We have witnessed miracles on the part of this man.' They retort, 'He is a sorcerer.' We say, 'Come, let us invoke God's curse on whomsoever is in error, leaving to Him the decision.' They reply, 'This is not permitted by our law.' We say, 'Let us kindle a fire and enter into the midst together.' They answer, 'You are mad.' We further say, 'Consider the godliness, piety and self-renunciation of those who believe.' They return us no answer." I propose to return the answer.

1. One characteristic of the Bahai leaders is *dishonesty in dealing with their history*. This sometimes takes the form of the suppression and concealment of documents, sometimes of the omission or perversion of essential facts or their presentation in such a way as to falsify history. In the writing of political history and in scheming for the triumph of a political party, we may expect crookedness in dealing with facts, but in the propagating of a new religion designed to supersede Christianity and Islam, and purporting to be an improvement on them, we do not expect to find dishonesty and misrepresentation. Yet this is exactly what we find, namely, "a readiness to ignore or suppress facts, writings or views (undoubtedly historical), which they regard as useless or hurtful to their aims."[385]

[380] "Life of Abbas Effendi," p. xxxvii.
[381] "New Hist.," p. 236; "Trav.'s Narr.," p. 82.
[382] "Bahai Proofs," pp. 63, 77.
[383] "The Bahai Religion," p. 111.
[384] Quoted in "New Hist.," p. 373; comp. p. 61.
[385] Professor Browne's Introduction to Phelps, p. xxi.

When Mirza Husain Ali (Baha Ullah) started out as a "Manifestation," it was necessary to get rid of certain facts and beliefs held by Babis. He must reduce the Bab from his position as the Point of Divinity—the Lord of a new Dispensation, as well as supplant and supersede the Bab's successor, Subh-i-Azal.[386] Thoroughly to accomplish this object (after the Babis leaders had been put out of the way), the history was rewritten. While claiming that the Bab gave testimony to Baha and taking to themselves the glory of Babi heroism and martyrdoms, the Bahais relegated the "Bayan" and other "revelations" of the Bab, not yet a score of years old, to dust-covered oblivion.[387] Subh-i-Azal avers that they wilfully destroyed them. He writes[388] that thirty or more bound books of the Bab were given in trust by him to his relatives (Baha and his family) as trustees. "They carried off the trust," and "making strenuous efforts, got into their hands such of the books of the Point as were obtainable, with the idea of destroying them and rendering their own works attractive." Professor Browne[389] informs us that it was very difficult to obtain a Babi book from Persian Bahais and next to impossible to get a glimpse of one at Acca, where the Bahais had them concealed. The "holy, divine books" were shelved from motives of policy.

A primitive Babi work of first importance was the "History," by Mirza Jani. This was an original narrative of events, at first hand, prepared in sincerity by one who shortly suffered martyrdom for the cause (1852). But its facts did not suit the Bahais. So it was superseded, first by the "New History"[390] (1880), and secondly by the "Traveller's Narrative" (1886). Both these histories purport to be written by European travellers. We might excuse their being anonymous, to avoid possible persecution, but to make pretense that the authors are travellers who have come from afar ostensibly to investigate, and into whose mouths are put praises of the religion, is but part of the insincerity noticeable in other things.[391] Mirza Jani's "History" passed out of sight, and it was only because a copy had been deposited by Count Gobineau in the Bibliothèque Nationale at Paris that it has reached our hands.[392]

Of the "New History" little need be said, except that it perverted the history and "carefully omitted every fact, doctrine and expression,"[393] not in accord with the policy of Baha.

[386] "New Hist.," p. 426.

[387] *Ibid.*, p. xxvii.

[388] "Trav.'s Narr.," pp. 342-343.

[389] Browne's "A Year Among the Persians," p. 530. "If, instead of talking in this violent and unreasonable manner, you would produce the 'Bayan,' of which ever since I came to Persia I have been vainly endeavouring to obtain a copy."

[390] Its authors were Mirza Husain of Hamadan, M. Abul Fazl, and Manakji.

[391] Numerous magazine articles, and even the "Life of Abbas Effendi" have been written by Bahais, as if they were outsiders making observations.

[392] In his Introduction (pp. xxxii.-v.) to Mirza Jani, which he has had printed in Persian, Professor Browne says, "But for Count Gobineau it would have perished utterly. This fact is very instructive, that so important a work could be successfully suppressed," and "that the adherents of a religion could connive at such an act of suppression and falsification of evidence." "This fact is established by the clearest evidence."

[393] "New Hist.," p. xxix.

Let us examine somewhat in detail how Abbas Abdul Baha treats facts in his "Traveller's Narrative." He is undoubtedly the principal author of this work.[394] The Persian Bahai, who sent Professor Browne the lithographed (Bombay) copy of it, wrote, "It contains the observations of His Holiness, the Lord, Mystery of God (May my personality be his sacrifice)." Professor Browne was also presented with a copy of it at Acca, which he published in Persian with an English translation. Of it he says,[395] "It was written to discredit the perfectly legitimate claims and to disparage the blameless character of his less successful rival" (Azal). "There is good ground for suspecting a *deliberate misstatement*[396] of facts and dates." He specifies[397] various points in which Abbas Effendi perverted the facts. Undoubtedly one of the aims of Abbas was to eliminate Azal. The latter had been regularly appointed by the Bab as his successor,[398] but he refused to make way for Baha. The Bahais tried to get rid of the question by suppressing all mention of him, even of his name, and "of all documents tending to prove the position which he undoubtedly held."[399] They would have consigned him to oblivion.[400] The "New History" makes but one doubtful reference to Azal.[401] Professor Browne says, "Abbas Effendi,[402] in order to curtail the duration and extent of Subh-i-Azal's authority and to give colour to their assertion that it was but temporary and nominal, *deliberately and purposely antedated* the Manifestation of Baha." And he continues to the present to misrepresent the facts. In "Answered Questions"[403] Baha is presented as the chief influence in Persia immediately after the Bab. Other Bahai writers repeat this error.[404]

[394] *Ibid.*, pp. xiv., xxxi.

[395] *Ibid.*, p. xiv.

[396] "Encyc. Brit.," article, Babism.

[397] "Trav.'s Narr.," p. xlv. It (1) belittles the Bab and glorifies Baha—making the former simply a forerunner; (2) belittles the sufferings and deeds of Babis, passing over remarkable events almost unnoticed and magnifies inferior deeds of Bahais; (3) debases Azal, disregards his position as successor, disparages and scorns him as lacking in courage and wisdom; (4) tries to curry the favour of the Shah of Persia and excuses his persecutions, putting the blame on Mullahs and Viziers, deprecating the resistance and wars of the early Babis.

[398] Count Gobineau (p. 277) says, "There was some little hesitation about the successor of the Bab, but finally he was recognized as divinely designated, a young man of sixteen, named M. Yahya (Azal). The election was recognized by all the Babis."

[399] "Mirza Jani," p. xxxii.

[400] *Ibid.*, p. xxxv. Professor Browne says, "When I was in Persia in 1887-1888, the Babis (Bahais) whom I met *feigned* complete ignorance of the very name and existence of Subh-i-Azal."

[401] Page 64, note.

[402] "Abbas Effendi *suppressed* all incidents and expressions not in accordance with later Bahai sentiment." "Of this I am certain that the more the Bahai doctrine spreads, especially outside of Persia, the more the true history is obscured and distorted" (Professor Browne in his introduction to "Mirza Jani," p. xxxvi.).

[403] Pages 36-38.

[404] One need not be surprised at this falsifying of claims and historical facts, for it is the testimony of the Bahai historian himself ("New Hist.," p. 5) that "the principal vice of the Persians is falsehood—so universal and customary and so familiar that truthfulness is entirely abandoned and ignored." "In matters relating to religion the Mullahs have shown

2. Another practice of the founders of Bahaism is *falsifying and changing the documents and texts of their Sacred Writings*, namely, those of the Bab and Baha, according to the exigency of circumstances. Subh-i-Azal made the accusation "that the Bahais had tampered with the Bab's writings to give colour to their own doctrines and views."[405] I pass this by, to notice how they have tampered with their own "Revelations." For example, take Baha's "Epistle to the Shah of Persia." Its original text was published by Baron Rosen.[406] It is embodied by Abbas Effendi in the "Traveller's Narrative."[407] The two do not agree. "Very considerable alterations and suppressions were made in the text by the author of 'Traveller's Narrative.'"[408] "The text has evidently been toned down to suit a wider audience and to avoid giving offense to non-believers."[409]

There is also another "Epistle to the Shah" which is contained in the "Surat-ul-Maluk." Its tone is strikingly different. The first is a careful diplomatic document which acknowledges the faults of the Babis, pleads pardon for the past and for religious toleration. It is monotheistic, representing Baha as a humble suffering servant, with no pretense to Divinity. The other "adopts a tone of fierce recrimination towards the Shah, and upbraids him for the Bab's death, saying, 'Would you had slain him as men slay one another, but ye slew him in such a way as the eyes of men have not seen the like thereof and heaven wept over him, and by God, the eye of existence hath not beheld the like of you; you slay the son of your prophet and then are of those who are joyful.'" He excuses the attempt on the life of the Shah, and threatens vengeance[410] on him. These two Epistles to the Shah have been a puzzle to the critics. This threatening, fierce letter seems so contrary to the policy of Baha. An adequate and not improbable explanation[411] would be that one letter was prepared for the perusal of his Majesty and the other for the Bahais, to impress

themselves to be ready liars and shameless forgers." The degree of reliability of this History may be judged from the following sentence, "When the people of Italy had proved the extent of the Pope's hypocrisy, guile and deceit, they so effectually deposed him and his children and his grandchildren that naught remained of him but the appearance" (referring to 1870-1871). I have received a pamphlet by A. J. Stenstrand, of Chicago, called "Third Call to Behaists." He writes (p. 27), "The Babi history as well as their sacred scriptures prove that a terrible corruption, changing and transposing of its meanings, has been going on in the hands of the Behaists." Again (p. 28), "We have plenty of proofs that there has been continual corruption, interpolation, changing, transposing and stealing away the sacred scriptures of the Babi religion in the hands of the Bahais."

[405] Cf. *Jour. Roy. As. Soc.*, 1892, p. 447.

[406] "The Alwah-i-Salatin," in Collections Scientifiques, St. Petersburg, 1877.

[407] "Trav.'s Narr.," pp. 108-164.

[408] *Jour. Roy. As. Soc.*, 1892, p. 313.

[409] *Ibid.*, p. 286.

[410] *S. W.*, Sept. 27, 1913, pp. 9, 10, "If thou dost not obey God, the foundations of thy government shall be razed, and thou shalt become evanescent—become as nothing. If no attention is paid to this book, thou shalt become non-existent."

[411] The same explanation will account for the opposite narratives of the trial of Baha before the Turkish Court at Acca. Mr. Laurence Oliphant reports that the Court put the question to Baha, "Will you tell the Court who and what you are?" "I will begin," he replied, "by telling you who I am not. I am not a camel-driver (alluding to Mohammed), nor am I a carpenter."

them with the boldness of their prophet.

Another example of this is seen in the suppression[412] of part of the "Lawh-i-Basharat" ("Glad Tidings"). Its fifteenth section commands Constitutional Government. When the Tablet was sent to Russia, this section was suppressed by Bahais. The Tablet was published in its mutilated form by Baron Rosen. Expediency, which rules Bahai practice, required that an incomplete "Divine Revelation" should reach Russia.

Playing fast and loose with the "Revelations" prevailed still more at the time of the bitter quarrel and schism on the death of Baha. Though Baha's Tablets are regarded as "Holy Books" in the highest sense, yet the Bahais commit the grave offense of changing them so as to misrepresent facts. Mirza Mohammed Ali and Badi Ullah, younger sons of Baha, in refuting the claim of Abbas Effendi to be Baha's successor, say, "Has Abbas dared to change the texts uttered by Baha Ullah? Most certainly, Yes. We have in our possession *many* texts of Baha Ullah which have been changed[413] by Abbas Effendi." Further, "he and his party have stolen the first paragraph of a sacred Tablet and have perverted its meaning, with deception."

Khadim-Ullah,[414] the lifelong amanuensis of Baha, asserts that Abbas actually rejected a "Sacred Tablet," written in the handwriting of Baha Ullah. Other Tablets are repudiated. For in "Hidden Words"[415] Baha Ullah refers to the "Fifth Tablet of Paradise" and the "Ruby Tablet." Abbas Effendi warns against accepting any such Tablets if they should be brought to light. What other reason for this can we imagine than fear that their contents would be against his claim. Enough has been said to show the truth of the charge that the Bahais deal dishonestly with the documents of their alleged revelation.

A peculiar instance of forgery occurs in the writings of Baha Ullah. In his Epistle to the Shah Baha quotes certain verses as from the "Hidden Book of Fatima." This book, the Shiahs believe, was revealed by Gabriel to Fatima, the daughter of Mohammed, disappeared with the twelfth Imam, and will be brought back by the

---

[412] "New Hist.," p. xxv.

[413] "Facts for Behaists," p. 27. We mention a few of the important ones. (1) The so-called Tablet of Beirut, which confirmed the claim of Abbas, and was said to be transcribed by Khadim Ullah. The latter declared it to be a forgery by Abbas Effendi. (2) Abbas omitted the middle part of the "Tablet of Command" to make it certify his claims. A complete copy in Baha's own handwriting showed the subterfuge. (3) He combined parts of two different Tablets, called it the "Treasure Tablet," and claimed that it certified his succession. The two Tablets were produced and proved the falsity of the claim.

[414] "Facts for Behaists," p. 55. Afterwards Badi Ullah, who had accused the party of Abbas of making additions to the writings, with a purpose changed sides in the quarrel and accused Mohammed Ali of the same things—"interpolating," "erasing," "transposing," "replacing," "clipping and joining fragments," of the Tablets of Baha Ullah, besides issuing "a false writing in his name." Mohammed Ali is also accused of "carrying away by way of the window" two trunks full of the "blessed writings." See "Epistle to the Bahai World," by Mirza Badi Ullah, pp. 3, 5, 12-17.

[415] "Hidden Words," numbers 20, 37, 48.

Mahdi at his coming. Professor Browne[416] wrote to Acca making inquiry about this "Book of Fatima" and the quotations from it. The authoritative reply which he received was, "That naught is known of such a book but the name, but Baha Ullah mentioned it in this manner to make known the appearance of the Kaim" (Mahdi). In other words, Baha was making a false pretense of quoting from the "Book of Fatima," as if he, as Mahdi, had brought it with him.

3. Bahais make *false representation of facts in political history*. The "Traveller's Narrative" perverts the truth for "political opportunism."[417] Contrary to the contemporary historian, Mirza Jani, and the European chroniclers, the Shah is represented as ignorant and innocent of and averse to the repressive measures taken by his government against the Babis. Let me give specific proofs of this.

At the first trial of the Bab, at Tabriz, according to Mirza Jani,[418] Nasr-ud-Din, then Crown Prince, whom he dubs "bastard," treated the Bab disrespectfully by rolling a globe towards him and taunting him with ignorance of it and by ordering him to be bastinadoed. The "Traveller's Narrative,"[419] per contra, says, "The heavenly-cradled Crown Prince pronounced no sentence with regard to the Bab, but the Mullahs ordered a bastinado." The former history states that the Prime Minister consulted, about the execution of the Bab, with the Shah,[420] who gave him full authority to act in the matter," and that he then communicated with Prince Hamza Mirza, Governor of Azerbaijan, who proceeded to make plans for it. Abbas' Narrative[421] states that "the Minister, without the Royal command and without his cognizance and entirely on his own authority, issued commands to put the Bab to death"; "that Prince Hamza utterly refused to have part in the trial and execution." Gobineau[422] confirms the original account, and states that Prince Hamza "took a leading part in the condemnation of the Bab." It is certain that contemporary Babis[423] held the Shah responsible for their persecution and were bitter against him. Mirza Jani records the death of Mohammed Shah, by saying that "he went to hell"; the "New History" affirms "that he passed to the mansions of Paradise." Nasr-ud-Din was no puppet king, he was fully cognizant of the affairs of state. Regarding the imprisonment of Baha, the "Traveller's Narrative"[424] says, "His Majesty, moved by his own kindly spirit, ordered investigation and the release of Baha Ullah." He had just ordered the execution of twenty-eight Babis, with horrid cruelties, after the attempt on his life. Regarding the torture and execution of Badi,

[416] "Trav.'s Narr.," p. 123.
[417] "New Hist.," p. vii.
[418] *Ibid.*, p. 353.
[419] "Trav.'s Narr.," p. 20.
[420] "New Hist.," p. 292.
[421] "Trav.'s Narr.," pp. 40, 41. Abul Fazl also is apologetic for the Shah, and says ("Bahai Proofs," p. 38), "Without seeking permission from the Shah, the Minister issued the order for his death."
[422] "Trav.'s Narr.," p. 259.
[423] In "New Hist.," p. xvii., Professor Browne says, "The Babis made no profession of loyalty, nor did they attempt to exonerate the Shah from the responsibility of the persecutions. To the Shahs, such terms as tyrant, scoundrel, unrightful king, are freely applied. The battle cry, 'Ya Nasr-ud-Din Shah,' is described as 'a foul watchword.'"
[424] "Trav.'s Narr.," p. 52.

who bore the Epistle to the Shah, it says:[425] "It was contrary to the desire of the Shah, and he manifested regret for it." This and much in that Epistle is written with the idea of conciliating the Shah and obtaining toleration. It is a sensible attitude, did they not maintain it with so much misrepresentation and hypocrisy. The real spirit of Bahais towards Nasr-ud-Din is seen in Baha's "Surat-ul-Maluk," and is one of "fierce recrimination." Confirmation of this comes from conversations with Bahais.

Another misrepresentation of history, which is universal among Bahais, is in belittling the plot to assassinate Nasr-ud-Din Shah in 1852. Abbas Effendi says,[426] "It was done by a certain Babi, by sheer madness, one other person being his accomplice." His sister, Bahiah Khanum, says,[427] It was "by a young Babi who had lost his reason." Kheiralla,[428] says, It was "by a weak-minded, insane believer." Similarly all their writers propagate a tradition that one irresponsible man made the attempt. It is permitted to doubt the Shiah historian, who gives a circumstantial account of how twelve Babis, including one high leader, laid the plot. But Count Gobineau[429] is entitled to credence when he says that there were a number of Babis in the plot and three took part in the attempt. A nephew of one of the accomplices told Professor Browne[430] that there were seven in the plot and three of them went out to commit the act. Why will not Bahai writers give the facts straight?

Another misrepresentation fostered by them is that of calling the Babi martyrs Bahais. Thus Abdul Baha says,[431] "When they brought Kurrat-ul-Ayn the terrible news of the martyrdom of the Bahais, she did not waver." Again he says,[432] "Thousands of His (*i. e.*, Baha Ullah's) followers have given their lives, and while under the sword shedding their blood they have proclaimed, 'Ya Baha-ul-Abha.'" He said[433] in Doctor Cadman's church, "The King of Persia killed 20,000 Bahais." Again,[434] "In all parts of Persia his enemies rose against Baha Ullah, imprisoning and killing *his* converts, razing thousands of dwellings." These are gross misstatements. In Kurrat-ul-Ayn's time there were no Bahais, only Babis. No such efforts as those described were ever made to crush Bahaism. The thousands who gave their lives were Babis. Perhaps some one remarks, "What's the difference?" Foreign writers may not know the difference, and an American audience certainly does not. But Abdul Baha, from whom I have quoted, makes a great difference. It arouses one's indignation to read Bahai literature, in which they claim credit for all that is noble in Babi annals, such as the martyrdoms, and yet they disparage and deny the Babis.

---

[425] *Ibid.*, pp. 104-106.
[426] *Ibid.*, pp. 49, 50.
[427] Phelps, p. 13.
[428] "Beha Ullah," p. 411.
[429] "Trav.'s Narr.," p. 53.
[430] *Ibid.*, p. 323.
[431] *S. W.*, Oct. 16, 1913, p. 210.
[432] *Ibid.*, July 13, 1913, p. 118.
[433] *Ibid.*, Sept. 18, 1912.
[434] "Some Answered Questions," p. 37.

Read Abul Fazl's "Bahai Proofs." He said[435] to Prince Naibus-Sultaneh, "The unseemly actions of the Babis cannot be denied nor excused, but to arrest Bahais for them is oppression, for these unfortunates have *no connection with the Babis,* who took up arms, *nor are they of the same religion or creed."* In another place he writes[436] repudiating the wars and disorders of the Babis, and affirming that they were guilty of many censurable actions, such as taking men's property and pillaging the dead, and engaging in conflict and bloodshed. If then the Bahais repudiate them, they must not appropriate their glory, for the old Babis, with all their faults, were at least heroic. Bahaism has, on the contrary, the spirit of *tagiya.*

I pass on to consider Abdul Baha's representations regarding Sultan Abdul Hamid. I present two quotations from Tablets addressed to American believers. The first says,[437] "Here one witnesses the fairness and impartiality of H. I. Majesty the Padishah of the Ottomans, who has dealt with the utmost justice and equity. In reality to-day, in the Asiatic world, the Padishah of the Ottoman Empire and the Shah of Persia, Muzaffar-ud-Din, are peerless and have no equals. These two kings have treated us with mildness—both are just. Therefore, pray ye and beseech for their confirmation in the threshold of the Almighty, especially for Abdul Hamid, who has dealt at all times in justice with these exiled ones." Abdul Hamid—a peerless, just one! Surely this would have remained among the *hidden things* had not one "Servant of God" (Abd-ul-Baha) revealed it to us about that other "Servant of God" (Abd-ul-Hamid). This "revelation" is dated 1906. After Abdul Hamid was deposed, Abdul Baha speaks[438] of "his oppression and tyranny," for the Sultan sent "an oppressive, august commission, that with all kinds of wiles, simulations, slander and fabrication of false stories, they might fasten guilt upon Abdul Baha. But soon fetters and manacles were placed around the *unblessed* neck of Abdul Hamid." Did the "Infallible Pen" err in the former character sketch? No, but Abdul Baha's oppression[439] of his brothers, in retaining their patrimony, resulted in a bitter quarrel and complaints, followed by an investigating Commission and Abdul Baha's imprisonment. On this account the whitewash scaled off from Abdul Hamid.

Another form of misstatement is their habitual way of speaking of the imprisonment of Baha and Abdul Baha. Abdul Baha says of Baha,[440] "His blessed days ended in the cruel prison and *dark dungeon."* "He passed his days in the Most Great Prison."[441] Abdul Baha continually speaks of himself in such words as the following, "Forty years I was a prisoner; I was young when I was put in prison, and my

---

[435] Pages 77, 78.

[436] Page 63.

[437] "Tablets of Abdul Baha," Vol. I, p. 46.

[438] *S. W.,* May 17, 1911, p. 6.

[439] Mrs. Templeton (previously Mrs. Laurence Oliphant), in "Facts for Behaists," tells of the unrighteousness of Abbas Effendi (Abdul Baha) in keeping from his brothers and stepmothers the pension money of the Turkish Government and the revenue of Baha's villages, and of his ostentatious charity in giving away part of these funds by distributing coins to a mixed crowd of beggars every Friday.

[440] *S. W.,* May 17, 1913, p. 74.

[441] "Tablets of Abdul Baha," Vol. I, p. 44.

hair was white when the prison doors opened."[442] "After all these long years of prison life." "My body can endure anything; my body has endured forty years of imprisonment."[443] Now, what are the facts?

In Phelps' Life, Bahiah Khanum[444] says, "We were imprisoned in the barracks at Acca two years (1868-70)." Then[445] "we were given a comfortable house[446] with three rooms and a court." After nine years of such restriction Baha Ullah moved to a beautiful garden outside the city and built there a Palace, called Bahja. He had the freedom of the surrounding country, visited Mount Carmel, and later spent a part of each year at Haifa.[447] Baha Ullah died in this Palace, not in a *dungeon*.[448]

As to Abbas Effendi, during the first brief period only he was restricted to the barracks. He was even temporarily put in chains in the dungeon[449] when accused of participation in the assassination of the Azalis. After that, for a period of *thirty years*, "he was permitted to go about at his pleasure, beyond the walls of Acca."[450] He built a fine residence[451] at Haifa, which I have seen. He journeyed to Tiberias and as far as Beirut. Only after his quarrel with his brothers and on their accusation was he ordered back to Acca, and even then he had the freedom of the city (1905).[452] Such are the facts about Abbas Effendi, whom Canon Wilberforce intro-

[442] *S. W., Ibid.*, p. 67.

[443] *Ibid.*, Sept. 8, 1912, p. 5.

[444] Phelps, p. 66.

[445] *Ibid.*, p. 70.

[446] This house was purchased by an American Bahai lady, that it might remain in Bahai hands.

[447] "Bahai Proofs," by Abul Fazl, p. 66. Remey, p. 23.

[448] Mrs. Grundy, p. 73 ff., "Ten Days," etc., speaks of the Palace of Joy as a very large white mansion. Professor Browne was received here (1890). He was conducted through a spacious hall, paved with a mosaic of marble, into a great antechamber, and entered through a lifted curtain into a large Audience Room.

Of the Garden of Baha, Sprague ("A Year in India," etc., p. 1) says, "It is a veritable garden of Eden, with luxuriant foliage and every fruit. Baha Ullah used to sit under the large spreading tree and teach his disciples." Mrs. Grundy says, "The Rizwan is filled with palm trees, oranges, lemons and wonderful flowers. A river, the Nahr Naaman, runs through it, in two streams, on which ducks and other fowls swim. On an island is an arbour under two large mulberry trees. A fountain plays in the midst. Under the arbour is a chair where Baha used to sit. No one sits in it any more. (Mrs. Grundy knelt at the foot of the chair.) The garden has a cottage, where Baha spent his summers." A Palace and a luxurious summer place were Baha's "Most Great Prison" during most of his years at Acca. Compare Laurence Oliphant's "Haifa," etc., p. 103, for a fine description of his "pleasure ground." How unfounded are such statements as Bernard Temple's (*S. W.*, p. 39, April 28, 1914). "All this while the founders were behind prison walls."

[449] Phelps, p. 75.

[450] *Ibid.*, p. 80.

[451] Dr. H. H. Jessup, who visited him in 1900, writes (New York *Outlook*, June, 1901), "Abbas Effendi has two houses in Haifa, one for his family, in which he entertains the American lady pilgrims, and one down town where his Persian followers meet him."

[452] Abbas Effendi in Acca at this time visited Mr. Remey ("Bahai Movement," p. 108). He received American pilgrims. Mrs. Goodall ("Daily Lessons," p. 6) speaks of "His bountifully spread table," the laughter and good cheer, and (p. 13) remarks, "One would never

duced in his church as "for forty years *a prisoner for* the cause of *brotherhood and love.*" In truth it was the quarrelling of the brothers, Azal and Baha, that led to the banishment from Adrianople to Acca, the murder of Azalis by Bahais increased its severity, the bitter hatred of the younger generation against each other brought back the restraint.

4. Another immoral practice of Bahais is *tagiya* or *ketman*, religious dissimulation. This is taught and practiced by Shiah Moslems,[453] and it is continued with all its offensiveness against good morals by Bahais. In it concealment, denial or misrepresentation by word or act is allowed for self-protection or for the good of the faith. It was formally permitted by Baha Ullah. In accordance with this practice Abdul Baha and his followers at Acca keep the Fast of Ramazan[454] in addition to the Bahai Fast at Noruz. Dr. H. H. Jessup[455] wrote, "He is now acting what seems to be a double part—a Moslem in the Mosque, and a Christ in his own house. He prays with the Moslems, 'there is no God but God,' and expounds the Gospels as the incarnate Son of God." Mirza Abul Fazl, a Bahai missionary, lately died in Egypt. At his public funeral[456] the Moslem *taziah*, with reading of the Koran, was held, though he was a strenuous worker for the abrogation of Islam. Most Bahais in Persia live in habitual *tagiya*. Fear of persecution is some palliation for this, but it is a great defect. Very far from the truth is the statement of Lord Curzon[457] that "No Babi (or Bahai) has ever recanted under pressure." Mr. Nicolas,[458] the French Consul at Tabriz, shows from the Bab's own writings that he himself denied his Manifestation at his examination at Shiraz and signed a recantation. At the execution[459] of the Bab in Tabriz (1850) two of his intimate disciples denied the faith. The explanation of the fact is remarkable and instructive. They were enjoined to do so by the Bab in order that they might convey certain documents to a safe place. In other words, they were to lie for the faith, by divine injunction. In another notable instance,[460] seven Babis stood firm and were executed at Teheran, while thirty recanted, being told by their leader to judge whether they were justified by family ties, etc., in renouncing the faith. "They determined to adopt a course of concealment, *tagiya*." Some years ago a Bahai was called before the Governor of Tabriz and questioned, "Are you a Bahai?" "I am a Mussulman." "Will you curse Baha?" "It is written in the Koran not to curse, I am not a Bahai." By payment of a peshkesk this answer was made acceptable. And no offense was recognized in conscience, for Baha had said, "If your heart is right with me, nothing matters." It were scarcely necessary to note that some Babis and Bahais have denied their faith, except to correct the mistake of travellers, but the fact that denial is permitted and approved is important. For *tagiya* is a deeply-rooted seed which bears evil fruits in

realize he was visiting a Turkish prison."

[453] Doctor Shedd says, "Concealment of religious faith is a common practice in Persia, and it is approved and recommended by Bahais."

[454] Phelps, p. 101.

[455] New York *Outlook*.

[456] *S. W.*, March 2, 1914.

[457] Phelps, p. xxxi.

[458] "Le Béyan Persan" (Paris), Introduction xvi.-xxiv., by A. L. M. Nicolas.

[459] "New Hist.," p. 252.

[460] "Trav.'s Narr.," p. 252.

their characters and conduct.

Even their propaganda is carried on in the same deceitful spirit. The Bahai conceals from the one he approaches his status and beliefs, insinuates himself into his confidence, suits the substance of his message to the preconceptions and prejudices of his hearer and leads him on, perhaps omitting to mention the real essentials of Bahaism.[461] One of their methods is to worm themselves into the employ of Christian Missions and clandestinely carry on their propaganda while they undermine the work of the Mission. Perhaps the Mission wishes a language teacher or a mirza. A Bahai presents himself. He talks well. In the course of conversation the missionary inquires his religious views. He appears liberal minded. Direct inquiry is made, "Are you a Bahai?" He replies, "No, *I am not*, but I am tired of Islam; I am a truth-seeker." The missionary employs him. After a time, maybe, he professes to be a Christian, and is baptized. Such were a certain Mirza Hasan and a Mirza Husain, who deceived the Swedish Mission and received salaries as Christian evangelists, but had been and continued to be Bahais and propagandists. I have heard that in a certain Station (not American) Bahais, without revealing their faith, accepted positions as cook, language-teacher, financial agent, etc., and so surrounded the new Mission that it was a Bahai more than a Christian establishment. Doctor Shedd[462] tells of an assistant he had with him in school work—a Persian, with whom he discussed religious topics freely. For years the man disavowed belief in Bahaism, but finally threw off the mask and became an active propagandist. After his dismissal he instigated the Persian pupils, whom he had previously secretly beguiled, and they complained to the Persian Government that "they, as good (?) Mohammedans, were offended by having to study the Christian Scriptures." Great is *tagiya*!

What else can we expect, since Abdul Baha instructs his disciples in pretense. A certain Madame Canavarro,[463] staying at Acca, expressed her desire to assist in spreading Bahaism among the Buddhists, and spoke of the difficulty of introducing it as a new religion. Abdul Baha replied, "At first teach it as truths of their own religion, afterwards tell them of me." She replied that she herself was imbued with the spirit of Buddhism. He answered, "What you call yourself is of no consequence." To a certain American lady who was afraid her friends would be repelled by the idea of a new religion, Abdul Baha advised, "Remain in the Church and teach Bahaism as the true teaching of Christ."

A striking instance of this religious dissimulation is seen in Hamadan.[464] There about two-and-a-half per cent. of the Jews have accepted Baha as the Messiah. But

---

[461] S. M. Jordan, of Teheran, says ("The Mohammedan World," Cairo, p. 130), "We are honestly open in our methods, while they are the reverse." Doctor Shedd says, "Christian Mission work is openly Christian, that of Persian Bahais is professedly Mohammedan." "Bahaism, as offered to a Jew, a Christian or a Mohammedan, varies greatly."

[462] *Missionary Review*, October, 1911.

[463] Phelps, p. 154.

[464] Miss A. Montgomery, in *Woman's Work*, 1913, p. 270, says of these Bahais, "This sect of Moslems, thirty years ago, were afraid to appear to be what they really were, they exercised the privilege of falsehood their deceitful faith grants them, and called themselves Christians."

many of these continue in the outward forms and associations of the Jews.[465] Others professed to be Christians, and were protected as such by the Shah's government. After a decade or two it became evident that they were hypocrites, cloaking their Bahaism under the Christian name.

This Oriental dissimulation takes on a different phase in Western Bahaism. The principle of the latter is stated thus, "Adhere to any religious faith with which you are associated."[466] "No religious relation[467] should be severed, but these relations should become as avenues for giving forth the message of the Bahai faith." This idea is delusive; it is self-deception, ignorance, or worse. No Christian can give allegiance to Baha as incarnate God and accept, as he then must, Islam,[468] Babism and Bahaism as successively true, and as higher revelations abrogating Christianity, and still be loyal to Christ. Bahaism is not a philosophy like Tolstoism, nor a theory of economics like the "single tax"; it is a religion as much as Mormonism is.

A plain example of Bahai *tagiya* is in connection with the organization known as the "Persian-American Educational Society." This was organized at Washington, D. C., under the patronage of Mirza Ali Kuli Khan, Persian Chargé d' Affaires. Its organizing body, committee to draft its constitution, its executive, are Bahais, yet its circular sets forth seventeen purposes for its existence without naming the propagation of Bahaism as one of them. It appealed for funds on general philanthropic and educational grounds, never mentioning its religious motive. It introduced the names of President Taft, Secretary Root, and other prominent men in such a way as to lead the public to understand that the movement had their intelligent endorsement. To its real purpose, viz.: aiding existing and establishing new Bahai schools in Persia and the Orient,[469] I am making no objection. It is the *concealment* of this purpose which is objectionable when contributions are asked from the general public. It claims to be *unsectarian*, because its schools take in pupils of all sects and religions. So do the schools of Christian Missions, but they are none the less Christian schools, and the "Orient-Occident" schools are distinctively Ba-

---

[465] A European Jew reports as follows (1914), "The Jewish Bahais in Hamadan are few in number (exactly fifty-nine besides children). They have not yet broken with Judaism. They go to the Synagogue and follow outwardly our religious practices. They deny *in public* that they are Bahais from fear of the Mussulmans, who detest the new religion. But the continual attacks of the Bahais against the Jews will exasperate our co-religionists, who will cast them out finally. At present the practical result is hatred and disdain, and bitter dissensions between fathers and sons, sisters and brothers, husband and wife."

[466] Phelps, p. 96. The Report of the Bahais to the United States Census Board says, "One may be a Bahai and still retain active membership in another religious body."

[467] Remey's "The Bahai Movement," p. 97.

[468] Bahaism says, "Christians who do not believe in the Koran have not believed Christ."

[469] The name of the Society has been changed to the "Orient Occident Unity," and a commercial department added. Its contributions are acknowledged, and its work reported through the *Star of the West* as Bahai work. An American, who imported a machine flour-mill to Persia, under its auspices, told the Consul that the object of his coming was not the mill but propagating Bahaism. In the *Jam-i-Jamsied,* Calcutta, March 28, 1914, Dr. E. C. Getsinger boasts to the Parsees, "The American Bahais have established schools in Persia, and have sent American teachers to those schools."

hai. They *disclaim proselytizing*. The claim is simply false. Bahai schools are hotbeds of proselytizing, and must be so by their nature. Their law[470] says, "Schools must first train the children in the principles of the religion." Dreyfus[471] adds, "There is no fear of a prescription, emanating from such authority, ever being disregarded." The Bahai school in Teheran worked under cover for some years. Remey says,[472] "This institution is not generally known as a Bahai School. However, it is in the hands of the Bahais. From the directors down through the teachers and students, the majority were of our faith." Similarly in Bombay,[473] the Bahai teacher concealed his faith. "The Zoroastrian parents of his pupils suspected him of Bahaism and so took their children out."

But to find the supreme example of Bahai *tagiya* we have to go to the fountain-head. Abdul Baha himself, oblivious to its moral obliquity, lays bare the fact in his "Traveller's Narrative."[474] We have seen that Subh-i-Azal, the half-brother of Baha Ullah, was appointed by the Bab as his successor. According to Abdul Baha, this appointment was a dishonest subterfuge on the part of Baha, arranged by him through secret correspondence with the Bab, in order that Baha might be relieved of danger and persecution and be protected from interference. So "out of regard for certain considerations and as a matter of expediency, Azal's name was made notorious on the tongues of friends and foes even to jeopardizing his life, while Baha remained safe and secure, and no one fathomed the matter." Abul Fazl[475] states the position of the "Traveller's Narrative" as follows, "The Bab and Baha Ullah, after consulting together, made Azal *appear* as the Bab's successor. In this manner they preserved Baha Ullah from interference." This account shows the low ideas of honour and truthfulness in the minds of Baha and Abdul Baha. And although their explanation is not true (but an invention of their *tagiya*—*corrupted* minds), it shows to what straits[476] they were put to explain away the succession of Azal, the legitimacy of which Azal still, in his ripe old age, maintains. Abdul Baha published to the world Baha's deceitfulness, but only made the matter worse for him.

Of a piece with this was the action of Baha's trusted agent, Maskin Kalam, in Cyprus. This Bahai was sent by the Turkish Government with Azal. "He set up a coffee-house at the port where travellers must arrive, and when he saw a Persian land he would invite him in, give him tea or coffee and a pipe, and gradually worm out of him the business that had brought him there. If his object were to see

---

[470] "Words of Paradise," p. 53.

[471] "The Universal Religion," p. 139.

[472] "Observations of a Bahai Traveller," 1908, p. 77.

[473] Sprague's "A Year in India," p. 16.

[474] Pages 62, 63, 95, 96.

[475] "Bahai Proofs," p. 52. See also Browne's "Mirza Jani's History," pp. xxxiii.-vi.

[476] The Bahais are impaled on the other horn of the dilemma also, for, as Professor Browne says ("Mirza Jani," p. xxxiii.), "The difficulty lies in the fact that Subh-i-Azal consistently refused to recognize Baha's claim, so that the Bahai is driven to make the assumption that the Bab, who is acknowledged to be divinely inspired and gifted with divine knowledge, deliberately chose to succeed him one who was destined to be the 'Point of darkness,' or chief opponent, of 'Him whom God should manifest.'"

Subh-i-Azal, off went Maskin Kalam[477] to the authorities, and the pilgrim soon found himself packed out of the Island." This account is given by a faithful Bahai. Afterwards Maskin Kalam retired to Acca and spent his old age as an honoured guest of Baha.

[477] "A Year Among the Persians," p. 517.

IX

ITS RECORD AS TO MORALS (CONTINUED)

Boast of Love—Hatred for Shiahs—For Persecutors—For Mullahs—
Abusive language—Vindictiveness—Addiction to alcohol and
opium—Testimonies.

> In their teachings they speak constantly of knowing the truth,
> but never of speaking the truth. In his book Kheiralla never men-
> tions veracity among the virtues nor lying among the vices. Reli-
> gious duplicity, *tagiya*, is a Persian peculiarity and some Moham-
> medan sects among which are our "truth-knowing" Bahais have
> raised *tagiya* to a pious privilege. Baha, the crafty chief, requires
> policy in consideration of expediency, often at the expense of good
> faith. Until the final triumph of the religion he has sanctioned
> feigned conformity. They have divine authority for duplicity.
> This is to them a pious means to a pious end. Since Baha's influ-
> ence has become paramount, they have adopted the plan of secret
> propaganda which does not hesitate, in case of need, at denying
> their faith under oath. Among Mohammedans they are primitive
> Islamites, among Christians they claim to be primitive Christians.
> If I had not taken their "private lessons," the supposition of such
> astounding duplicity would have appeared incredible or beyond
> even the Oriental proverbial duplicity.—*S. K. Vatralsky, "Amer.*
> *Jour. of Theology," 1902, pp. 73, 74, 76.*

BAHAIS particularly boast of love as one of their characteristics. They often
quote the words of Baha "to consort with all religions with spirituality and fragrance." Phelps claims for them[478] "a peculiar spirit, which marks them off from
other men,—whose essence is expressed in one word, Love. These men are Lovers; lovers of God, of their Master and teachers, of all mankind." Dreyfus, with
a forgetfulness or ignoring of facts that is astounding, says, "Their conduct is so
perfect, their harmony so complete that although they have been there at Acca for
forty years, no judge had yet to intervene for them in any dispute." Chase says
"Bahaism removes religious rancour."[479] Let facts speak. Let me array them first
by showing the relation of the Bahais to the Moslems, and then to the Azalis (see

[478] Page 112.

[479] Yet Phelps, p. 158, and Chase themselves inveigh against orthodox Christianity
with bitterness and scorn.

chapter on "Religious Assassination") and finally to each other (see chapter on "The Quarrel over the Succession").

The Babis and Bahais show great hatred and animosity against the Shiahs of Persia, abuse and revile them and heap maledictions and curses upon them. These evil feelings are shown specially against the Mullahs and the rulers. The Babi and Bahai historians indulge so much in diatribes and maledictions that Professor Browne wearies of translating them and omits pages of abuse.[480] More than enough is at hand to show the rancorous spirit of the new religion.

First take a short backward glance at the Babis. Professor Browne says:[481] "The Babis entertained for the Kajar rulers a hatred equal to that for the Mullahs." Mohammed Shah and Nasr-ud-Din Shah are called "bastard" and "scoundrel" and Mohammed Shah is consigned to hell at his death. The Shiahs are called "foul Guebres" and the Mullahs heaped with abuse. "They hated the Mohammedan clergy with an intense and bitter hatred" and anticipated the fulfillment of the prophecy "when the Kaim or Mahdi should behead 70,000 mullahs like dogs." The Bab called Haji Kazim Khan, chief of the Sheikhis, "the Quintessence of Hell Fire and the infernal tree of Zakkum." He even at times emphasized his words with blows.[482] "When a prisoner in the household of Anti-Christ—that accursed one (*i. e.*, the Shah), the Mullah of Maku showed him some discourtesy, whereupon the Ocean of Divine Wrath was stirred and He (the Bab) brought down his staff with such vigour on the unclean form of that foul creature that the august staff broke in two. He then ordered Aga Sayid Hasan (his scribe) to drive out that dog from the room, though the accursed fellow was a person of great consideration." "The Bab took leave of his jailer, Ali Khan, with the words, 'Ay maalun' ('Accursed One')."[483] It is unnecessary further to enlarge on the feelings of the Babis towards the Shiahs, for the sanguinary wars and persecutions explain them and they made no secret of their feelings of hatred.

I pass on to the Bahais, whom Abul Fazl claims were reformed and transformed by Baha. Baha himself it is, who in the "Ikan" calls the Shiahs "a foul, erring sect," who said of his Turkish guards, "Shame upon them! God shall consume their livers with fire, and verily he is the fiercest of avengers" (Lawh-i-Rais) and who exultingly celebrated, in a hymn of triumph, the death of Fuad Pasha,[484] the vizier who had exiled him, and consigned him to hell "where the heart boils and the tormenting angel melts him." Baha's winsome words about the mullahs are, in the "Ikan," "1278 years have passed and all these worthless wretches have read the Koran every morning and have not yet attained to a single letter of the purport of it."

The spirit of *love* (?) is shown by Mirza Abul Fazl, the preacher and apologist for Bahaism, in his discussion (1873) as recorded in the "New History."[485] His

---

[480] "New Hist.," pp. 320 f, 281, 289.

[481] "*Ibid.*, pp. xvii. and 354.

[482] "Mirza Jani," pp. 131-132.

[483] "New Hist.," p. 352.

[484] *Jour. Roy. As. Soc.*, 1892, p. 271.

[485] Pages 173-190.

abusive language runs on page after page. The mullahs of Persia are called mischief-makers, dolts, a pack of scoundrels, tyrants, fools, plunderers of men's properties and wives, sectarian zealots steeped in prejudice and thinly disguising their greed of worldly lucre under a veil of sanctity, sprung from the rustic population and the scum of the towns, ignorant of the decencies of society and neglectful of good breeding, with wickedness, worldliness, rapacity and selfishness which are incurable and folly that exceeds all bounds and surpasses all conception, with stupidity, overweening arrogance and presumption absolutely unparallelled, hiding the truth in falsehood, circulating false reports, possessing malignant hatred, malice, spite and great injustice, and notoriously eager to shed blood, yet with cowardice like a timid girl.

He avers further that they are lacking in patriotism, nullify sovereign authority, encroach upon and usurp the power of kings, dismiss viziers, invite the people to rebel, cause national decay, set their feet upon the necks of all mankind, menace the order and well-being of the government, devour public wealth and substitute treason for service. "Perish their homes of folly whose learning is all pretense, their colleges which never yielded a man of sense." This is a condensation of the Bahai philosopher's amiable (!) description of the chiefs of his national religion. The author of the "New History" almost surpasses him in abuse.[486] He compares the mullahs to a "host of foul reptiles who befoul and pollute the pure water of life so that it waxeth loathsome and abominable.... They are fraudulent and sophistical hypocrites ... inwardly reprobate and outwardly devout, clothing themselves in the garb of spurious asceticism and simulated piety: fabricators of 'authentic' traditions." Later Haji M. Haidar Ali,[487] writing by command of Abdul Baha, says of Persia, "The old religious sects ... degenerated into ferocious wolves and mad dogs, even surpassing the ravenous man-eating beasts." Apropos of the martyrdom of Aga Sayid Jafar of Abargoo, "Our Great Lord and Master Abdul Baha revealed the following in a Visiting Tablet" to be *chanted at the tomb*: "Hell is for such as rejected thee, fire for such as sentenced thee to death, infernal flame for such as betrayed thee, and the hellish gulf for such as shed thy blood."[488] These quotations show the vindictive spirit of the Bahai leaders. Any one who is acquainted with Bahais in Persia knows that this is the spirit that animates them, that they revile the Mutasharis and Sheikhis and especially their mullahs. They are brotherly and helpful to their own particular sect of Bahais, vindictive to all who have opposed them. Doctor Frame quotes a Persian as saying this of the attitude of Abdul Baha, "He is very kind towards his friends and bitter towards his enemies." In view of all that has been brought forward, how can Mr. Phelps aver "that they have no trace of bitterness or resentment for their sufferings." The habit of Bahais in denying that they have animosity against other religions reminds me of one of their own stories. A certain mullah said to his friend, "If you notice in me any objectionable habit please inform me." "I perceive no fault in you," answered his friend, "save a habit of using abusive language." "Abusive language!" cried the mullah. "What rascally knave calls me abusive? What shameless ruffian have I

---

[486] Pages 4-5, written 1880.
[487] "Martyrs of 1903," p. 3.
[488] "Visiting Tablets," p. 12, N. Y. Bahai Board of Counsel.

abused that he should dare accuse me?"

In the statements of Bahais which I quoted above, they laid claim to superior chastity and sobriety. In the chapter on "Bahaism and Woman" I have noticed their defects in regard to the treatment of women. In regard to sexual immorality, they are neither better nor worse than Persians of the middle class to which they mostly belong. Bahai law follows the Moslem law in prohibiting the use of alcohol as a beverage, as did the law of the Bab. The Bab prohibited opium and tobacco. Azal follows the Bab in these restrictions, while Baha exempts tobacco from the prohibition. A good many Moslems, especially of the cities and upper classes, are addicted to alcohol, and have been through the centuries of Islam. My observation leads me to believe that Bahais are more addicted to the use of intoxicants than Moslems are. Regarding the relation of Bahais to wine and opium, we have an impartial witness who writes his experience without prejudice or motive. Professor Browne, in his "A Year Among the Persians," tells of his social intercourse with the Babis, Azalis and Bahais. His prolonged stay in Kirman was largely spent among the Bahais. He became so intimate with them as to be considered one of them by many in the city. He joined in their convivialities and he gives us a simple narrative of everyday events and experiences. Read the volume from page 475 to 540 and see how many of the Bahais lived in the habitual use of wine and opium. It is shocking and shows what goes on behind their doors. No other one has had opportunity to see and reveal their hidden life. One and another and another of the Bahais is referred to by name and occupation as addicted to intoxicants.[489] Sheikh Ibrahim "is a drunkard and a libertine"; Usta Akbar, the pea-parcher, "returned in a state of boastful intoxication, talking blasphemous nonsense"; the son of the Bahai postmaster "wants money to get drunk and play the libertine"; Haji Shirazi is "a drinker and a libertine" and a reviler; another is a victim of copious libations of beer; another a drunkard and blasphemous in his cups.

Regarding the use of opium they appear to be worse. It seems to be a common habit among them. See pages 499, 500, 505, 520, 524, 525, 540. Of certain dinners Professor Browne says, "All present were Babis (Bahais) and we sat sipping our tea and whiffing opium." "We sat talking late and smoking opium." "The wildest ascriptions of Deity to Baha were made when intoxicated with wine and opium: then they praised the 'Beloved.'" "The poor lad, the son of the telegrapher whom I had seen smoking opium, was dead." "A Bahai dervish was engaged in smoking an opium pipe." The Prince secretary, an Azali Babi, "was a confirmed opium smoker." Browne even joined the Bahais in the use of opium and almost became a victim of the habit. On one occasion[490] they secretly filled his pipe with hashish (Bhang). He recognized the taste and refused it. Why did they do so? Would they possibly have shown him visions with the hope of persuading him of the truth of Bahaism? Maybe some such incidents are the basis of the Moslem accusations against the Bahais of using hashish on neophytes. The point of the above citations is plain. Bahaism does not exercise the transforming power that is claimed for it. The Persian Bahais are yet in the bonds of iniquity. The boasts of Bahais are

[489] Pages 436, 517, 524, 540.
[490] Pages 520-521.

ungrounded. What of Abul Fazl's question,[491] "Have you ever heard of a Bahai accused[492] of drinking wine?[493] None are accused of evil deeds or bad morals." Again Sprague says, "The conditions of the Millennium are already visible among these people," and Thornton Chase declares, "It brings men to a higher conception of duty and life than has been the heritage of the churches." How blind to facts is such faith!

---

[491] "Bahai Proofs," p. 79.

[492] The testimony of Mr. Getsinger that he saw the son of Baha Ullah under the influence of liquor is given in Chapter XI.

The testimony of Professor Browne as to their habits is borne out, in a general way, without his personal experience, by others who have had long residence in Persia. Rev. W. A. Shedd, D. D., of Urumia writes, "Does the religion bring about a change of life and character? The reports given by Bahai travellers are glowing, but long residents in Persia have no such a tale to tell. The Bahais are not noticeably more honest, more truthful, more sober nor more reliable than others" (*Missionary Review*, Oct. 1911). J. D. Frame, M. D., of Resht says (*Moslem World*, July, 1912), "The real test of a religion is its influence upon life. Repeatedly we have challenged the Bahais, 'Show us from your personal lives a power to regenerate the lives of men.'" Rev. S. M. Jordan of Teheran writes ("The Mohammedan World," p. 179), "By neither Moslems, Jews, nor Christians are they considered morally superior to the Moslems, while in some respects they rightly are judged less so." The Rev. J. H. Shedd, D. D., writes, "The Bahai freedom runs to license, and hence as a reform leaves men worse rather than better. Mr. Browne found himself in the meshes of the opium habit in Kirman by yielding too freely to their influence. There is undoubtedly a generous fellowship in the Bahai community, but there is no moral principle.... There are no high and strong characters developed to lead the world in true reform, no high motives to virtue are developed. The seeds of its own destruction are in the system and the best argument against it will soon be its fruits" (R. E. Speer's "Missions and Modern History," p. 182).

[493] "Bahai Proofs," p. 82.

X

RELIGIOUS ASSASSINATION

Strife between Baha and Azal in Bagdad—Baha goes to Kurdistan—
Dissension at Adrianople—Testimony of an eye-witness—Attempted assassinations—Plots and counter plots—Bahais assassinate Azalis at Acca—Other assassinations—In Bagdad, in
Persia—Attitude towards taking of life—Suicide commended—
Psychological attestation—Traditional custom—Assassination
practiced in Islam—Testimonies—Azali hatred

The religion now entered upon the phase of intestinal dissensions, bitter animosities, schisms, and internecine strife. The pages of its history are henceforth filled with tales of dissension and
disruption; of anathemas and accusations; of heresy and apostacy
reiterated and reciprocated with increasing bitterness; of fratri-
cidal assassinations and persecutions.—*Professor Browne in "New
History," p. x.*

Subh-i-Azal is the Khalifa of the Bab and the Bahais are in bad
faith when they deny it.—*Nicolas, p. 20.*

When inspiration and revelation failed, Baha did not disdain
to benefit by the pointed argument of the dagger and the subtle
persuasion of poison.—*Vatralsky in "Amer. Jour. of Theology."*

We cannot tolerate iniquity in God nor in one claiming to be
God and we cannot conceive of God incarnate subject to the limitations of racial moral ideals.—*R. E. Speer, p. 146.*

IN general Bahais claim that they and their leaders have been exemplars of
love and harmony. Specific declarations of their excellence in this regard have
been quoted. M. Abul Fazl[494] writes: "During the long years from the arrival of
Baha Ullah in Bagdad to the present day they have not committed that which
would disturb a single soul. They have been killed but they have killed no one."
Mr. Horace Holley[495] says: "For forty years no judge has had to settle a dispute
between them." It behooves us to inquire how the conduct of Baha and his adherents shows up in this regard during the first period of their exile. It is evident
that in Persia Baha had no sincere love for his brother Azal, for he planned to

[494] "Bahai Proofs," p. 12.
[495] "The Modern Social Religion," p. 167.

secure safety for himself by putting Azal's life in jeopardy. (See Chapter VIII.) It is further plain that early in the exile jealousy, envy and hate manifested themselves, even while Baha was outwardly obedient to Azal. In Bagdad, says Bahiah Khanum, "disharmony and misunderstanding arose among the believers—discord—strife—contention."[496] Therefore Baha went off to Kurdistan. He refers in the "Ikan" to the dissensions,[497] "Such an odour of jealousy was diffused, banners of discord hoisted, enemies endeavoured to destroy this servant,—hardships, calamities and sufferings inflicted by Moslems were as nothing compared with what hath been inflicted by the believers." His opponents say that he wished to introduce innovations, relax the law and put forward on his own account a claim to be a Manifestation and being resisted in this, he "got angry."[498] After they were removed to Adrianople the quarrel waxed hotter. Abul Fazl describes it as one of "interior fires of dissension and jealousy between the rival leaders, far exceeding the jealousy of outsiders.[499] Mohammed Jawad Kasvini says[500] there were "all manner of intrigues, falsehoods and untruths." I have received from a Moslem convert to Christianity an interesting account of conditions then and there. He was at that time a *peesh-khidmat* to the Persian Minister at Constantinople. He was at Samsun when Azal and Baha and their parties embarked and was introduced to them by Haji Rajab Ali Khan, brother-in-law of my informant. He saw them day by day and became a serious inquirer. Afterwards he went to Adrianople bearing presents to Baha. He found Baha and Azal living in separate rooms of the same house under guards. The two brothers were in dispute over the supremacy, and the *murids* had been won over by Baha. He narrates, "I entered one day. I heard words of angry disputation and revilings. Yahya said, "Ay! Husain Ali, you are vile! Do you not remember your sodomies? You are defiled. Your wife is a bad one!" Husain Ali answered, "Ay, cursed one! Your son Nur Ullah is not your son but son of Sayid——. You yourself are a sodomite, an adulterer." Such like revilings they hurled at each other. I called Maskin Kalam and said to him, "What are these words and doings? If Baha is true why does he talk so? Why do these brothers revile each other? What a fool I am to come so many miles to hear such revilings from a divinity!" We then went to the room of Ishan. My companion said to Ishan, "Why do they curse so?" I said, "I wish to ask a question." He said, "What is it?" I said, "You say they do not work miracles, but must there not be personal power and influence in words?""[501]

The condition at Adrianople culminated in a series of crimes, which now come before us for examination.

Charges have been made, in detail, against the companions of Baha Ullah of

---

[496] Phelps, pp. 19-20.

[497] Pages 178-181.

[498] "Trav.'s Narr.," pp. 356-358.

[499] "Bahai Proofs," p. 51.

[500] Manuscript "Life of Beha Ullah," p. 20.

[501] Professor Browne, afterwards in Persia, found the attitude of the Bahais towards the Azalis "unjust and intolerant" and reprimanded them for "their violence and unfairness." They cursed and reviled in the presence of Professor Browne ("A Year Among the Persians," pp. 525-530).

assassinating the Azalis, the followers of his rival Subh-i-Azal. Most of the information regarding the matter is to be found in the books and translations of Professor Browne, the great authority on Bahaism in the Anglo-Saxon world. I wish to present and weigh the evidence in hand regarding these accusations.

1. The first charge is *that Baha Ullah attempted to poison Subh-i-Azal, his half-brother* and predecessor. This charge is found in the "Hasht Behesht," a history of Babism, by Aga Sayid Javad,[502] a prominent Mullah of Kirman and a leading disciple of the Bab. The occurrence took place when Azal and Baha were both at Adrianople under surveillance of the Turkish authorities. Baha, so it narrates,[503] ordered that there should be placed before him and "Azal a dish of plain food, with one side of which he had mixed some poison, intending to poison Azal. For hitherto the apportioned breakfast and supper had been from the house of Mirza Husain Ali (Baha Ullah). When that poisoned dish was placed before them, Baha pressed Azal to take of it. By a fortunate chance, the smell of onions was perceptible in the food, and Azal, being averse to onions, refused to taste it. Though urgently pressed, he refused, saying: 'It smells of onions.' Baha, supposing his evil design was suspected, and to disguise the truth, ate a little from the other (unpoisoned) side in order that Azal's suspicions might be dispelled and that he might eat of the poisoned side. Now, inasmuch as the poison had to some extent diffused itself to the other side, it produced some slight effect on Baha, causing him sickness and vomiting, so that he summoned his physician." This account was confirmed by Mirza Abdul Ali, the son of Subh-i-Azal, to Professor Browne, when he visited him in Cyprus in 1888.[504]

The daughter of Baha, Bahiah Khanum, gives a contradictory account of the same affair.[505] She says that the feast was at Azal's house and that rice for both was served on the same plate, having been prepared in Azal's house. "The portion of rice intended for my father was flavoured with onions, of which he was very fond. The servant, by direction of Azal, placed this portion towards my father. He ate some of it, but fortunately not very much. He preferred the rice prepared for Azal, and ate of it. Soon after eating he became ill. The physician declared that he had been poisoned. He was so desperately ill for twenty-two days that the physician said he could not live." Mirza Abul Fazl, a Bahai writer, says,[506] "Azal sought to poison Baha Ullah, and attempted to do so twice, but failed to accomplish his design." "He repeatedly planned to murder Baha." Baha himself alludes to these events in the "Sura-i-Haykal."[507] "My brother warred with me. He desired to drink my blood. He took counsel with one of my attendants tempting him unto this. We went out from among them and dwelt in another house. Neither did we see him afterwards."

Thus we have brother against brother, each accusing the other of attempting fratricide. How shall we settle the question of veracity? Mr. Phelps makes a plea for

[502] "New Hist.," p. 200, Note 4.
[503] *Jour. Roy. As. Soc.*, 1892, p. 296, by Professor Browne. Also "Trav.'s Narr.," p. 359.
[504] "Trav.'s Narr.," p. 369.
[505] Phelps, "Life of Abbas Effendi," pp. 40-44.
[506] "Brilliant Proof," p. 11.
[507] Chicago Edition, pp. 20-23; and "Trav.'s Narr.," pp. 368, 369.

Baha, but his words lack foundation. He says that Azal's story "is a *transparent* fabrication because it assumes an impossible ignorance on the part of Baha Ullah that Azal disliked onions, as well as the impossible hypothesis that Baha Ullah would knowingly partake of food in which poison had been placed." But neither of these "impossible" things are a part of the story. The first objection can only be taken, if at all, to Professor Browne's abridged account in the "Traveller's Narrative," and not to the original in "Hasht Behesht," which distinctly states that onions had communicated their flavour to the other side of the platter, contrary to intention; and, secondly, Baha supposed when he ate (according to the "Hasht Behesht" account) that the poison had not communicated itself to his side of the platter of rice. Those familiar with Persian *pillau*, or boiled rice, in which each grain is separate and dry, will see that it would ordinarily be quite possible to put onions and poison on opposite sides of the platter without either reaching the other side. Each man would help himself, according to Persian custom, from the side of the dish next to him. Moreover, it was customary to prepare the food for Azal in the kitchen of Baha.'[508] Up to the time of the incident they had both continued to live in the same house. This is evident from Baha's words in the "Sura-i-Haykal," where he says, "We went out, dwelt in *another house, neither did we see him afterwards*." This agrees with the "Hasht Behesht." In this and several other particulars the narrative of Bahiah Khanum is defective or misleading. Mr. Phelps' plea, on account of the character of the Bahais, begs the question. This charge and subsequent ones to be discussed, involve the integrity of Baha's character and that of his immediate disciples. The history shows no more reason to believe Baha than to believe Azal, but rather less.

2. The next charge of the Azalis is as follows:[509] "Shortly after this, another plot was laid against Subh-i-Azal's life, and it was arranged that *Mohammed Ali, the barber, should cut his (Azal's) throat while* shaving him in the bath. On the approach of the barber, however, Subh-i-Azal divined his design, refused to allow him to come near, and, on leaving the bath, instantly took another lodging, and separated himself entirely from Mirza Husain Ali and his followers."

On the Bahai side, Bahiah Khanum says,[510] "One day in the bath Azal asked the servant (of Baha) 'whether it would not be easy for an attendant who was not faithful to Baha to make away with him while shaving him.' The servant replied that this was certainly the case. Azal then asked whether, if God should lay upon him the command to do this, he would obey it? The servant understood this to be the suggestion of such a command, and was so terrified by it that he rushed screaming from the room. This occurrence was ignored by my father, and our relations with Azal continued to be cordial."

Here we have two stories in direct contradiction to each other. It may be observed that the attendant or barber, who was that day serving Azal in the bath, as is agreed by both parties, was a partisan of Baha,[511] without doubt the same barber, Mohammed Ali, who subsequently murdered the Azalis,[512] and who was

[508] Phelps, *Ibid.*, p. 40.
[509] "Trav.'s Narr.," p. 359.
[510] Phelps, p. 39.
[511] Phelps, p. 38.
[512] "Trav.'s Narr.," p, 361.

decorated by Baha with the title Dallak-i-Hakikat,[513] "The Barber of the Truth." It was much more natural that Azal should be suspicious of him than try to tempt him to kill Baha.

In either case, what do we see? Behold, these two "Manifestations of God" accusing each other of attempting assassination. They were brothers, both eminent disciples of the Bab, the "Point of Divinity" of the "new Revelation," both "revealers of inspired verses." The heart of each was full of hatred and envy and of desire to overreach the other. Neither is worthy of credence, both being steeped in Persian deception from childhood. Possibly, at that time, each was ready to compass the death of the other. The subsequent history, however, casts back its reflection upon the murder-plots at Adrianople, and in its lurid light the character of the Bahais grows darker. As a consequence, the charges of the Azalis against the Bahais become probable and are easily accepted.

3. The *proved assassination of Azalis by Bahais at Acca*. The quarrels and plots at Adrianople led to complaints of each party against the other before the Osmanli Government. For the sake of peace and safety they were separated. Azal was sent as a prisoner-pensioner to Famagusta, Cyprus. Baha was removed to Acca, Syria. The "Hasht Behesht" says:[514] "With the latter were his family, about eighty of his adherents, and four of Subh-i-Azal's followers, to wit, Haji Sayid Mohammed of Ispahan, Aga Jan Bey, Mirza Riza Kuli of Tafrish, and his brother Aga Mirza Nas-rullah."

These Azalis were murdered by the Bahais in Acca. Of this crime there are many who give testimony, (*a*) The "Hasht Behesht" says:[515] "Before the transfer was actually effected, however, Mirza Nasrullah was poisoned by Baha, at Adrianople. The other Azalis were assassinated shortly after their arrival at Acca, in a house which they occupied near the barracks, the assassins being Abdul Karim, Mohammed the barber, Husain the water-carrier, and Mohammed Javad of Kasvin" (all attachés of Baha).

(*b*) Subh-i-Azal independently confirmed this account in conversation with Professor Browne.[516]

(*c*) Bahai testimony also confirms it. Professor Browne heard the story at Kirman from Sheikh Ibrahim, a Bahai, who had suffered imprisonment and torture for the faith, and who had seen some of the perpetrators while on a pilgrimage to Acca. He said,[517] "The Babis were divided into two factions. So high did feeling run that the matter ended in open strife, and two Azalis and one Bahai were killed" at Adrianople. "The Turkish Government sent seven[518] Azalis to Acca with Baha. They—Aga Jan, called Kaj-Kulah, Haji Sayid Mohammed of Ispahan, one of the original companions of the Bab, Mirza Riza, a nephew of the last, Mirza Haydar Ali of Ardistan, Haji Sayid Husain of Kashan, and two others whose names

[513] *Ibid.*, p. 362.
[514] "Trav.'s Narr.," p. 361.
[515] *Ibid.*, p. 361.
[516] *Ibid.*, p. 371.
[517] "A Year Among the Persians," pp. 513-517.
[518] Possibly he counts those who afterwards left their allegiance to Baha.

I forget—lived all together in a house situated near the gate of the city. Well, one night about a month after their arrival at Acca, twelve Bahais (nine of whom were still living when I was at Acca) determined to kill them and so prevent them from doing any mischief. So they went at night, armed with swords and daggers, to the house where the Azalis lodged, and knocked at the door. Aga Jan came down to open to them, and was stabbed before he could cry out or offer the least resistance. Then they entered the house and killed the other six." In consequence, "the Turks imprisoned Baha and all his family and followers in the caravanserai, but the twelve assassins came forward and surrendered themselves, saying, 'We killed them without the knowledge of our Master or of any of the brethren. Punish us, not them.' So they were imprisoned for a while; but afterwards, at the intercession of Abbas Effendi (Abdul Baha), were suffered to be at large, on condition of remaining at Acca and wearing still fetters on their ankles for a time."

(*d*) Mr. Laurence Oliphant gives an account of the Bahais at Acca in his "Haifa, or Life in Modern Palestine."[519] He substantiates the account of the assassinations, and narrates how Baha Ullah was called before the Osmanli Court to answer on the charge of complicity in them. He further states that after one session, Baha "purchased an exemption from further attendance at court *with an enormous bribe.*"

(*e*) The defense, unable to escape the force of the damaging testimony or to deny the facts against such testimony, can only offer some excuses in extenuation. Bahiah Khanum[520] reduces the number of Bahais who made the attack on the Azalis to three, asserts that their intention was to threaten death and frighten but not to kill them, that but two Azalis were killed and also one of the Bahais, that the provocation was that the Azalis had slandered Baha Ullah, forged letters in his name, which incited the Government against him and were threatening to kill him, and further that Baha was not cognizant of their intention. But Professor Browne shows that Baha regarded the murder with some complacency at least,[521] and refers to it in the "Kitab-ul-Akdas," saying, "God hath taken away him who led you astray," viz.: Haji Sayid Mohammed, one of the murdered men, who was Azal's chief supporter. He also confirms the fact that Abbas Effendi interceded for the murderers and secured their freedom from adequate punishment. Just as Brigham Young[522] condoned and secured immunity from punishment, if he did not justify or instigate the crimes of his sect. Bahiah Khanum herself shows us that the murderers acted for the religion, and not from any private or personal motives; in other words, committed "religious assassination," after the traditional oriental custom.

The same is shown and more facts brought out in the defense made by Mohammed Jawad Gasvini.[523] He writes that the three persons mentioned above published tracts which were calculated to excite the populace against Baha and his adherents. One, Nasir Abbas of Bagdad, came from Beirut to kill them but was

[519] "Haifa, etc.," p. 107; "Trav.'s Narr.," p. 370.

[520] Phelps, p. 75.

[521] *Jour. Roy. As. Soc.*, 1889, p. 519; "Trav.'s Narr.," pp. 94, 370.

[522] "Brigham Young," by Cannon, p. 271. "Brigham failed to punish or even condemn those criminals who served him too well."

[523] Manuscript, pp. 41-48.

enjoined by Baha not to do so. Then "Some believers organized a secret meeting to put an end to these evil doers. The author was among them and was of their opinion." Baha again restrained them, so the author avers. But, he continues, "The following seven persons secretly determined to put out of the way the aforesaid intriguers" (here follow their names and occupations). "These seven began to consort with the intriguers very cordially, pretending that they were in accord with them and with their belief, and continued to do so for some time. But one afternoon they entered their residence, which was situated opposite the residence of the governor of the city of Acca, and there they killed the said Sayid Mohammed, and Aga Jan, and Mirza Riza Kuli. This took place in the year 1288 A. H., *i. e.*, 1870 A. D. When the Government heard of the tragedy it arrested the said seven and arrested all the followers of Baha Ullah who were in Acca." All, including Baha Ullah, Abbas Effendi and the other brothers were imprisoned. Baha was released after three days, after being interrogated by the court. Sixteen of the Bahais were confined in prison for six months and the seven for terms of seven to fifteen years, afterwards reduced by one-third. Thus twenty-three out of about forty male believers were found guilty of the assassinations or of complicity in the plot.

4. Various and *sundry other assassinations for the faith.* According to the Azali historian, these murders were followed by many others. Certain disciples separated themselves from Baha. Of these some fled from Acca,[524] "but the Khayyat Bashi (chief tailor) and Haji Ibrahim were assassinated in the caravanserai of the corn-sellers and buried in quicklime under the platform. Another, Haji Jaffar, importunately pressed his claim for a debt of 1,200 pounds which Baha owed him. (I wonder whether it was incurred to meet the 'enormous bribe.') Thereupon Baha's amanuensis, Mirza Aga Jan Kashani, instructed a disciple, Ali of Kasvin, to slay the old man and throw his body out of the window of the upper room which he occupied in the caravanserai." It was then reported "that he had cast himself out and died, yielding up his life to the Beloved." "All the prominent supporters of Subh-i-Azal, who withstood Baha, were marked out for death,[525] and in Bagdad, Mullah Rajab Ali Kahir and his brother Haji Mirza Ahmad, Haji Mirza Mohammed Riza and several others fell one by one by the knife or the bullet of the assassin." The following others are specified with the place and name of the assassin,[526] "Aga Sayid Ali the Arab, one of the original 'Letters of the Living,' was killed in Tabriz by Mirza Mustapha of Nirak; and Aga Ali Mohammed by Abdul Karim; Haji Aga of Tabriz met a like fate, as did Haji Mirza Ahmad, the brother of the historian Haji Mirza Jani.[527] Another, whose faith had grown cold, was Aga Mohammed Ali of Ispahan, who was residing at Constantinople.[528] Mirza Abul Kasim was sent from Acca with instructions to "bleed that block of heedlessness whose blood is in excess." He robbed his victim of £350, with part of which he bought and sent goods to Acca. Another instance was Mirza Asad Ullah "Deyyan," who

---

[524] "Trav.'s Narr.," p. 362.
[525] "Trav.'s Narr.," p. 359; *Jour. Roy. As. Soc.,* 1889, p. 519; 1892, pp. 995-996.
[526] "Trav.'s Narr.," p. 363.
[527] *Ibid.,* p. 332. Also "New Hist.," p. 391.
[528] "Trav.'s Narr.," p. 363.

claimed to be a "Manifestation."[529] "Mirza Husain Ali (Baha), after a protracted discussion with him, instructed his servant, Mirza Mohammed of Mezanderan, to slay him, which was accordingly done." Count Gobineau confirms this account.[530] Concerning these crimes we have also the independent testimony of Subh-i-Azal, who mentioned most of these instances by name and added several others. Azal said to Captain Young, a British officer in Cyprus,[531] "About twenty of my followers were killed by the Bahais." He confirmed it in an autograph letter to Professor Browne, saying, "They (*i. e.*, the Bahais) unsheathed the sword of hatred and wrought what they would. They cruelly put to death the remnant of my friends who stood firm." In the "New History"[532] Professor Browne names over the list of those assassinated, and adds, "Of the more prominent Azalis, Sayid Javad, of Kerbela (or Kirman), seems to have been almost the only one who long survived what the Azalis call 'The direful Disorder.'" In Kirman, Professor Browne said to the Bahais,[533] "From a statement of one of your own party, it appears that your friends at Acca, who complain so much of the bigotry, intolerance and ferocious antagonism of the Mohammedans, and who are always talking about 'consorting with men of every faith with spirituality and fragrance,' could find no better argument than the dagger of the assassin wherewith to convince the unfortunate Azalis."

5. The conduct of the primitive Babis and their leaders, and *their attitude towards the taking of life*,[534] has a bearing on the question of the conduct of the Bahais, for up to the time of the residence at Adrianople they were identical. The history of the Babis is a bloody one. The "first bloodshed which took place in Persia (in connection with the Babi movement) was the murder of a Shiah Mujtihid by one or more Babis." It was a "religious assassination." The circumstances were as follows,[535] When the Bab, as captive, passed through Kasvin, *en route* for Maku, he wrote a letter asking succour from Haji Mohammed Taki, an orthodox Mujtihid, who was the father-in-law of the celebrated Kurrat-ul-Ayn. "The Haji tore the letter into fragments, and made some unseemly remarks." When this was reported to the Bab, he said, "Was there no one to smite him on the mouth?" The Bahai historian (1880) continues, "Wherefore the Lord brought it to pass that he was smitten in the mouth with a spear head that he might no more speak insolently." Shortly afterwards a certain Babi,[536] named Salih, hearing the Mujtihid curse and revile Sheikh Ahmad, the teacher of the Bab, entered the mosque and slew him at the pulpit. The Bahai historian continues, "This was the consequence of the Haji's conduct to the Bab, and agreeable to the tradition of the Imams, 'whosoever curseth us ... is an infidel,' and so he deemed it incumbent on himself to slay him."

[529] *Ibid.*, pp. 357, 365.

[530] "Religions et Philosophies dans l'Asie Centrale," pp. 277-278.

[531] *Jour. Roy. As. Soc.*, 1889, p. 996.

[532] Page xxiii.

[533] "A Year Among the Persians," p. 530.

[534] The Bab asked his fellow prisoner to kill him ("Mirza Jani," p. xlvii.).

[535] "New Hist.," pp. 274, 275; "Trav.'s Narr.," pp. 198, 199, 311.

[536] The "Kasas-ul-Ulema," the Shiah history, says, "Certain Babis, stung by his words, fell upon him early one morning as he was praying in the mosque, and with knives and daggers inflicted on him eight wounds from which he died two days later" ("Trav.'s Narr.," p. 198).

A variation of this story is found in a work by an American Bahai, Mary H. Ford, called "The Oriental Rose."[537] She narrates that Kurrat-ul-Ayn heard the Mujtihid cursing the Bab, and gazing upon him she exclaimed, "How unfortunate you are! For I see your mouth filled with blood!" "The following morning, as he was crossing the threshold of the mosque, he was struck upon the mouth by the lance of a hidden assailant. The attack was followed up by five or six other assassins, who beat the life out of his mangled body." "The strange insight of Kurrat-ul-Ayn had foreseen it." "The assassination removed a serious obstacle from her pathway."

From these narratives, both from the pens of "Friends," it is evident that the Bab and Kurrat-ul-Ayn each spoke words which were direct instigations and incitements to their fanatical followers to commit murder. The chief murderer fled and "joined himself to the people of God" at Sheikh Tabarsi. Disregarding his crime, they welcomed him to their ranks as a "follower of God, and he attained to martyrdom."[538]

We can admire the courage and devotion of the Babis, but certainly their hatred and fanaticism carry them on to retaliation and revenge which are far from pure religion. Witness their deeds! Farrukh Khan, a prisoner of war, was first skinned alive and then roasted,[539] and twenty-two prisoners of war were put to death at the same time, at Zanjan. At Sheikh Tabarsi, by order of Janab-i-Kuddus, His Excellency the Holy, the enemies slain in battle were decapitated and their heads set on posts around the ramparts.[540]

The attempt to assassinate Nasr-i-Din Shah (1852) shows also the murderous spirit of the Babis. From seven to twelve[541] Babis were engaged in the plot, and four of them started out to take part in the assault. It was not, as is commonly represented by Bahais, the act of an unbalanced, weak-minded individual, but the revengeful plot of a number. The spirit of vengeance was very strong within them. Of this we have a witness from a very unexpected quarter, namely, the celebrated Bahai apologist, Mirza Abul Fazl. He writes,[542] "Numerous historical and tangible evidences can be furnished to prove that it was the pen of Baha Ullah which protected from death his own enemies, such as Subh-i-Azal, Nasr-i-Din Shah and certain great doctors and divines. Otherwise the Babis *would not have allowed a single one of these people to have escaped alive.*" He certainly must include Bahais, for the Babis would not have desired to kill Subh-i-Azal. But the assertion of M. Abul Fazl, that Baha was as the "Prince of Peace" among a lot of untrained, untamed disciples, will not stand investigation. For Baha's history shows the contrary.

6. *Baha also commends suicide for his sake.* It is narrated by Abdul Baha[543] that rather than be separated in exile from Baha, "Haji Jafar was moved to lamentation,

---

[537] Pages 61, 62.

[538] "New Hist.," pp. 82, 278.

[539] "New Hist.," p. 115 and note, p. 411.

[540] *Ibid.*, p. 73; "Trav.'s Narr.," p. 178.

[541] *Ibid.*, p. 323.

[542] "The Brilliant Proof," p. 11.

[543] "Trav.'s Narr.," pp. 100-101.

and with his own hand cut his throat." Baha, in the Lawh-i-Raiz, alluded to this event, saying, "One from amongst the Friends sacrificed himself for myself and *cut his throat with his own hand for the love of God*. This is such that we have not heard from former ages. This is that which God hath set apart for this dispensation." Another disciple attempted suicide about the same time.[544] This "old and faithful follower seized a knife and exclaiming, 'If I must be separated from my Lord, I will go and join my God,' cut his throat. With the aid of a physician, his life was saved. Again when the ship bearing the exiles reached Haifa, Abdul Ghaffar, finding himself to be separated from his Lord, determined to sacrifice his life, and threw himself into the sea from the steamer, exclaiming, 'O Baha! O Baha!'" The sailors rescued him.[545] This tendency to suicide reveals an astonishing degree of fanaticism among the Bahais. But suicide is so rare among the Persian Shiahs that these reports arouse suspicion and call for further investigation. I was informed of one person whom the Bahais at Acca reported as a suicide, but who in reality had been murdered by them. Of another, named Haji Mirza Riza, who would have written a history favourable to Azal, the latter wrote to Professor Browne that "they (the Bahais) sought to slay him, and at length gave out that, on the first night of his imprisonment, he had bound a cord about his throat and destroyed himself and so became a martyr."[546] The celebrated Nabil, Bahai poet and historian, is reported to have committed suicide by throwing himself into the sea, shortly after the death of Baha Ullah. "He could stay on earth no longer—he loved and yearned so for Baha Ullah."[547] As this same Nabil had himself claimed to be the Manifestation,[548] it was very convenient that he should make away with himself at that time, instead of renewing his pretensions.

These instances of suicide are cited as proofs of the truth of the religion by M. Mohammed Husain Shirazi, who says,[549] "More faithful and devoted (than the early Christians), some martyrs of our day have killed themselves with their own hands out of devotion to their Lord Baha." Again Baha sent Badi, the messenger, to the Shah, with the "Epistle" from Acca, assuring him beforehand that he was going to death.[550] The letter could easily have been sent through one of the foreign consulates without sacrifice of life.

Doctor Jessup says:[551] "They teach unscrupulous persecution of those obnoxious to them. I had a friend, a learned Mohammedan of Bagdad, called Ibrahim Effendi, of scholarly bearing, refined and courteous—a brother of the wife of Abbas Effendi. His father, a wealthy man, died when he was young and his uncle determined to bring him up as a Babite (Bahai). But the boy refused to accept it. His uncle then robbed him of his property," and threatened him. He fled and came to Beirut. He professed Christianity and was baptized at Alexandria, Egypt. While at

[544] Phelps, p. 50.
[545] Manuscript Life, p. 36.
[546] Compare "History by Mirza Jani," p. xvi.
[547] "Notes taken at Acca," by Mrs. C. True, p. 27.
[548] "Trav.'s Narr.," pp. 357-358.
[549] "Facts for Behaists," p. 42.
[550] "Oriental Rose," p. 186.
[551] "Fifty-three Years in Syria," pp. 637, 605.

Beirut, "he went down to Acca to visit. One night he found that his life was in great danger if he stayed through the night and he escaped to Beirut in great terror."[552]

7. *Psychological attestation of the accusation* against the Bahais, of assassination, is seen in their doctrine of the power and prerogative of the "Manifestation," and the inference made by the Bahais from that doctrine. This is set forth in the Tablet of Ishrakat,[553] "Verily He (Baha) hath come from the Heaven of the Unseen, and with Him the standard of 'He doeth whatsoever He willeth,' and the hosts of power and authority. As to all else save Him: It is incumbent upon them to cling unto that which he hath commanded." "Woe unto those who denied and turned away from Him." "The Most Great Infallibility" is applied only to one (the Manifestation), whose station is sanctified above commands or prohibitions. He is proof against error. Verily if he declares heaven to be earth, right to be left, or south to be north, it is true, and there is no doubt of it." "No one has a right to oppose him, or to say, 'Why or wherefore'; and he who disputes Him is verily of the opposers." "He doeth whatsoever he willeth, and commandeth whatsoever he desireth."

In like manner Abdul Baha states the authority of the Manifestation,[554] "He is not under the shadow of the former laws. Whatever he performs is an upright action. No believer has any right to criticize." "If some people do not understand the hidden secret of one of his commands or actions, they ought not to oppose it."

These principles are boldly interpreted and applied by the Bahais to the subject under discussion. Sayid Kamil, a Bahai of Shiraz, said to Professor Browne[555] with a look of supreme surprise, "You surely cannot pretend to deny that a prophet, who is an incarnation of the Universal Intelligence, has a right to inflict death, openly or *secretly*, on those who stubbornly opposed him. A prophet is no more to be blamed for removing an obdurate opponent that a surgeon for an amputation of a gangrenous limb." This opinion prevailed among the Bahais. At Yezd they said,[556] "A divine messenger has as much right to kill and compel as a surgeon to amputate." The Bahai missionaries maintained[557] that, "A prophet has a right to slay if he knows it necessary; if he sees that the slaughter of a few will prevent many from going astray, he is justified in commanding such slaughter. No one can question his right to destroy the bodies of a few that the souls of many may live." A Bahai acquaintance of Doctor Frame, of Resht, told him[558] "without any appearance of shame, that he paid so much to have a persecutor removed."

8. In connection with all the above facts, it must be kept in mind that *"reli-*

[552] Doctor Kheiralla believes that assassination is to be feared at the present time. He told me that a prominent follower of M. Mohammed Ali had been poisoned at Jiddah. Doctor Pease said to me, "Until now Doctor Kheiralla is afraid of assassination. A Bahai told me, 'We want only one thing from Kheiralla, *i. e.*, the translation of the "Kitab-ul-Akdas," then we will get rid of him.'" When Hasan Khorasani came to Chicago, Kheiralla was warned from Syria to beware of him and he put himself under special police protection.

[553] Chicago Edition, 1908, pp. 11-14.

[554] "Answered Questions," by Barney, pp. 199-201.

[555] "Trav.'s Narr.," p. 372; "A Year in Persia," p. 328.

[556] *Ibid.*, p. 406.

[557] "A Year in Persia," p. 306.

[558] *Moslem World*, 1912, p. 237.

gious assassination has been freely practiced since the beginning of Islam, and that the prophet Mohammed gave it the sanction of his example on numerous occasions." Professor Browne,[559] who thus emphasizes this fact, and gives instances from the Moslem biographies of Mohammed, points out its bearing on our judgment regarding the assassinations alleged against the Bahais, and concludes, "In Asia a different standard of morality prevails in this matter." Certain facts regarding the Imams revealed in the dark annals of Islam show what historical precedents the Babis and Bahais had back of them. Consider the deaths of the twelve Imams. Ali was[560] assassinated with a dagger, Husain killed after battle, nine other Imams were *poisoned*, and the last one mysteriously disappeared.

To sum up. Our investigation has led to the conclusion that the Bahais were guilty of these assassinations as charged. The evidence is both direct and circumstantial, with names and places. Some of the witnesses are still living. Some have given their testimony in writing, some in conversation with Europeans, who have reported it accurately to the world. The environment in which they lived, and the historical and theological traditions on which they fed, strengthen the direct proofs.

The answer to these charges by Mirza Abul Fazl in his "Brilliant Proof"[561] is, that we should hear both sides, and that it is not right to accept the witness of enemies against the Bahais, which is as that of Protestants against the Catholics and *vice-versa*. Our reply is, that both sides have been heard, and examined, and that some of the most damaging testimony is from Bahais themselves. It should be noted that the testimony is altogether from the followers of the Bab, of various kinds and not from Moslem writers. Mr. Phelps, like many Bahai writers, would ignore the charges. He says,[562] "I do not think that it would be time well employed to advert to them in detail." He pronounces them "incredible" and "flatly in contradiction to the spirit, lives and teachings of Baha Ullah and his successor," and destined "quickly to fade away and be forgotten, if left to themselves." No indeed! Lovers of truth will not overlook and forget such a record. They will judge Bahais by their deeds, not by their professions.

The conclusions of Professor Browne, who was undoubtedly a favourably-inclined judge, who investigated impartially and heard the testimony on both sides, has the greatest weight in determining the judgment of the world.[563] In the "Traveller's Narrative," his first volume on Babism and Bahaism, he states that it is only with great reluctance and solely in the interest of truth, that he sets down these

---

[559] "Trav.'s Narr.," pp. 371-373.

[560] *Ibid.*, p. 296.

[561] A Reply to Rev. P. Z. Easton's article in the *Evangelical Christendom*.

[562] "Life of Abbas Effendi," p. 43.

[563] Mr. A. J. Stenstrand, of Chicago, was convinced by the facts. He wrote, "When I studied the Babi history and read about the terrible cruelty and assassinations which the followers of Beha perpetrated upon Subh-i-Azal's supporters which made no resistance, this broke the backbone of my Behai faith." In conversation he told me that Doctor Kheiralla had informed the Chicago assembly that the account of the assassinations as narrated by Professor Browne was true and that the Manifestation had a right to slay them."

grave accusations against the Bahais, and adds,[564] "If they are true, of what use are the noblest and most humane utterances, if they are associated with such deeds? If they are false, further investigation will, without doubt, conclusively prove their falsity." In the "New History," which was published two years later, after further investigation and calm deliberation, he wrote,[565] "At first not a few prominent Babis,[566] including even several 'Letters of the Living' and personal friends of the Bab, adhered faithfully to Subh-i-Azal. One by one these disappeared, most of them as, I fear, *cannot be doubted, by foul play on the part of too zealous Bahais.*"

----

[564] Page 364.

[565] "New Hist.," p. xxiii.

[566] One of these was the author of "Hasht Behesht." If the Bahais had the longer dagger, the Azalis did not lack the bitter pen. Professor Browne translates from this work as follows, "The misleadings of black darkness brought me into the city of blood (Acca). I met Abbas Effendi, the whisperer of evil thoughts, one of the manifestations of infidelity. Afterwards I saw the rest of the Wicked One's followers. Their words and arguments consist of a farrago of names, baseless stories, calumnies, falsehoods and lies, and not one of them had any knowledge of the first principles of the religion of the 'Bayan.' They are all devoid of knowledge, ignorant, short-sighted, of common capacity, hoodwinked, people of darkness, spurned of nature, hypocrites, corrupters of texts, blind imitators. God hath taken away from them His light and hath left them in the darkness of the Wicked One and hath destroyed them in the abysses of vain imaginings." He was admitted to audience with Baha and narrates, "When I came there and looked upon the Arch-Idol, that Greatest Talisman, that personified Revolt, that rebellious Lucifer, the envious Iblis, I saw a form upon the throne and heard the lowing of the Calf (Baha—Golden Calf). Then did I see how the light of the Most Great Name shone on Ahriman the accursed, and how the fingers of the demon wore the ring. (Alluding to the theft of Solomon's ring by the demon.) For they had written the name Baha-ul-Abha on divers writings and called it 'the Most Great Name.' Thereat there came to my mind the verse of Hafiz:

> Efficient is the name divine: be of good cheer, O heart!
> The div becomes not Solomon by guile and cunning art."

XI

THE QUARREL OVER THE SUCCESSION

Claim to love refuted—Death of Baha—Titles of sons—Quarrel over
will—Abbas assumes Pontiffship—Brothers protest—Bitter
schism—Boycott, anathema—Appeal to Turkish government—
Results in restriction of liberty—Quarrel and schism in Persia—In
America.

> The confusion, the reaction, and the spiritual division usually
> attendant upon a prophet's death were in this case happily avert-
> ed (!?).—*Holley, a Bahai, "The Modern Social Religion," p. 169.*

> The last schism and the bitterness to which it gave rise lead
> me to inquire, where is the compelling and constraining power
> which they regard as the essential and incontrovertible sign of the
> divine word as in the text, "Associate with all religions with spiri-
> tuality and fragrance," when they can show such bitter animosity
> against those of their own household.—*Professor Browne.*

> Whosoever claimeth a mission before the completion of a full
> thousand years from this manifestation is a lying impostor; who-
> soever interpreteth or explaineth this text different from what is
> obviously revealed, is bereft of the Spirit of God and His mer-
> cy.—*"Kitab-ul-Akdas."*

THE claims of Bahais in regard to the conduct of Abdul Baha must be further
considered. Mr. Phelps describes him as a man "who proves that self can be utterly
forgotten: that all-embracing love can be substituted for egotism: the recorded love
of Buddha and Christ may indeed be realized." M. Asad Ullah writes: "He sees
the Moslem, the Christian and the Bahai, all with one eye,—he is equally kind to
all." Mr. Sprague affirms: "Abdul Baha manifests universal love in every word and
act." Mr. Chase says: "Bahaism does bring men into loving unity with each other."
Abdul Baha said in his address at Denver, Col., "All other nations ... inquire as to
the character of this love. What love exists among the Bahais! What unity obtains
among these Bahais! What agreement there is among these Bahais! All envy it."[567]
Again let the light of history shine forth and these claims be justified or refuted by
the facts.

Baha Ullah died at Acca in May, 1892, in his seventy-fifth year. The death of
[567] *S. W.*, Nov. 4, 1913, p. 230; Phelps, pp. 255, 133.

the father was the signal for a bitter quarrel among his sons. The occasion was the succession to the leadership. The cause, no doubt, lay partly in that jealousy which results from a polygamous household. This polygamy was the occasion of misfortune even at the time, for the Persian consul at Bagdad, named Mirza Buzurk Khan Kasvini, had desired to wed one of the women and vented his disappointment on the Bahai community by making accusation against them before the Persian and Turkish Governments.[568]

Baha Ullah had twelve children. The four sons who grew to manhood received "great swelling" titles. Abbas was entitled "The Greatest (Azam) Branch of God" and regarded as the "return" of Jesus; Mohammed Ali, "The Mightiest (Akbar) Branch of God" and the "return" of Mohammed; Ziah Ullah, "The Purest Branch and as Abraham" (died 1898); Badi Ullah, "The Most Luminous Branch and as Moses."

Abbas Effendi was the son of Aseyeh. The other three were sons of Ayesha or Madh Ulya. Abbas Effendi claimed the succession, basing his right and title on the Will of Baha, called the Kitab-il-Ahd and on previous declarations. His right was disputed by the other brothers. I have a manuscript by a lifelong Bahai which gives the following account: "Nine days after the 'ascension' of Baha, Abbas Effendi desired nine of the chief men to come to the house of Mohammed Ali Effendi. He opened the will. It was in Baha's own handwriting and two pages long. The nine men saw it. On the second page, over a part of the writing, Abbas had put a blue paper that it might not be read, and he refused to have it read. On the same day, the whole congregation (men) gathered to the palace of Baha. Mirza Majd-i-Din (Abbas' sister's son) rose and read the will up to the blue paper. Later the women were called to the Kasr Bahja and the will was again read, but the concealed portion was not made known. It was evident that it was for his own selfish purposes that Abbas concealed it, because the future authority did not pertain to him. From Persia and India many wrote, saying: 'Show the last portion; it is the writing of His Holiness.' He refused. To this day it is concealed."

Abbas assumed authority as the Supreme Ruler of the new dispensation, the Centre of the Covenant, and the Infallible Interpreter of its teachings. His claim is clearly set forth in a Tablet[569] wherein, speaking in the third person, he declares: "All Bahais must obey the Centre of the Covenant and must not *deviate one hair's breadth* from obedience to Him." "He should be looked upon as authority by all." "Obedience and submission must be shown Him and the face turned to Him completely." He was given such titles as[570] "His Holiness the Master," "Our Lord," "The Centre of the Cause of God," "Dawning Place of the Divine Light," "Dayspring of the Light of the Covenant." Indeed his first Apostles to Persia bore the message, "I am the Manifestation of God. My paps are full of the milk of Godhead. Whosoever will, let him come and suck freely."

His claims to headship were strenuously opposed by his brothers and some of the nearest disciples. A bitter quarrel began as a consequence and has raged to

[568] "Trav.'s Narr.," p. 84, note 2.
[569] *S. W.,* July 13, 1912.
[570] Abul Fazl's "Bahai Proofs," pp. 109-122.

the present time. Letters were sent by each party to the Persian Bahais, involving them in the quarrel. Mohammed Ali composed a book, called the "Ityan-i-Dallil," presenting proofs of the invalidity of Abbas' claims, from the writings of Baha. They charge[571] Abbas with concealing and annulling Baha's will, perverting his teachings, changing the writings of Baha, publishing expurgated and interpolated editions of them, and attempting to suppress the authorized Bombay editions. Specifically they accuse him of publishing a Lawh-i-Beirut, a Tablet in which Abbas is greatly exalted, and attributing it to Baha, though it is spurious; that he has inserted verses into letters written in the hand of Baha's amanuensis and published them as genuine; has omitted verses from the "Tablet of Command"; made up the "Treasure Tablet" from parts of several others; appropriated to himself Tablets pertaining to Mirza Mohammed Ali; and commanded to destroy all Tablets of Baha which have not his (Abbas') seal upon them.[572]

Per contra the party of Abbas accused his brothers of intemperance and profligacy[573] and of heresy, covenant-breaking and fraud. Mr. Hadad reported M. Mohammed Ali and Badi Ullah as "being profligate and wanton, frequenting wine shops and being spendthrifts." Mr. Getsinger said he had seen Badi Ullah in the street intoxicated and being helped home by two servants, that he and his brother had taken and pawned the effects of Baha, rugs, hand-bags, etc., and a pearl rosary belonging to Baha which was valued at $10,000 (!) and had squandered the money." Abbas said to Mrs. Grundy,[574] "Mohammed Ali has appropriated many papers and tablets written by the Blessed Perfection (Baha). It is possible for these writings to be altered, as the meanings in Persian are greatly changed by a single dot here and there. Before His Ascension, the Blessed Perfection said to me, 'I have given you all the papers.' He put them in two satchels and sent them to me. After His Ascension, Mohammed Ali said, 'You had better give me the two satchels to take care of.' He took them away and never returned them." He said that Mohammed Ali deceives, "for the Will was also written by Mohammed Ali's own hand from dictation of the Blessed Perfection. By violating the Covenant (Will) he has become a *fallen* branch. All the beautiful blossoms upon the Tree of Life were destroyed by Mohammed Ali."

Abbas proceeded to the use of boycott and anathema. He[575] ordered that no one of the Acca community should send any letters anywhere without first showing them to him, and commanded the Bahais in Persia not to receive any letters that were not sealed by him, but to send them back to him, and that in writing to Acca they should send their letters open. These restrictions on freedom gave great offense. Abbas also prohibited his followers from associating with his brothers and their followers, strictly ordering them "not to sit, meet, speak or correspond

---

[571] See "Facts for Behaists."

[572] We can well believe that these accusations are true, in view of what we know from Professor Browne of the way Abbas Effendi perverted facts of the history of the Bab and Subh-i-Azal, in the "Traveller's Narrative" of which he was the author ("New Hist.," pp. xiv., xxxi.).

[573] "Facts for Behaists," pp. 8, 9.

[574] "Ten Days in the Light at Acca," p. 63.

[575] Persian Manuscript.

with them, not even to trade or associate with them in any profession."[576] Khadim reports that "once in his own house, Abbas rose up and furiously attacked" his stepmother, who, in return, reviled him and fled from the house, wailing. "At the sacred tomb he used cruelly to treat the brothers and sisters."[577] "On one occasion he repeatedly struck his youngest (half) sister in the presence of her little ones and many believers," scolding her "with a loud voice, uttering many harsh words."[578] On another occasion he "insulted and beat Khadim (Mirza Aga Jan, Baha's amanuensis) at the sacred place" and afterwards "ordered his followers to imprison and cruelly beat him, which they did."[579] He sent adrift Abdul Gaffar Ispahani, called Abdullah, one of the first believers on Baha, in such destitute condition that he died of hunger and was buried in a potter's field at Damascus.[580]

"Alas! Alas!" exclaims Mirza Aga Jan, "Abbas Effendi has caused his followers to display such vehemence of hatred and rancour, the like of which has never been shown by barbarous nations, and even by the most ignorant tribes."[581] Of Abbas, Mrs. Templeton[582] writes: "His pride, alas, is great.... He seems to be blinded.... With regard to business matters Abbas Effendi has not been just to his brothers, who have suffered a good deal in consequence."[583]

Abbas Effendi cut off the living of his stepmothers, brothers and their dependents. Baha Ullah and his household had a stipend from the Turkish Government, as Azal and the Babis in Cyprus had, and it was not an ungenerous allowance.[584]

"The family had an income from the Government, as well as a revenue from three villages."[585] "These funds Abbas Effendi appropriated and with these made his charitable gifts (?) leaving the forty dependents of the younger brothers to live as best they could."[586] This excluding the protesters from their share of the income and offerings embittered the strife, at the same time weakening their ability to propagate their contention. Bitterness and enmity increased; recriminations and accusations inflamed the passions of both sides.

Mirza Abul Fazl, the philosopher of the movement, gives, as a partisan of Abbas Effendi, an account of these times in his "Bahai Proofs."[587] He describes the "ruinous discords and divisions," "the world-consuming flame of jealousy and hatred of the people of error," "the hard hearts of the men of hostility," "the animosity and groundless pride," "the senseless hatred, degradation and shame of the violators of the covenant." He gives the opprobrious title of *Nakhazeen* to Mo-

---

[576] "Facts, etc.," p. 45.
[577] *Ibid.*, p. 59.
[578] *Ibid.*, p. 60.
[579] *Ibid.*, p. 25.
[580] Persian Manuscript.
[581] "Facts," p. 54.
[582] Mrs. Templeton was Mrs. Laurence Oliphant and had resided at Acca and in intimate relations with the family of Baha for ten years.
[583] "Facts," pp. 6-7.
[584] "Trav.'s Narr.," p. 378.
[585] Mrs. Templeton's letter to Doctor Pease in "Facts," p. 9.
[586] Mrs. Templeton, p. 9.
[587] Pages 116-118.

hammed Ali's party. He continues, "The evil intrigues, calumnies, false pamphlets and accusations, evil tongues and cursings of the Nakhazeen divided the community and filled it with foul odours." Several outside parties tried to act as mediators and bring about a reconciliation. Among these were the British Consul at Haifa and Mrs. Templeton. The younger brothers agreed to the terms. Abbas Effendi was formally requested to show the Will before impartial witnesses and all were to abide by its word. "This he resolutely refused to do and he must stand condemned for this before all impartial men."[588] After the failure of these efforts at reconciliation, the anger and bitterness waxed hotter. To quote Abul Fazl again: "The Nakhazeen cursed and insulted the visitors to the tomb of the Blessed Perfection," so that there was danger of its desecration. "Consequently Abbas Effendi asked the local (Turkish) Government to supply a guard to accompany and protect" his party. Abbas also went to Tiberias and made complaint to the Government there.[589] As a result of all these conditions, "The people of hostility and violation," says Abul Fazl, "availed themselves of political machinations," in other words, Mohammed Ali's party, "those dwellers in hellfire,"[590] appealed to the "fanatical men of those lands," *i.e.*, those same Turkish Authorities. Mohammed Ali formally complained to the Governor of Damascus, Nazim Pasha, sending Mirza Majd-ud-Din as his special messenger.[591] They accused Abbas of retaining their stipends, of confiscating their patrimony, including the father's gold watch which had been donated to Mohammed Ali. Above all, according to the interesting narrative of Abbas' sister, Bahiah Khanum,[592] they made accusation that the shrine which was being erected on Mount Carmel "was intended as a fort, in which Abbas and his followers would intrench themselves, defy the Government, and endeavour to gain possession of this part of Syria." To use the words of Abbas, they said that "he had hoisted the banner of independence; upon that he had inscribed 'Ya Baha-ul Abha': that he had summoned all to assemble that he might found a new monarchy." Therefore "an inquisitorial body (a Commission) was appointed by the Government. To them the copartners of my brothers confirmed them (the reports) and added to them."[593] After the report of the Commission and in consequence of these charges and counter-charges of the "Greatest Branch of God" and the "Mightiest Branch of God," a telegram was received from the Sultan to the Governor "issuing a firman, decreeing the original order, by which Baha's family were confined within the walls of Acca." After *nine* years of quarrelling (*nine* being the sacred number of Bahais) this order was put in force, 1901 A.D. They were still confined to Acca in 1906 when I visited Haifa. I saw the shrine and the fine residence of Baha at Haifa, just beside the English Mission. It deserves to be emphasized that the *cause of the Bahai leaders being restricted to Acca* was not religious persecution by Moslems but *their own quarrellings.*

---

[588] Mrs. Templeton.

[589] See "Facts, etc.," Khadim's letter.

[590] Page 136.

[591] "An Epistle to the Bahai World," by M. Badi Ullah, p. 19, and Mr. Howard MacNutt's Interview with Badi Ullah, *S. W.,* July 13, 1912.

[592] Phelps' "Life," p. 81.

[593] "Letters to the Friends in Persia," pp. 2-3. Comp. "Tablets of Abdul Baha," Vol. I, pp. 45-47.

So completely had the suspicions of Abdul Hamid's government been aroused by their accusations against each other that the death sentence was feared. Pilgrimages were stopped and terror rested on the followers.[594] Abdul Baha wrote to his American disciples of these conditions in the following hyperbolic words: "Verily, by God, I would not change this prison for the throne nor for all the gardens of the earth. Verily I hope to be suspended in the air, and that my breast may become the target to be pierced by thousands of bullets: or that I may be cast into the bottomless seas or thrown into the wilderness.... If I could taste the cup of the great martyrdom, my greatest desire would be fulfilled. This is my utmost aim, the animation of my spirit, the healing of my bosom, the sight of my eyes." But when the establishment of the Constitution in Turkey gave him freedom, he was quick to take advantage of it. He went to Egypt and took up his residence there.[595]

The history I have narrated above refutes these various pretensions of Bahaism, its claims, its "great swelling words" more forcibly than logic or the judgments and opinions of myself and others. The conduct of Abdul Baha and his followers towards the brothers and their followers, as well as that of Bahais to the Azalis, contradicts their fine professions of toleration and love to all religions and all men. Well may we exclaim with Professor Browne: "Where is the restraining power, when they can show such *bitter animosity* against those of their own household!" The numbers of Bahais living at Acca then was about ninety,[596] and of them thirty[597] or forty[598] were of the opponents of Abbas.

In Persia, where Bahais number a hundred thousand, a small, but influential minority rejected the authority of Abbas Effendi. These were placed under the ban, anathematized, and ostracized. For example, one of them, Mirza Jalil of Khoi, was driven out of his house, which was destroyed by Shiahs, instigated by new Bahais. Another adherent of Mohammed Ali, Mirza Khalil of Tabriz, was completely ostracized, according to command received from Acca. His daughter, who was married to a new Bahai, was allowed to visit her parents only once a year, though living in the same city, and when she died they did not give them word till six days after the funeral. Another Bahai libelled this man to his employers in hope of injuring him.

Another result in Persia was the permanent estrangement of a considerable number of Bahais who lapsed into scepticism.

Abbas Effendi, influenced by the opposition, put a veil over his high claims and instructed his followers to speak of him as simply Abdul Baha, "the Servant of Baha," which is usually translated by them "the servant of God." The protesters replied, "Rather let the title be Abdul-Hawa, 'the servant of air,'" *i.e.*, windy and bombastic. But notwithstanding his disavowals Abdul Baha allows himself to be assigned a position both inconsistent with his own words and with the teachings

---

[594] "Daily Lessons," by Goodall, pp. 27-29 and the "Bahai Movement," pp. 106-108.
[595] "Tablets," Vol. I, pp. 4, 94.
[596] Phelps, p. 109.
[597] Abul Fazl, p. 118.
[598] Mrs. Templeton, "Facts, etc.," p. 9.

of Baha. Mr. Phelps, his disciple and biographer, says,[599] "Abdul Baha, styled 'Our Lord,' 'Our Master,' is regarded with a love and a *veneration* second only, *if indeed second*, to that which they bestow upon Baha Ullah. He is classed as the third or last of the Divine Messengers of the present Dispensation." The Bab, Baha and Abbas constitute, as it were, the Bahai trinity. Abdul Baha commended and approved for publication an ode written by Thornton Chase in which he is glorified with the following epithets among many others.

"O Thou Enlightener of the Spirits of Men! Thou Heart of the World!

"Thou Physician of Souls! Thou Prince of Peace!

"Thou Right Arm of the Almighty! Thou Lord of the Sabbath of Ages!

"Thou Mystery of God!"

Another disciple, Mrs. Grundy,[600] writes, "Abdul Baha is the Bazaar of God, where everything humanity needs may be found without money and without price." Mr. Remey (a Bahai) writes,[601] "The Divine Spirit is manifested in Abdul Baha—*the Branch*. He is the unique channel through which the Power of God is conveyed to each individual believer. He is the intermediary. The spiritual well-being of every Bahai depends on his connection with Abdul Baha."

The outcome of this quarrel in America is told in the following chapter. An interesting sequel is the recantation of Mirza Badi Ullah. Doubtless helped thereto by poverty, he made his submission to Abdul Baha, and published a confession, called "An Epistle to the Bahai World." Concerning it Doctor Pease told me that Badi Ullah is not the author of the whole of that which is published in English under his name. The Epistle says, I Badi Ullah "turn my face to the appointed station, Abdul Baha—May the life of all existent beings be a sacrifice to Him." Against M. Mohammed Ali, with whom he had associated himself for a decade, he makes accusation of untrustworthiness, of purloining the papers and books of Baha and interpolating and falsifying them, of cursing and execrating Abdul Baha through jealousy. He turns on his former supporters and says, "they (the Nakhazeen) have no God save passion, no object save personal interest."[602] Doctor Jessup says:[603] "Badi not long ago was threatening to kill Abbas, and assassination is an old fashion of Persian fanatics…. He has become reconciled but I would not guarantee that his main object is not to gain his share of the money." Better had Badi stuck to his former plan when he petitioned the Governor of Damascus and the Sultan to be sent as a prisoner to Rhodes. Doubtless then he would have had an independent pension.

---

[599] Page xxxiv.

[600] "Ten Days at Acca," p. 105.

[601] *Star*, Sept. 8, 1913.

[602] Page 28.

[603] "Fifty-three Years in Syria," p. 687.

XII

BAHAISM IN AMERICA

First notices of—Kheiralla—His converts—Writings—An American Azali—Pilgrims to Acca—Quarrel and schism—Abdul Karim—Abul Fazl—Methods of propaganda—Publications—Orient Occident Unity—Abdul Baha visits America—Press agents—Photographs, movies—Addresses—Attitude of public—Communion service of Bahais—Bahai Temple, Mashrak ul Azkar—Memorial vase—Influence in America—Chicago congregation—Number in U. S. A. exaggerated—Statistics of other religious fads—Christian liberalism excessive.

I speak from the point of view of Persian Bahaism and not from that American fantasy which bears its name.—*Nicolas, "Béyan Persan," Vol. I, p. II.*

Abbas is an elderly and venerable man, very similar to a score of venerable Druse and Moslem Sheikhs I have met.... The Lord deliver them (American Christians) from the delirious blasphemies.... The claim that the Acca Sheikh is God is quite enough to condemn them.—*H. H. Jessup, "Fifty-three Years in Syria," p. 638.*

Pray for my return to America and say: O Baha Ullah! Confirm Him in the servitude of the East; so that He may not spend all his time in the Orient; that He may return to America and occupy His time in the Western world.—*Prayer of Bahais.*

It is doubtless this mystical, allegorical character of Bahaism which attracts a certain type of mind in America, in the main probably, the same type which follows after spiritualism, esoteric Buddhism, Swamis from India, theosophy, and other movements which play around the edges of the occult and magical, and help to dull the edge of present realities with the things which are neither present nor real.... Indeed it is probably this soft compliance with anything and the absence of the robustness of definite truth and solid principle which makes Bahaism attractive to many moral softlings in the West.... It will run a brief course and amount to little in America.... The novelty will soon be over and the people who did not have sufficient discernment to discover the truth that will satisfy them in Christianity, will not find it in Baha Ullah or

Abbas Effendi.—*R. E. Speer, "Miss. and Mod. Hist.," Vol. I, pp. 143, 162-168.*

BAHAISM, as distinguished from Babism, was, to a certain extent, introduced to public notice in America by Christian missionaries, who reported about it as a movement likely to break the solidarity of Shiahism and facilitate the evangelization of Persia. With the same thought in mind, Professor Browne's translations of "The New History" and "The Traveller's Narrative" attracted attention. In the Congress of Religions, at the Chicago Exposition in 1893, the eminent missionary, Rev. H. H. Jessup, D. D., described Baha Ullah as "a famous Persian sage,—the Babi saint, named Baha Ullah (the glory of God), the head of that vast reform party of Persian Moslems, who accept the New Testament as the word of God and Christ as the deliverer of men; who regard all nations as one and all men as brothers."[604] Shortly after the Exposition a Syrian, named Ibrahim G. Kheiralla, began a propaganda in favour of Bahaism. He was of Christian parentage, born in Mount Lebanon, and educated in Beirut College. At Cairo, under the tutelage of Mirza Karim of Teheran, he accepted the Bahai faith. He was engaged in business, to which he joined faith healing and lecturing. He was given a fake degree of Doctor of something by a night school in Chicago. This he rightly despised, but considered that he was entitled to the degree because M. Mohammed Ali had addressed him as Doctor! I had several interviews with him. He showed me a trunk full of Bahai manuscripts and documents, and allowed me to read his translation into English of the "Kitab-ul-Akdas." He is a man of strong mind, acute argumentative faculties, fine conversational powers and altogether an interesting personality. He first taught Bahaism in secret lessons, as a religion of mysteries, a secret order, a doctrine for truth-seekers only, not for the masses. "The secret teaching gives us the key to the truth."[605]

Mr. S. K. Vatralsky was among the private pupils at Kenosha. He did not become a believer, but learned the esoteric doctrine and published an interesting account of the cult under the title, "Mohammedan Gnosticism in America."[606] Of the method used he writes, "In their secret lessons they allegorize and explain away; in public by means of mental reservation and the use of words in a double sense, they appear as they wish to appear." Doctor Kheiralla published in 1897 a booklet called "Bab-ed-Din, The Door of the True Religion—Revelation from the East." It has two parts (1) On the Individuality of God and (2) A Refutation of the Christian doctrine of the atonement. Later (1900), in conjunction with Mr. Howard MacNutt, he published "Beha Ullah" in two volumes. It is the theology and apologetics of Bahaism. Its Preface informs us that its purpose is to "demonstrate that the Everlasting Father, the Prince of Peace, has appeared in human form and established His kingdom on earth." The propaganda met with considerable success in Chicago and its vicinity. In 1897 Doctor Kheiralla went to New York City and in a short time "140 souls" were persuaded. In this same year two of his pupils were married in his house in Chicago, receiving his blessing. These were Mr. and Mrs.

[604] "Parliament of Religions," p. 640; I. G. Kheiralla, "Beha Ullah," p. ix.

[605] "Bab-ed-Din," by I. G. Kheiralla, pp. 9, 13, 18.

[606] *American Journal of Theology*, 1902.

E. C. Getsinger. They "taught seekers" in Ithaca, N. Y., and afterwards in California. There they converted Mrs. H— —, a woman of great wealth, to the faith. Mr. Vatralsky narrates that Doctor Kheiralla converted no less than 2,000 Americans during the first two years of his labour. Of these 700 were living in Chicago (Doctor Kheiralla told me 840), between 250 and 300 in Wisconsin, about 400 in New York, the rest in Boston, etc. In his "Beha Ullah" Doctor Kheiralla says, "Over seven years ago I began to preach the message. Since then thousands of people of this country have believed and accepted the glad tidings of the appearance of the Lord of Hosts, the Incarnation of Deity, and the glorious message is rapidly spreading in the United States." Speaking of this period Mr. Vatralsky writes: "It would not have had its success, had it come flying its own native colours. It has succeeded because, like a counterfeit coin, it has passed for what it is not."

A curious incident occurred on May 6, 1906. Mr. August J. Stenstrand was exscinded from the "First Central Church of the Manifestation," because he rejected Baha Ullah and accepted Subh-i-Azal. He was led to this step by investigating the history as recorded in Professor Browne's translations. He subsequently published three pamphlets, "Calls to Behaists" (1907, 1910, 1913) setting forth the claims of Azal. I had interesting interviews with him in 1914.

In the winter of 1898-99 pilgrimages were organized to visit the shrine and leaders at Acca.[607] One party consisted of Mrs. H— —, who bore the expenses, Doctor and Mrs. Kheiralla, Mr. and Mrs. Getsinger, Mr. Hadad and others. The pilgrimage turned out unfortunately. They found the "holy household" divided. They saw only Abbas Effendi and one sister. They were kept from even a sight of the others. Doctor Kheiralla was bold enough to dispute with Abbas Effendi and he told me that for this reason the latter conceived a grudge against him. Of this Dr. F. O. Pease writes: "Doctor Kheiralla had some discussion with Abbas in the presence of native guests and teachers at which Abbas took umbrage."[608] The Getsingers accused Kheiralla of immoral conduct and Abbas Effendi reported these stories to Mrs. Kheiralla and her daughter, with the result that they repudiated Kheiralla. Certain financial irregularities of the party further disgusted Mrs. H— —and chilled her faith. So animosity and dissension sprang up.

Mr. Getsinger, on his return to America, announced that he was to be the representative of Abbas Effendi, because Doctor Kheiralla's teachings were erroneous and his conduct immoral. Doctor Kheiralla responded with counter charges against his accuser, of a private and personal nature, and declared him qualified for the Ananias club by his accounts of himself in California. The Chicago and Kenosha assemblies were rent asunder. In the correspondence, some of which I have in my possession, they hurl at each other such terms as falsehood, lie, malevolence, injustice, maliciousness, deluding, laying traps, etc. Thornton Chase was accused of dishonesty in money matters. Doctor N— —, the treasurer of the "Assembly" in Chicago, was denounced for embezzling its funds. Mirza Abdul Karim arrived from Acca to quiet matters but he poured oil on the flames. Kheiralla was first informed that if he would submit and coöperate, "he would nev-

---

[607] "Bahai Movement," p. 101; *S. W.*, p. 38, 1914.

[608] An open letter to the Abbab in America, by Doctor Pease.

er want anything." He writes:[609] "Abdul Karim promised me plenty of money, and when I refused, he denounced me and prohibited believers from buying or reading my book." He ordered a social and business boycott against him and his party. Stenstrand says,[610] "They have ousted, given bad names, and thrown mud at each other both in their sermons and in print worse than any Christian or heathen religions have done." The spirit of Abdul Karim may be seen from one of his addresses: "O nakhiz (violator), thou spotted snake, thou shalt be seized with a great torture and punishment and thou, O sister serpent, who art wagging thy sinuous way and trailing thy deceitful slime over another region, know thy fate." He declared that he would call to God for vengeance against Kheiralla. Hasan Khorasani, too, threatened him, saying, "He would be smitten of God in two weeks," and "a sword shall cleave the sky and cut his neck." He was greatly frightened. Doctor Pease said to him, "Do not be afraid, you have nothing to fear." Kheiralla answered him, "I know these Orientals better than you do. I know what they did to the Azalis." Before they came to the next discussion, he had policemen concealed in his house for his protection. The upshot of the whole matter was that protesters repudiated Abbas Effendi, after a conference in Chicago on May 27, 1900, finding "increasing evidence of falsity and double dealing in him." Indeed, says Doctor Pease, "Why should we not inquire whether Abbas is not *a* son, if not *the* son of perdition." They entered into correspondence and became one with the party of M. Mohammed Ali. After this the controversy took on a doctrinal aspect and all questions of Abbas' supremacy and misconduct were thrashed out between the American Behaists and Bahais. This controversy from the side of the Behaists is contained in "The Three Questions" and "Facts for Behaists" (Chicago, 1901); from the other side in "Letters of Abdul Baha Abbas to the Friends in Persia" and "An Epistle to the Bahai World," by M. Badi Ullah, after his recantation. The details of the schism have been given already. To heal the schism different leaders were sent to America successively by Abbas Effendi. Following M. Abdul Karim, came M. Asad Ullah, 1901. He published, in New York, "The Sacred Mysteries" in which he anathematizes the Behaists. He organized a "House of Justice" in Chicago, a step which had been previously taken by the other party. Next came the learned Mirza Abul Fazl, 1901-1902. But their efforts were unavailing though each was willing to acknowledge the faults of his predecessor. The quarrel gave a great setback to the cause. Doctor Pease wrote in 1902:[611] "About 1,700 have left us because of the dissension and false teaching, and because they would not engage in religious scandal. The whole number in the country is now 600 or 700. Of these 300 are Behaists; the others are Abbasites of one sect or another, holding belief that Abbas is Lord and Master." Doctor Kheiralla says, "Many grew cold, few remained." With this agrees the word of Thornton Chase:[612] "We have seen too many, when the first winds of testing blew, show faith of shallow depth." Abdul Baha says:[613] "Chicago, in comparison with the cities of America, was in advance and numerically contained more Bahais, but when the stench or vile odour of the

[609] "The Three Questions," p. 23.
[610] "Third Call to Behais," p. 3.
[611] Letter to M. Badi Ullah.
[612] "Before Abraham was I am," p. 1.
[613] *S. W.*, Sept. 8, 1913, p. 174.

Nakhazeen was spread in that city there was stagnation." In Chicago Bahaism never recovered from these quarrels. In 1914 Mr. F. A. Slack, "Spiritual Guide of the Behaist Assembly of Kenosha," wrote to me "of the bitter invectives and false accusations and persecutions we are subjected to" by the followers of Abbas Effendi. The Behaists had dwindled to 40, according to their own report to the U. S. Census in 1906, while the Bahais reported 1,280 in U. S. A. of whom 492 were in Illinois, 23 in two Assemblies in New York State, 58 in New Jersey, 52 in Pennsylvania. One of the largest Assemblies was in Washington, D. C., with 74 members, white and coloured. These organized local "spiritual assemblies" were 27 in 1913, a very small increase.[614] There are also "assemblies of teaching" for the women. There are Annual Conventions with delegates from the different groups. These conventions are "unique and peerless among the assemblies of mankind," in the mind of their imaginative reporter, "because of the divine favour of Baha Ullah which gathers them together.... All other meetings in the world are for worldly or selfish purposes. These alone are spiritual."[615] They also hold a summer conference at Eliot, Maine.

The Bahai propaganda is carried on by means of these assemblies, by parlour meetings, by personal intercourse and by letters (tablets) from Abdul Baha. Their publicity bureau is most active and supplies many articles to magazines and newspapers. They make use of the Chautauquas, Peace Congresses, etc., to promulgate their peculiar tenets. Their press at Chicago publishes the *Star of the West*, formerly the *Bahai News*. It is issued monthly, that is, every nineteen days, according to the Bahai calendar. For example, the issue of September 27, 1914, is dated Masheyat 1, Year 70. It is printed in English and Persian, the latter being lithographed. It is confined to Bahai subjects, giving many of Abdul Baha's "revelations." Their literature, so far issued, is (1) The Works of Baha Ullah, in six or more books. (2) The Tablets and Addresses of Abdul Baha. (3) The Apologetics of Bahai writers, American or translations from the Persian. (4) Journals of pilgrims to Acca. (5) Tracts and reports. Of his own Tablets, Abdul Baha says:[616] "In course of time, the light of these Tablets will dawn, the greatness, the importance will be known. The truth I say unto thee, that each leaflet will be a wide-spread book, nay rather a glistening Gem on the Glorious Crown. Know then its value and hold great its station." These Tablets are, for the most part, letters to individuals.

Besides the Bahai Publishing Society, another agency is the Orient-Occident Unity,—first organized in 1909 as the Persian American Educational Society. It has a commercial side, but its main object is to promote Bahaism by assisting or opening schools and hospitals in Persia and other Oriental countries. It has started mission work in Teheran, Tabriz, Meshed and other points in Persia and in Burmah. They seek to strengthen Bahaism in Persia where it is small and weak in comparison with other sects. The work of the American Bahais there is of little importance. "But the presence of American Bahais in Persia or the value of an American newspaper is not their direct influence, but the impression they give

---

[614] *S. W.*, Sept. 8, 1913, p. 127.
[615] *S. W.*, May 17, 1914, pp. 51-52.
[616] "Tablets," Vol. I, p. ii.

that America has largely accepted Bahaism."[617] In the United States this Unity poses as philanthropical, not revealing in its constitution, circulars and appeals for funds its Bahai connection. This concealment is inexcusable and cannot be too strongly condemned. Christians and Jews should not be asked to contribute to any cause under false pretenses, nor should prominent statesmen, educators and philanthropists be thus led to give their quasi endorsement to the Society.[618]

In 1912 Abdul Baha Abbas, after a sojourn in France and England, visited America, arriving April 12 and departing December 5. America has not lacked its own prophetic product, as witness Joseph Smith, Mary Eddy, John Dowie, Crowdy and Indian medicine men. But Abdul Baha, except for Hindu Swamis, was the first Asiatic revelator America has received. Its hospitality showed up well. The public and press neither stoned the "prophet" nor caricatured him but looked with kindly eye upon the grave old man, in flowing oriental robes and white turban, with waving hoary hair and long white beard.[619] His visit was noticed, as has been the case with many distinguished foreigners, but did not create any special sensation. His own press agents were active and aggressive, furnishing many articles for newspapers and magazines. The reporters took the exaggerated statements of the Bahais without sifting. He performed his part fairly well and allowed himself to be interviewed and photographed with the patience of an actress. He posed for the "movies" man and spoke for the phonograph records. He sat for an oil painting and approved of his bust in marble.[620]

Abdul Baha's tour comprised a number of the chief cities of the northeast, followed by a rest at Green Acre Conference, Eliot, Maine, and then a trip to Canada and California. His meetings and addresses were of two kinds: for the public and for the Bahais. He spoke to the churches, liberal and evangelical,[621] Socialists, Theosophists, etc.; to Woman's Clubs, Suffragists, Colleges, Historical Societies, Peace

---

[617] J. D. Frame, M. D., *Moslem World*, 1912, p. 243.

[618] Sec.'s Report, June, 1911; October Bulletin, 1911; *S. W.*, May 17, 1911, July 13, 1913, Nov. 4, 1913, March and June, 1914.

[619] The "Kitab-ul-Akdas" commands that the hair should not be allowed to grow below the level of the ear: why does not Abdul Baha keep this law?

[620] Myron Phelps states (p. 97) that Abbas Effendi wishes no photographs of himself taken. This is certainly a mistake as years ago they were circulated in Persia and purchasable in the bazaar. The account of his posing for the motion pictures is amusing. When requested to pass before the camera, he at once replied, "Khaili khob" (very good). The Bahais present were very much upset and protested that his picture would be scattered all over the country in the movies. He replied, "Busiar khob" (still better). Later, in June, an extended motion picture was taken. The scenes were somewhat spoiled by Abdul Baha not remaining in focus and disarranging the scenario. These films, with words, are being used in the Sunday services of the Bahais and are to be used in the Orient in connection with the voice record on the Edison talking machine.

[621] Mr. Remey said to him: "We expected an attitude of hostility towards you from the clergy and theologians. We did not expect the churches and religious societies would open their doors" (*S. W.*, March 21, 1913, p. 18). Doctor Cadman of Brooklyn explained his inviting Abdul Baha to preach in his pulpit by saying, "Christian people can afford to be absolutely free and catholic in their extension of liberty and courtesy to other people." Yet most Christians were grieved and consider it disloyalty to Christ.

Societies and at the Conference on International Arbitration, at Lake Mohonk.

Abdul Baha's principle in his public addresses was "to talk about things upon which we agree and say nothing about things upon which we differ."[622] Thus he spoke much of the Fatherhood of God, but failed to mention that he regarded Baha Ullah as "the Manifestation of the Father." He spoke of brotherly love extensively yet never about the violent quarrels that abound in Bahai annals. He said much of religious unity[623] but did not state how the movement had increased the number of sects in Persia and in America. He spoke much on "Universal peace," though Babi history, which they boast of, has some of the cruelest and bloodiest conflicts of arms recorded in history. He dwelt much on the principle of arbitration, though he had refused to arbitrate his dispute with Mohammed Ali. Even while he was in America, a grandson of Baha Ullah, who lives near Chicago, sent a request for an interview to lead to a reconciliation. Abdul Baha ignored the request. He discoursed at length on woman's rights and equality, but omitted to inform the public that Baha Ullah had three wives and carefully concealed his women in an oriental haram. Besides all these, he erroneously attributed to Baha Ullah the origination of teachings which have been the age-long possession of Christendom.

The meetings with the believers were of a different character. To them his message was: "Teach Bahaism; work for the cause; spread the faith; build the Temple." With them he celebrated the Unity Feast. This has some of the features of the *agape* of the ancient Church and some of the Lord's Supper. Often a variety of food is partaken, Persian pilau being a favourite. When all were seated Abdul passed through the rooms, speaking:[624] "Abdul Baha is now walking among you commemorating Baha Ullah. Blessed are ye who are the servants of Baha Ullah. In the utmost of love I greet each and all of you. This is like the Lord's Supper. Material food is prepared for you. The manna from heaven is present for you. May your hearts be exhilarated in the kingdom of Abha. The labours of Baha Ullah have not been in vain." After the Feast, he raised his hands and pronounced his blessing upon them. This is called the 19th day Unity Feast and is celebrated at the beginning of every Bahai month. When Abdul Baha is not present the Tablets are read and praises to Baha, as to God, are chanted.

One incident was the establishment of the Day of Thornton Chase as a memorial anniversary. Chase is the first American Bahai to be canonized. Abdul Baha visited his grave at Los Angeles, and ordained a saint's day in the Bahai calendar, October 19th. He said:[625] "This revered personage was the first Bahai believer in

---

[622] *S. W.*, March, 1913, p. 18.

[623] The striking lack of unity among the Bahais is evident from a Tablet of Abdul Baha written shortly before his visit to America (*S. W.*, May 17, 1811). "In view of the differences among the friends and the lack of unity among the maid servants of the Merciful, how can Abdul Baha hasten to those parts? Is it possible? No, by God!" "Your worthless imaginations, backbiting, and faultfinding enable the Nakhazeen to spread a noose for you." The Americans could reply, "Physician, heal thyself," for the worst anger and discord have been between the brothers at Acca. And he himself continues to cry out, "Hold aloof from the violators."

[624] *S. W.*, Oct. 16, 1913, p. 203.

[625] *S. W.*, Sept. 27, 1913, p. 187.

America. He served the cause faithfully and his services will be ever remembered throughout ages and cycles."[626] "He was of the blessed souls.... He witnessed the light of the kingdom of Abha and wrote proofs and evidences of the Manifestation." Thornton Chase certainly had a surprising faith in Abdul Baha.

A special event was the dedication of the grounds of the Bahai Temple, the Mashrak-ul-Azkar (the Dawning-place of Praises). This took place in the midst of the Rizwan Feast, on May 1, 1912, in the presence of the Bahai Temple Unity composed of delegates from all the "spiritual assemblies" in America, convened in its fourth annual convention. A site of five acres has been purchased in the village of Willmette, a suburb of Chicago. Abdul Baha, using a golden trowel, broke ground and others of the different races, who were present, used picks and shovels and prepared a place into which Abdul Baha put a stone. He said: "The mystery of this building is great. It cannot be unveiled yet, but its erection is the most important undertaking of this day. This Temple of God in Chicago will be to the spiritual body of the world what the inrush of the spirit is to the physical body of man, quickening it to its utmost parts and infusing a new light and power.... Its results and fruits are endless." Of the structure he said: "The Mashrak-ul-Azkar will be like a beautiful bouquet. The central lofty edifice will have nine sides, surrounded by nine avenues interlacing nine gardens where nine fountains will play. There will be nine gateways and columns, with nine arches and nine arched windows and nine caissons nine feet in diameter. Nine will also be carried out in the galleries and dome. Further, its meetings are to be held on the ninth of each month."[627] Thus the Bahai sacred number will be exhibited everywhere. "Behold!" exclaims the Bahai reporter. "What a priceless piece of ground is this site, dedicated by the hands of the Orb of the Covenant and blessed by his holy feet."[628] But in another place Abdul Baha urges them to hasten the completion of the building, complaining[629] "America has not been working enough for it." "Money comes slowly," says the treasurer; "pledges were tremendous—as big as our eyes saw at the time and afterwards we could collect[630] only a small proportion." After six years of strenuous pleading and effort, they have paid for the ground. The ladies evidently preferred to spend their money in jaunts to Acca, with Paris and Cairo en route, rather than to put up an extravagant temple in Chicago for 200 people who are scattered in that city—a temple in which the believers in New York and Los Angeles may never worship. The cause for haste is "to fulfill a great prophecy, that in the day of the Branch shall the temple of the Lord be built" (Zech. vi. 12). And Abdul Baha is already more than seventy. When finished, "It will have an effect on the whole world." "It will be dedicated to the worship of Baha Ullah and his words only are to be read in it."[631]

[626] Similar phrases addressed to his living disciples sound like flattery and appeals to their vanity, such as, "Your names will go down through the ages." "Kings and Queens will never be talked of as you will be" (*S. W.*, Dec. 13, 1913, p. 274, etc.).

[627] *S. W.*, June 5, 1914.

[628] *S. W.*, Dec. 31, 1913, p. 272.

[629] *S. W.*, Aug. 1, 1913, p. 136-138.

[630] "The Oriental Rose," p. 11, says that $5,000 have been sent from the Orient for the Temple.

[631] "Daily Lessons," p. 17.

After a sojourn of about eight months, Abdul Baha returned to England, whence he telegraphed: "Thanks to Baha Ullah, I arrived safely." As a souvenir of the visit, the American Bahais presented a silver vase to the shrine of Abdul Baha Ullah at Acca, "the Holy City." Of this Mr. Remey writes:

"The Holy Tomb in which this vase is to repose (we ardently hope) for hundreds, perhaps thousands of years already contains precious offerings, vases and many wonderful things placed there by people from all over the world. Among this ever-growing collection at the Threshold of the remains of the Earthly Tabernacle of Him who manifested forth to a dying world the very Fatherhood of the Eternal of Him, who for us is the Sublime King of Kings, must stand this silent token, as a measure of the response from the hearts made glad by this ineffable sacrifice of Him who, giving up all thoughts of self, came to us (*i. e.*, to U. S. A.) in our need, The Centre of the Covenant, His Holiness Abdul Baha."

The visit of Abdul Baha did not leave any great impression. His personality had no deep influence. He appeared conspicuous neither for intellectuality nor spirituality. Many a distinguished traveller has got hold of the public ear and heart to a greater extent. I was in Baltimore when he was there. He caused scarcely a ripple on the surface. His addresses were tame and full of platitudes. It was told me that his visit led to doubt and coldness on the part of some adherents. He was, as Canon Wilberforce said, "not an orator, nor even a preacher," practiced in public address. One of the distinguished clergymen whose pulpit he occupied said to me, "The man has no special message. He is a faker." Another liberal thinker, who has given publicity to this doctrine, after an interview, pronounced him a fraud. Some of the American disciples, especially the ladies, idolized him, even to the extent of bringing down upon them the reprobation of some English disciples. One of the latter wrote:[632] "There seems to be a tendency in America and elsewhere to focus too great attention on Abdul Baha rather than upon the Manifistation."

What of the progress of Bahaism in America? It is making no marked progress. In some sections it seems to have gone forward, as on the Pacific coast and around New York and Washington. It has decreased in the South and in the headquarters of the movement, Chicago. The organization at Atlanta has disappeared from the list. The South will not take kindly to the advocacy by Abdul Baha of the miscegenation of the races. He recommends that efforts be made towards the intermarriage of the coloured and white races as the ideal panacea for the present estrangement.[633]

I understand that a Washington negro has married an English Bahai woman, the courtship having occurred when both were pilgrims, and under the encouragement of Abdul Baha. Of the condition of the cause in Chicago I can speak from personal investigation. I attended the regular Sunday service in St. John's room, eighteenth floor of the Masonic Hall. It was a pleasant May day. About sixty were present—twenty men and forty women. I questioned the men and found that six of them were Bahais and fourteen, like me, were visitors. The man next to me on the right was a member of an ethical culture society that meets on the twelfth floor.

[632] *S. W.*, Dec. 11, 1911.
[633] L. G. Gregory, "The Heavenly Vista," pp. 13, 15, 25, 31.

I asked the man on my left to what organization he belonged. He replied, "To the kingdom of God." I inquired what was his opinion of Abbas Effendi. He pulled from his pocket a much used New Testament and pointed to the verse in Revelation which refers to the beast and said, "That is he." I conversed with several of the Bahai ladies, two of whom acted as instructors of the meeting. The Sunday-school held at an earlier hour, I learned, was a class in Esperanto. To my question as to the number of Bahais in Chicago, she replied "that Baha Ullah has told us that there must be a falling away before the triumph," from which I inferred that conditions were not prosperous. The next man, a Bahai, told me the number was about one hundred and fifty. The leader, Mrs. C. True, told me about three hundred. One of the opposing sect told me there are only sixty, while his sect has lost all organization and numbers only forty in the whole country. But if we take the number at the highest estimate given, the number is less than fifteen years ago.

I go into particulars regarding this point, because there is a false impression abroad, in Europe and Asia, an impression that is carefully fostered. Take this incident. In Persia a Bahai affirmed before the crowd that one-half of Chicago was Bahai. A Bible colporteur disputed the statement and proposed to telegraph to the Mayor of Chicago and inquire, and whichever side was wrong should pay for the telegram. The Bahai declined. In distant India a similar impression is created for effect. Mr. Getsinger wrote in the *Jam-i-Jamseed* of Bombay:[634] "The Bahai faith has spread in America by leaps and bounds, *the number being beyond computation.*" Strange exaggeration, if you give it no worse name! Some such a one was no doubt interviewed by the "wayfarer" of the Continent and told him that there were one million in the United States.[635] But that well-informed reporter put the number at 3,000. *The Star of the West* (Feb. 7, 1912) says: "There are several thousand Bahais in the United States." My own conclusion is that there are 2,000 in twenty-seven organizations. In 1906 they reported to the Census 1,280 members in twenty-four organizations. Most of the members are women. (See Chap. VII.)

That the Bahai propaganda has nothing special to boast of in the United States is evident when we compare its results with those of other religious fads. The Dowieites of Zion City (followers of John Dowie who claimed to be the prophet Elijah) report seventeen organizations in ten states with 5,865 members; the Crowdyites (Crowdy was a negro cook who in 1906 claimed to be a prophet) report forty-eight organizations and 1,823 members; Theosophists eighty-five and 2,336 members; Vedantists (Swamiists) four and 340 members; Spiritualists 455 with 35,056 members; Christian Scientists 638 and 85,000 members. Well may the Egyptian *Gazette* say: "If Bahaism has found favour in the United States, it cannot be forgotten that countless other 'religions' have become popular there which would not have been taken seriously in any other country in the world." Yet, aside from the Mormons, how few they number altogether.

Is it not marvellous that clergy of various Protestant churches, even of the Church of England, have given the use of their edifices for its anti-Christian pros-

---

[634] *S. W.,* April 28, 1914.

[635] The *S. W.* of March 2, 1912, reported one organization in Montreal, one in Hawaii, one in England, two in Germany, viz., Stuttgart and Zuffenhausen, and one in Cape Town.

elytism? Roman Catholic churches have not been open to it. And this happened not only when Abdul Baha was a guest among our people but is continued since. Surely such latitudinarianism must grieve the heart of Christ even as it shocks His faithful followers and gives boldness to those who would hurl Him from His mediatorial throne. It is unnecessary now to catalogue the various Protestant pulpits and platforms in Great Britain, and in America where, with readings from the Bahai "revelations" and flattering introductions, place was given to the "false Christ." But the disloyalty still continues. Lately a missionary was a speaker at a Woman's Foreign Missions Society and was preceded by a lady advocating Bahaism. In a late number of the *Star of the West* (April 9, 1914) is a picture of the St. Mark's-in-the-Bowerie Episcopal Church, New York, with a notice that an audience room had been granted in the parish house for Bahai meetings every Sunday. This was followed by a letter from Abdul Baha rejoicing in this opportunity "to promulgate the principles of Baha Ullah," and by a request for the prayers of all Bahais that "through this opened door many hearts may be turned to the 'Branch,'" *i. e.,* Abdul Baha. Another issue contains an announcement[636] of the marriage at Montreal of the editor, Doctor Bagdadi, to Zeenat Khanum, both Persian Bahais of Mohammedan antecedents. The narrative declares: "The minister who officiated astonished all [even the Bahais] by reading from the Bahai writings!"

The Bahais still continue to proselyte through Ethical Culture and Theosophic Societies and on the platform of peace congresses. Is it not full time that Christian people and churches should cease to give countenance to this system which is an enemy of the cross of Christ, and which has already deceived several thousands of our fellow Christians?

---

[636] *Star,* May 17, 1914, p. 57.

BIBLIOGRAPHY

Consulted by the Author

(1) Non-Bahai Writers

E. G. Browne: "The Babis of Persia," *Jour. Roy. As. Soc.*, July, Oct., 1889.

"Babi Manuscripts," *Jour. Roy. As. Soc.*, April, July, Oct., 1892.

Art. "Babism" in "Encyclo. Brit.," "Enc. of Religion and Ethics," and "Enc. of Islam."

Introductions and Appendices to translations of Babi-Bahai books.

"A Year Among the Persians."

"Literary History of Persia."

A. L. M. Nicolas: "Sayyid Ali Mohammed dit le Bab" (Biography).

R. E. Speer in "Missions and Modern History," Vol. I, Chap. III, pp. 121-182, "The Religion of the Bab."

"Haifa or Modern Life in Palestine," by Oliphant.

Canon Sell "Babism" (Tract 1895), "Bahaism" (Tract 1912).

Critical Magazine Articles.

American Journal of Theology, Jan., 1902, "Mohammedan Gnosticism in America," S. K. Vatralsky.

North Amer. Rev., June, 1912, J. T. Bixby; April, 1901, Prof. E. D. Ross.

Outlook, June, 1901, Dr. H. H. Jessup.

Open Court, June and July, 1910 and 1904, Dr. P. Carus.

Moslem World, July, 1912, Dr. J. D. Frame.

Mission. Rev. of World, Oct., 1911, Dr. W. A. Shedd.

Oxford Magazine, May, 1892.

(2) *Babi or Bahai Writers*

By the Bab:

"Béyan Persan" (Fr.), 4 Vols, trans. by A. Nicolas.

By Baha Ullah:

"Akdas," MS. Trans., by I. G. Kheiralla.

"Ikan," "The Seven Valleys," "The Hidden Words," "Surat-ul-Hykl," "Words of Paradise," "Glad Tidings," Tablets—of the World, of Ishrakat, Tarazat, Tajallayat (Chicago).

By Abdul Baha:

"The Episode of the Bab or the Traveller's Narrative" (trans. by Browne).

"Tablets of Abdul Baha," Vol. I; Addresses in Paris, London and America; "Some Answered Questions," recorded by L. C. Barney; Letter to the Friends in Persia, etc.; The Covenant or Will of Baha Ullah.

By Persian believers:

"Kitab-ul-Nuktatul Kaf," by Mirza Jani, with Introductions by Browne.

"New Hist. of the Bab," trans. by Browne.

"The Sacred Mysteries," Asadullah.

"School of the Prophets," Asadullah.

"Bahai Proofs," Abul Fazl.

"The Brilliant Proof," Abul Fazl.

"Martyrdoms in Persia in 1903," Haider Ali.

"Epistle to the Bahai World," Badi Ullah.

By Western believers:

"The Universal Religion," M. H. Dreyfus.

"The Bahai Revelation," Thornton Chase.

"Before Abraham was, I am," Thornton Chase.

"The Bahai Movement," C. M. Remey.

"Universal Principles of the Bahai Movement," and "Peace," and "The Covenant," C. M. Remey.

"Observations of a Bahai Traveller," C. M. Remey.

"A Year Among the Bahais of India and Burmah," and "Story of the Bahai Movement," Sydney Sprague.

"Dawn of Knowledge and the Most Great Peace," P. K. Dealy.

"The Revelation of Baha Ullah," Mrs. S. D. Brittingham.

"God's Heroes," Barney-Dreyfus.

"Abbas Effendi; His Life and Teaching," M. Phelps.

"The Oriental Rose," M. H. Ford.

"The Modern Social Religion," Horace Holley.

"Bahaism, the Religion of Brotherhood," F. K. Skrine.

"The Reconciliation of Races and Religions," T. K. Cheyne.

"Bahaism in Its Social-Economic Aspects," H. Campbell.

"Prayers and Communes," and "Songs of Prayer and Praise."

Narratives of Pilgrims to Acca:

"In Galilee," T. Chase.

"Unity Through Love," H. MacNutt.

"The Heavenly Vista," L. G. Gregory.

"Ten Days in the Light of Acca," Mrs. Grundy.

"Daily Lessons Received at Acca," Mrs. Cooper.

"My Visit to Abbas Effendi," Mrs. Peeke.

"Table Talks With Abdul Baha," G. T. Winterburn.

"My Visit to Acca," Mrs. Lucas.

"Flowers from the Rose Garden of Acca," Mrs. Finch.

"Notes at Acca," Mrs. True.

Periodicals:

The Bahai News, and *The Star of the West*, from 1910 to 1915

Reports and Bulletins of the Persian-American Educational Society.

By Behaists:

"Beha Ullah," 2 Vols, I. G. Kheiralla.

"Bab-ed-Din," "The Three Questions," and "Facts for Behaists," I. G. Kheiralla.

"Life of Baha Ullah," MS., Mohammed Javad Kasvini.

By Azalis:

"Call to Behaists" (Nos. I, II and III), Stenstrand.

INDEX

Burmah *X, 11, 31, 52, 119, 127*

C

Canonized *121*
Canon Wilberforce *32, 84, 123*
Census *87, 119, 124*
Chicago *10, 14, 19, 31, 39, 46, 47, 48, 58, 64, 69, 70, 79, 97, 105, 106, 115, 116, 117, 118, 119, 121, 122, 123, 124, 127*
Christian Commonwealth *Ix, 32*
Christian Missions *Ix, 52, 86, 87*
Civil Laws *11*
Claims Of Bahaism *4, 7, 25, 29*
Claim To Love *108*
C. M. Remey *22, 36, 66, 73, 127*
Conditions Of Discipleship *7, 11*
Constantinople *59, 66, 67, 68, 71, 96, 101*
Converts From Islam *52, 73*
Count Gobineau *77, 78, 82, 102*
C. True *104, 124*
Cyprus *3, 66, 70, 88, 97, 99, 102, 111*

D

Daniel *34, 39*
Divorce *20, 62, 69, 70, 74*

E

E. C. Getsinger *87, 117*
Educational Society *119*
Education Of Girls *62*
Effulgences *46, 63*
Elijah *37, 38, 124*
Emperor Of Germany *11*
Episode Of The Bab *10, 127*
Epistle To The Bahai World *80, 112, 114, 118, 127*
Esperanto *20, 124*
Eternity Of Matter *15*

F

Fast *44, 49, 85*
Feasts *25*
Forgery *80*

G

Glad Tidings *19, 20, 26, 46, 50, 58, 63, 80, 117, 127*

Lector House believes that a society develops through a two-fold approach of continuous learning and adaptation, which is derived from the study of classic literary works spread across the historic timeline of literature records. Therefore, we aim at reviving, repairing and redeveloping all those inaccessible or damaged but historically as well as culturally important literature across subjects so that the future generations may have an opportunity to study and learn from past works to embark upon a journey of creating a better future.

This book is a result of an effort made by Lector House towards making a contribution to the preservation and repair of original ancient works which might hold historical significance to the approach of continuous learning across subjects.

HAPPY READING & LEARNING!

LECTOR HOUSE LLP
E-MAIL: lectorpublishing@gmail.com